Joining Forces

Joining Forces

Police training, socialization, and
occupational competence

Nigel G. Fielding

Routledge

London and New York

First published in 1988 by Routledge
11 New Fetter Lane, London EC4P 4EE

Published in the USA by Routledge
in association with Routledge, Chapman & Hall, Inc.
29 West 35th Street, New York NY 10001

Filmset by Mayhew Typesetting, Bristol, England
Printed in Great Britain by Biddles Ltd., Guildford

British Library Cataloguing in Publication Data

Fielding, Nigel
    Joining forces: police training,
    socialization, and occupational competence.
    1. Police training — Great Britain
    I. Title
    363.2'2'0941   HV8195.A2

    ISBN 0-415-00683-X

Library of Congress Cataloging in Publication Data

Fielding, Nigel.
    Joining forces: police training, socialization, and occupational
    competence / Nigel G. Fielding.
        p.   cm.
    Bibliography: p.
    Includes index.
    ISBN 0-415-00683-X (pbk.)
    1. Police training — Great Britain. 2. Police training — United
States. 3. Police professionalization — Great Britain. 4. Police
professionalization — United States. I. Title.
HV8195.A4F54 1988
363.2'07'1041 — dc 19

To Jane and Jessica

Contents

Preface

This book is about people joining a unique occupation and about the ways they, with others, seek to develop competence in meeting its demands. Pursuit of this theme brings the work and opinion of many others into the wings, but the recruits remain at centre stage. This is intentional. It is increasingly possible to immerse oneself in social and behavioural studies of policing and yet to remain with a 'Spitting Image' view of the police world. To be sure, data, detail, and analysis refine the caricature, yet alone they leave us little wiser about the persona behind the spoof.

Of course, the relative mystery of the job, and its long-established arm's-length relationship with the inquisitive, play their own part. The limits of the understanding of even the well-informed are obvious in the shock that commentators express at each latest revelation of police misdeed and malpractice. In the hectic world of police research, too, the recurrent questions of personal motivation and 'sell-out' to policy interests or 'the state' reflect a continuing ambivalence about relationships with the police. Detachment is not sought only on the police side. But the detachment necessary to independence in research also has an analytic cost. Policing becomes one of those subjects about which one may know a lot but understand little. In a hard-nosed research environment, the research vision tends towards a myopia born of detailed data without an appreciation of the people it only partly describes.

This book cannot claim to be a gentle skim above the data, either. These are the facts of police training and the indices of the recruits' progress through it. But readers will find, more than is usual, an effort to enable the police themselves – recruits, trainers, colleagues – to find their own voice in the text. Interviews and narrative description are extensively used to make good the neglect of those questions which bring the study of a working group alive. What kind of people want to be police? What kind of people are the police? How do they see their role? Do they think it changes them? Does it affect their family and friendships? Do they appreciate the training? What are their criticisms of it? What do they think of equal opportunities and the other policies the force has adopted? Do they take community policing seriously? Do they see weaknesses in their own police work? How do they develop a tactical and strategic sense of competence? How do they define good policing?

It should be plain that these concerns are central to the achievement of any reform in operational policing which goes deeper than the paper it is printed on. Certainly Harris, the American pioneer in studying police training, knew this, as did Rubinstein, whose 1973 book is still in the first rank of ethnographies of police work. But, if I am reciting my 'influences', I must advertise one principal scholarly inspiration for the present work, William Ker Muir's intense and penetrating study of the police as 'streetcorner politicians'. More than any other student of the police, Muir kept his sustained focus on the human experience of being a police officer, and the central issue of what is 'good policing'. There have been remarkably few studies of what is good policing (in the UK or in the US, where all three studies so far mentioned originate). Nor has the matter of how officers form an appreciation of what is good police work been much at issue. There has been no shortage of comment and anecdote from a cynical perspective about versions of police work which are 'good' for the officer's interests, or the force's. Indeed, this is the essential preoccupation of studies of informal organization, about which there is more below. But the ways that officers construe the good, seek to pursue their conception of it, and reconcile their abilities with the mandate, have been neglected. While one trusts that these have been preoccupations of the managers of the police service (under present arrangements, 'trust' is all we can do, and the very nature of these matters makes the platitude the first and last line of response), movement in both the research world and the polity means it cannot remain so circumscribed a concern.

Public debate, to which official, semi-official, and renegade research is responsive, has grown increasingly explicit about the definition of 'good policing'. In the 1987 British general election, the control of operational policing was an explicit and party political issue. That the processes which gave rise to this are part of the wider socio-economic and political context is obvious. Others (Reiner 1985) have concentrated effectively on this and I defer to their achievements by not doing so here. But the implication that is clear to researchers in the field is that we need to know much more about how officers identify specific achievements as desirable, recognize certain skills as related to those achievements and therefore worth refining, and set about practising and improving those skills in their work.

The place of training in this should be becoming more apparent. There have been many studies of the kind of policing we get. There have been some studies of what kind of policing we want. There have been few studies of how to get it. Short of massive organizational reform, training is still the best way to get the policing we want. I use 'best' in respect of it being most amenable to rapid adjustment, most readily inspected, and most effectively measurable in its achievement. In an absolute sense, of course, there is no 'best' means to bring about the good, only 'least bad' methods. We are dealing with human beings, after all, and the police are as innovative, thoughtful, and intransigent as any other occupational group. But training is a means which touches every officer, both at the outset and in service. It is centrally directed, in appearance and often in fact, and its curricula are subject to expert and political external review. Closer to the concerns of this book, however, training gives officers the warrant to speak explicitly about their ideals, intentions and procedures. In all these respects, training enjoys a sharper and clearer relation to what happens in routine policing than the welter of consultative committees, lay visitors' schemes, multi-agency panels and other devices currently being explored as a means to get the police to do, or to listen to, what we want.

Like other symbolic institutions, the acknowledgement of scholastic and personal debts is no less real for its being conventional. The co-operation received from the training establishment of the force in question, the instructors, experienced constables, and, especially, probationers was literally crucial to the analysis as well as the data-gathering. Their goodwill, tolerance and humour also kept the researcher going in terrain that sometimes felt unfamiliar and remote. I am especially indebted to Tony Leonard, now Deputy Chief of another force, for his sociological insight as well as his very considerable contribution to access and data collection. In its wisdom, the then Social Science Research Council which invested in this work also approved consultation with Professor Peter Manning of Michigan State University and Wolfson College, Oxford. His combining an ethnographer's insight into the minutiae of organization with the theoretician's grasp of system-wide relations gave me more than I, or the SSRC, ever had a right to expect. There is room for another debt. That is to Professor John van Maanen, who came over from MIT for a year on a Senior Fulbright Scholarship. I cannot imagine more conducive discussions at a time when the manuscript was being shaped, and what I owe is only glimpsed from the yardage scored by John in the list of references. Finally, this book is dedicated to Jane Fielding, my partner in all things, and to Jessica, who sustains us both.

1
Situating the police

The connection between the changes individuals undergo in training and the contemporary debate over policing is direct and compelling. Our understanding of the changes recruits undergo in training fundamentally affects our ability to anticipate the decisions they will make as police officers. Formal socialization concerns the planned efforts of the organization to transform recruits into novice members, while informal socialization occurs in contacts with existing members. The prime source of formal socialization is the training school and the prime source of informal socialization is the occupational culture of police officers. Socialization does not just include imparting factual information but attitudes about the organization, its system of authority, its work and a host of other features. Much of this is learnt from informal sources.

The influence of formal elements is greatest at the beginning of the socialization process. Training is an important time for the organization to secure the commitment of recruits to the values it endorses; this is when the 'official line' is retailed with the greatest assurance. Trainers are understandably preoccupied with the elements of socialization they can directly affect, and increasingly recognize that, while they are important, the informal elements are largely outside their control.

Because the distinction between formal and informal influences is not only entrenched in the research literature but makes sense to trainers there has been a tendency to assume that socialization develops in linear fashion: first, the recruits are exposed to the formal influences and persuaded by them, later the recruits are exposed to informal influences and learn to be sceptical about the organization, its senior officers, and the official line. In this book it is argued that, while formal and informal influences undoubtedly operate, the situation is complicated by the individuals' attempts to make their own sense of their experience as police officers. Socialization is a process of identity transformation. If formal and informal sources of socialization together only account for some aspects of the officers' decision-making, then our ability to anticipate the action they will take in particular circumstances will be impaired. We need to know how recruits experience and respond to formal socialization and how they resolve conflicts between the procedures taught in formal socialization and those derived from informal sources. Further, whatever our reservations about formal socialization, training remains the most direct and intensive way by which the organization can seek to influence its members' adjustment to the police role. If policing is to respond to the need for change attested to by the current debate over every aspect of policing, training must work from a more refined appreciation of the experiences individuals undergo in joining the force.

The principal repository of informal organization is deemed to be the occupational culture (Manning 1977). To assess the degree to which recruits and novices actually mediate formal and informal influences one needs to understand the character of occupational culture. The occupational culture has been characterized as extremely powerful. Indeed it is often depicted as so uniform and sustained an influence as to exercise a monolithic authority which degrades the ability of senior officers to manage and subverts attempts to exact greater accountability of constables for their actions (Fielding 1981). While it is undoubtedly powerful, it is open to question whether it is as solidary and universally compelling as it is sometimes made to appear. Equally dubious is the characterization of the individuals drawn to a police career as being of a similar and authoritarian bent. In emphasizing that individuals reach their own resolutions of formal and informal socialization influences, both the typification of occupational culture as homogeneous and the characterization of police as people of similar disposition will be criticized. If we are to appreciate the determinants of the decisions officers make in police work we will have to look elsewhere than merely to formal organization and informal culture.

Such a focus requires data showing how police recruits get to grips with their experiences in training and on the street. Data sensitive to shifts of perspective and recruits' sense of identity were gathered by qualitative and quantitative research based in a force training establishment (for a discussion of methods see Appendix I). Some 125 recruits were followed through their two-year training, being interviewed and completing sociometric tests at regular intervals. The findings were augmented by interviews with instructors and officers responsible for recruitment and training, the 'tutor constables' supervising trainees in their first postings, and experienced constables. Observations of training sessions added valuable information about the mode of instruction.

To establish the analytic framework, Chapter 2 reviews the concept of socialization, highlighting features distinctive of socialization into the police. Factors influencing decisions to join are examined. The recruits' highly idealistic motivation and perception of policing as a form of social service are emphasized. Their increasing sense that the career choice has heavy consequences for their self-identity is demonstrated. Chapter 3 offers a profile of police training, discussing recruits' experiences of local (training establishment) and regional (District Training Centre) input as the basis of their recognition of a disjunction between formal and informal practices and culture. The theme is sustained by experience in their first field postings, and anxiety over the prospect that they may not make the grade. The chapter closes with a commentary on resignation and the growing realism about the organization and its work.

Chapter 4 pursues this theme, documenting the changes recruits undergo as they negotiate the hard realities of police work – the shift system, the paperwork, the conflict between crime control and social service, the prospect of being armed with guns. Chapter 5 considers their responses to their status as constables, examining both divisions between officers and the ties that bind them. Divisions provoked by differences of ambition, different loyalties, different perspectives on women in the police, the rights of police as employees, and the discipline system, are considered. Chapter 6 analyses the ways constables develop competence in their work and examines the lessons of the study for the relationship between constables and citizens. The focus on competence supports a concluding critique of the current means of training, with recommendations for change in mode and content to bring it into line with the demands of modern society.

Focusing on competence obliges us to be explicit about what police should, and should not, do. At root, the numerous competencies required of police hinge on their ability to conduct themselves sensitively in interaction with others. There are descriptions of such skills in the research literature, but commentaries on police training seldom start from them. Bittner's (1967) and Muir's (1977) police are massively competent social actors. They recognize in the people they police and the colleagues with whom they work the full range of human purposes and potential actions. Recruits may lack the finely honed view represented in such accounts, but if they are to survive in the occupation their performance must indeed become orientated to the processes of sensitive observation and negotiation on which competent officers mostly rely for the construction of local public order. These universals are moderated by dramatic variations in the locality policed. Placing the young WPC in her home neighbourhood in kindness to her ailing mother renders very different experience to the former military cop posted to a declining steel town. Yet out of divergent police experiences, and diverse recruit backgrounds, a force of interchangeable 'personnel' is to be formed. This book considers the varying influence of the formal and informal bases of occupational socialization on recruits during training and, identifying their limited relevance, suggests that the practice of policing is understood only by attention to the officers' construction of a police role out of their own situated experiences.

This radically descriptive appreciation of the police role reflects the character of the 'essential' knowledge held by officers. As Bittner remarked of officers' local knowledge, 'new facts . . . are added to the texture, not in terms of structured categories but in terms of adjoining known realities . . . the content and organisation of the patrolman's knowledge is primarily ideographic and only vestigially, if at all, nomothetic' (Bittner 1967). The experienced officer's preference for accumulative and unanalytic forms of generalization, where description is preferred to axiom when reflecting on experience, informs the outsider's sense that the essential nature of policing is elusive and incapable of generalization, a sense that causes novices to despair. The pervasive reign of anecdotes marks discussions of policing. Recruits remain uncomfortable until realizing that use of a small number of analytic categories (e.g. 'rubbish work', 'good collar') under the assault of endlessly disconfirming and just plain different episodes is the officers' way of expressing that the police occupation cannot be pinned down because it is formed by the chaotic variation 'out there' in society. The preference for 'playing by ear' in patrol work has given training a special problem, encouraging recruits to think 'anyone can do it', and training the excuse to make only the law and the organizational rules explicit. Both ignore that, 'in saying that "he plays by ear" . . . he is making his decisions while being attuned to the realities of complex situations about which he has immensely detailed knowledge' (Bittner, 1967: 715).

While officers are inclined to see all their actions and decisions as wholly contextual, 'almost idiosyncratic in form', this is misleading, 'for they do alter their behaviour and adjust their actions in line with their reading of social situations, personal advantage and organisational rules' (Manning 1980: 96). The reluctance to verbalize which impedes accurate instruction is a mark of the tactics officers use in planning their own career path under the constraints of their working situation. One of the elements of the informal code recruits must learn is to hold their tongue. Cain quotes an experienced constable's comment that 'on this job you must never let on how much you know' (Cain 1973: 199). The mechanism is sublimely cautious; for example, 'their introduction to easing facilities and infringements was gradual, and after each step they were carefully watched to see if there was any "come back"' (ibid).

Such informal elements are vital in the process of organizational socialization. It is generally seen as occurring in a four-stage sequence of pre-entry, admittance, change and continuance phases (van Maanen 1973). Were one to construct a variable-centred socialization model one would need to account for change over time (conventional stages being anticipatory, formal and informal), include a description of the process by which change occurs (e.g. the influence of reference groups), specify the structural factors which mediate the influence of the reference group (e.g. organizational hierarchy) and note individual differences between recruits (demographic and biographical variations). (See Bennett and Greenstein 1975). Yet the individual remains the mediator of these artificially separated influences on action; their determinate character is the principal flaw of such models. This is why it is fruitful to look at the accounts rendered by novice police as they begin to perceive and define social situations from the perspective of social control. The focus is the contrast between early understandings of the police role and subsequent reformulations consequent on experience.

The occupational culture and organizational context of police work

At a time when labelling theorists and radical criminologists felt they had transcended models of criminal behaviour as determined, irrational, and pathological, accounts of police behaviour based on similar tenets were still predominant. It is remarkable that the 'humanizing' of deviance so clearly preceded the extension of a similar perspective to the premier agency of social control. Until recently the police have been depicted as acting in accord with a personality remarkable for the extremity of its authoritarianism, aggression, and cliquishness. The wrangle over the existence of a 'police personality' continues; old hostilities have been revived by research on the gruesomeness of cops' thoughts on race (Colman and Gorman 1982).

Yet a major survey of the 'police personality' admitted that, while the researchers began by assuming that police are 'very unusual people', isolated by 'their authoritarian mentality', the evidence was that 'policemen may be rather ordinary people . . . We cannot even be sure there is such a thing as a police personality, however loosely we define it' (More 1976: 125). In time this fuss may properly be consigned to sideshow status, as studies of the police are increasingly oriented to the same complex matters of aetiology applicable to the study of deviance. That is, as Punch (1979) suggested, the performance of the police role will increasingly be approached as 'a situational and interpretative predicament in its own right'. Rather than the presumption that policing attracts malicious individuals of a punitive and reactionary bent, such work begins from the assumption that the work the police are given to do, and its institutional placing, largely accounts for the character of police practice.

Recognition that police work is embedded in an organizational context and mediated by location in an occupational culture, both of which much complicate the equation of 'bad policing' with 'bad cops', was a direct consequence of the pursuit of naturalistic research methods. The strength of occupational culture became explicable as a response to their working situation. It seemed both natural and pervasive. '(A)ll occupations develop ideologies to defend their perquisites, rationalise their errors and fallibilities, spin out myths of sacredness, immunity and self-righteousness, and transform symbolically all that the practitioner sees and does' (Manning 1978: 136). The occupational culture became an analytic preoccupation.

The power of attraction of police reference groups was particularly emphasized by Harris (1973). Integration into the police reference group, and through it the occupation, was by three prevalent influences. First, the novice was impelled to seek out the reference group comprising other recruits for guidance and support in the face of 'administrative and job-related depersonalisation'. A second motivator of affiliation was the ambiguity and ambivalence of the formal organization's messages about the police role. The near-cosmic breadth of the police role is daunting, and worry over this may not be met by formal training's concentration on the law and administrative procedure, the former presenting its own sources of ambiguity and the latter a stupefying concentration on petty detail.

> The rookie shares the widely held opinion that policemen have special skills to see things. If only he knew what these abilities were . . . 'When you go on the street, you will develop a sense about these things,' one instructor said. The mysterious skills hinted at are not made explicit by the examples that the instructors offer – 'Watch out for "people walking late at night"' . . . Always illustrations of heroics and cleverness from a diminishing past when acuity paid off.
> (Rubinstein 1973: 219)

Third, the reference group was a redoubt to assuage feelings of isolation, danger, and low esteem generated by encounters with the public at its worst. This emphasis on occupational reference groups played on the distinction of formal from informal aspects of organization.

The important point for studies of police organizations is that whether or not the formal tenets of the organization pertain, they are thought to do so by members and clients. The rules may not always be followed, but action is still oriented to them. If one builds on this approach one may describe the articulation of formal and informal bases of action without having to see action as inscribed in organization or as random (Bittner 1965). The organization's essence is its repository of approved vocabularies to permit organizational action. 'Thus the formal organisational designs are schemes of interpretation that competent and entitled users can invoke in yet unknown ways whenever it suits their purposes'

(Bittner 1965: 249–50). Ability to invoke the justificatory vocabularies naturally varies with organization experience, so there are consequences for practice in the organizational naivety of, for example, probationer PCs. While Bittner (1965) acknowledges that 'members will bring different biographical experiences, different levels of technical or rhetorical skill and different cross-cutting commitments to this task' (p. 15), he emphasizes the unifying and warranting function of the organization's mandate (Hughes 1971) or charter, 'the concept to which organisation members orient in their dealings with each other and with nonmembers to establish the limits of legitimisable action' (Strong and Dingwall 1983: 19). Charter issues are implicit in the numerous decisions on the exercise of discretion made by constables. They limit the legitimation of action by restricting the range of legitimizable discourse; only certain motives, justifications, and kinds of evidence may be used. Two points are notable – that organizational success is much to do with ability to think up accepted justifications for action, and that control over the interpretation of charters and discourse expressing their meaning may be used to disbar particular motives, justifications, and inferences.

Training represents a distinct locus for the rehearsal and negotiation of the police organization's charter. Another relevant occasion calling forth charter-oriented accounts is that of assessments. While most organizations practise personnel evaluations and suffer public complaints, the police and particularly constables are continually under this kind of scrutiny, from supervisors and public. Bittner emphasized the inapplicability of strict legal codes as guides for decisions on peace-keeping matters, identifying the officer's refinement of organized common-sense perspectives on the locale which substitute for the penal code in regulating social order. One ground for the cynicism officers feel about paperwork stems from their development of a detailed local knowledge. No one is better equipped to adopt a sceptical stance towards organizational statistics, particularly performance measures; officers appreciate that statistics are produced by agencies with special interests in recording actions relevant to their purposes. The fact that an encounter with a person must be transformed into an event in an officer's report whose original character cannot then be recovered is hardly lost on officers. Paper is less and less a satisfactory index of activity as the officer becomes increasingly informed by a rich body of particularized local knowledge; there is no easy congruence between legal category and the characteristics, forms of behaviour, and typical motives ascribable on the basis of situated knowledge.

Apart from the problem of 'translation' this gives officers, there is another problem bearing implications for the character of enforcement. The officer's ability to construe action as 'deviant' is contingent on the prior ability to construe action as 'normal'. One must be able to describe a normal environment in order to describe normative departures from it. The quality of the officer's interpretive apparatus is crucial in determining the visibility of offence. Manning (1980) argues that drug squads secure autonomy by cultivating public concern about the drug problem. But the symbol works on agents as well as public (1980: xii). The imagery attaching to enforcement not only communicates instrumental messages but 'also expresses selves, an organisational line or rhetoric, a set of strategies and subjective meanings'. As a process of change in self-identity, socialization features individual accommodations to experience of such work. It is a long-term and open-ended process.

Thus the sources of influence on police recruits change during the two-year probationary period, necessitating a processual model of the development of police attitudes. While the police reference group is still a prime source of influence, its constitution changes. In particular, as probationary officers are dispersed throughout the constabulary, the recruit reference group is broken up and its influence reduced. The effect of the tutor constable wanes as the probationary officer gains experience of the working environment. Consequently, attitudes, particularly general attitudes on complex issues, cannot simply be 'read off' from agencies of socialization. Van Maanen's work on American police training confirms the far from straightforward impact of formal socialization (1975, 1976) and emphasizes the impact of the first enforcement-related public contact the recruit experiences. He suggests that the outcome of the encounter increases the salience of the police reference group for the individual. The enforcement encounter acts as a catalyst that makes 'structural' factors like social isolation, danger, role ambiguity, public hostility, and an adversary relation with other agencies suddenly real and important for the novice.

Experience also features in the trend Butler and Cochrane found towards

> a personality which needs to be independent of others in decision making (autonomy), to argue one's point of view (aggression), and away from the need to recognise guilt or having done something wrong (abasement) and to do new and different things (change).
>
> (1977: 446)

It is particularly important, in the light of the quarrels over 'the police personality', that these tendencies towards conservatism and increasing emphasis on self-esteem are seen as the result of the officer's working experience. Indeed these authors see a 'constant battle' in the police role between competing sets of values, rather than a simple modification of one set of values and beliefs in the light of occupational socialization.

McNamara (1967) identified the conflicting goals as law enforcement versus service, prosecution of offenders versus legal and procedural constraints, individuality versus bureaucratic control, and maintenance of authority versus presentation of self. An 'occupational culture' conceived as a buffer and alternative source of esteem seems an inevitable response to such dilemmas. Socialization into the police is marked by increasing self-orientation and social isolation, indicating the need for police to protect themselves from the stress of the police role by affiliation to occupational culture.

However, this does not imply that the occupational culture is the same in every locale or force. Proponents of this line of analysis were understandably inclined initially to emphasize similarities rather than variation in order to establish the concept (Banton 1964; Manning 1972; Salaman 1974; Westley 1970) and there are some remarkable similarities between police in very different societies (Bayley 1975: 370). Nevertheless there are differences in culture not only between forces but within the same force; the most cautious version discerns two 'cultures of policing', based on rank (Reuss-Ianni 1983). Clearly the concept of occupational culture may be taken further by arguing that it is not undifferentiated but comprised of several cultures formed around adjustments to the occupation. Thus the initial conception of a coherent source of formal socialization and a solidary occupational culture supplying alternative, informal socialization influences, has been considerably refined. Consequently, the formal/informal model of socialization into occupations remains only partial unless account is taken of the mediation of these influences by individuals making their own adaptations, constructing an 'organizational reality' special to themselves from these various sources of influence. The research data reveals the resilience of recruits and their capacity to resist as well as embrace the influences arising from formal and informal sources.

Whereas Butler and Cochrane's police seem to be on the retreat, rather defensively withdrawing into their personal values, Manning's are more aggressive, coming out fighting in a he-man occupational culture and inclined to assert their own values instead of compromising with the others they are meant to reconcile. The latter conception seems more in accord with the vigour and temper of contemporary police groupings. It has the unmistakable character of a subcultural redoubt. Socialization into the culture may be seen as a form of career (Hughes 1958) in which 'career contingencies' are the facts on which mobility depends, including both elements of the job structure and changes in perspectives and motivations (Becker and Strauss 1956). Becker's early formulation insisted that withdrawal or reversal of the career path was possible. During the original enthusiasm for social reaction theories of deviance, the concept acquired an unwelcome and misleading air of determinacy, as if mere application of a deviant label by some social audience were enough to confirm the unfortunate individual in irrevocable alteration of self-identity. This was much out of keeping with the interactionist inspiration of Becker's work. In applying the concept, the sense of contingency in the original 'career' idea should be preserved. The occupation may present a range of conflicting 'structural factors' and occupational culture may pose its own imperatives, but the individual officer is the final arbiter or mediator of these influences. Socialization settings do not have unambiguous, natural properties beyond those individuals attribute to them.

On entry to an unfamiliar setting the person must actively construct an interpretative scheme to render the situation meaningful. In her study of police recruits Hopper (1977: 151) found that differences of background experience with law enforcement indicated differences in their 'long range perspectives on police work and the police world'. These different perspectives led to their facing different career contingencies. As Hughes (1958: 129) says, 'Career is . . . a sort of running adjustment between a man and the various facts of life and of his professional world.' The steady progress through each stage of career commitment can always be halted, and at any stage the officer can withdraw. This will have important consequences for self-identity (Becker 1964: 52), and for the character of the individual's practice of policing. An awareness that one's colleagues may draw on very different experiences to form their own adaptation to the police role does not subvert the notion of occupational culture. The great stress by police on the need to understand policing on the basis of experience implies a respect for the choices made by individuals in relation to their distinctive experiences. As the grounds for a tolerance of diversity within occupational culture this is a resource training could mobilize. Far from being a sign of individual or social breakdown ambivalence suggests a flexibility appropriate to careers whose demands are unpredictable and diverse (Merton and Barber 1976: 3).

The police college and the market

In Britain police training on a systematic national scale began in 1946. Between 1946 and 1973 the initial training, a thirteen-week course, was virtually unchanged. Following the 1971 Working Party report it was altered to ten weeks in 1973, which prevailed up to the present, with the addition of the Associated Police Studies lessons in 1981. A profile of the recruit training in the research force appears in Appendix II. Residential training has always been supplemented by the 'apprenticeship' with the tutor constable, and the probationary period has consistently been two years.

The research for this book was carried out in the Derbyshire police force. The Derbyshire Police Training Establishment runs a variety of in-service courses but also conducts recruit training. This county in the English Midlands can be divided on a west/east basis, into a traditional, rural, conservative population and an industrial, radical left population. In the latter, traditional *gemeinschaft* relations prevail, but the police felt able, prior to the miners' strike, to declare they were regarded as part of the community. A senior officer spoke of a sergeant who grew up as a friend of Dennis Skinner, the local and radical Labour MP; the point, he suggested, was that such ties negate the idea that police repress the working class (although pay and job security now make the police more credible as an aristocracy of labour than the miners). While the east side is not heavily urbanized it is highly industrial, with chemical, mining, textiles, and general manufacturing. Most of the beat postings are in the east. A chief inspector declared that policing in mining towns was 'pretty well as tough as any cop would want' (field notes, 8.3.82).

The force headquarters and training establishment (TE) are built around the Old Hall, a large country mansion set in some acres of parkland. The site was acquired for a very low valuation from a major company divesting assets. A tower block houses the headquarters staff, with the low-lying buildings of the TE alongside. The facilities at the complex are impressive, particularly the comprehensive TV studio, which allows officers to become proficient at presenting themselves in the media as well as making their own programmes. The library contains a wide range of references on criminal law, criminology, sociology and psychology, novels, and political literature. Holdings of the latter are so extensive they prompted a senior officer's joking remark that if Special Branch knew what they had they would probably 'do' the library. It is one of the few police libraries in the country with a professional librarian (*Ramparts* 1980: 3).

The library represented the focus of a deviant element in the police culture, and some emphasis was put on the liberal lifestyle and university education of the librarian. Otherwise, regimentation and routine procedure mark the superficial impressions a casual visitor gains. While loitering in the TE one is likely to hear dull parade ground signals filtering in from outside, and robust carol singing at Christmas. Waiting in the staff common room one may encounter a visiting lecturer, high-ranking officers from another force, or a teaching equipment salesman paying a casual and regular visit, selling his wares to anyone who will listen. There is a busy air among the instructional staff; despite it being not fully a backstage area one sees staff in various degrees of uniform and informal relations clearly operate in what is a small working group. It is more like a college than a police station. The chief similarity to the latter is at night, when the duty officer acts in a station sergeant role minding the store (field notes 10.1.80). People do unfamiliar duties with little training, but with a general willingness to 'muck in and have a go'.

Things have changed since training was wholly personalized. A chief constable's order for 21 December 1866 reads 'Constable Edward Marshall is to proceed to Chesterfield this day and to be drilled by Sergeant Lounds and taught his duties by Mr Wheeldon. He shall, in a month's time, be permanently located in Bakewell to be placed in charge of the county horse.' Now the total number of instructors, including civilian driving instructors and constable instructors of cadets is about forty. A 'qualified instructor' for general training must pass a Home Office course at the central planning unit at Harrogate. Those for mountaineering, canoeing, and so on must also pass recognized courses, e.g. mountain rescue school. Bar the top two officers all the TE staff were qualified instructors. The instructors active in training courses were a much smaller subgroup of thirteen, comprising a chief inspector, two inspectors, eight sergeants, and a constable (AVA technician). As well as probationer training and specialist courses the TE is involved in refresher courses for 'senior constables', aimed at the 'integration' of the force at PC level, with the various specialisms being related to the one central role of patrol officer; beat patrol is projected as the prime work role (field notes, 16.5.83).

Among the small band of police training instructors (PTIs) there were several stalwarts for whom training was a good, safe job. Despite the ethos of frequent transfers and the allusions to getting back to operational duties – the 'sharp end' – the longer-serving PTIs were happy to function where they were. The police have a pension scheme which allows retirement at forty-seven, and some PTIs would probably remain in the TE until then. The TE might also function as the last posting for higher officers not directly involved in teaching. One PTI of senior rank spoke of disillusion and early retirement and was following an OU course. An inspector and a chief inspector had LLBs and one also had an MSc in personnel management. The genuine bantering at meals reflected a team comfortable at working together, with the chief instructor referring to 'my men' warmly and without stiffness. They joked about one of the PTIs, an inspector, being extreme left-wing while another told a teasing anecdote about pushing a 'yobbo' off a bus so he fell flat out (he was trying to push past an old lady) and how old riot shields stored from a long ago purchase tended to splinter when struck, making a convenient edge for 'decapitation' (field notes, 28.7.81).

While this book is concerned with themes particular to this organization, these are cross-cut by those that recur in all organizations. One such is enterprise and innovation. While the TE represents a means of generating income from the specialist training offered to other forces, other facilities were being scrutinized for potential to render profit or savings. On one visit I accompanied an officer to lunch in the 'police bar' in the Old Hall. The bar was open for lunch for an experimental month; beer was at pub prices and the rolls were bought from the canteen. The principle was that the bar must not compete with existing facilities. There was a fruit machine in a corner gaining some custom. The clientele seemed to be sergeants and up, and civilian female clerical officers. There were a lot of references to the female presence and an air of somewhat forced joviality. The officer pointed out the role of the bar as a social gathering place, adding that it was not to make profit but needed to secure overheads to buy improved equipment. As well as marking an aspect of the internal economy of the police, the bar was clearly someone's pet project and needing to attract trade to confirm its worth. Others 'with an interest' in existing catering were also police officers but were at odds with such developments.

A discussion with a chief inspector about the way instructional programmes at one TE diffused through similar establishments led to an unexpected commercial perspective. A Derbyshire course had been particularly successful.

'We do have the community liaison officers course here, which is a national course backed by the Home Office. It has now even got inter-national status and we've had a Canadian mounted policeman and we've had two from Holland, one from France. We thought Australia were interested and we're hoping they still will be. Certainly the Home Office then push it out, they advertise it. That's why we get a lot of income from it. We only used to have one a year and this year we've had to run two.'   (81: 3,8)

This plainly promotes a competitive and commercial perspective, adding to those directed outwards to the demands of the public and inwards to what is valued and endorsed as 'knowledge' by the occupation. 'We've got 140 bedrooms and ideally we would like to fill them every week of the year.' The high cost of building training facilities (Surrey's cost £3.5 million) obliges forces that are close to full establishment to look for new markets. However, recognition of the market potential had not removed certain obstacles, including a management new to this approach and local government which was not geared to turning a profit on police education.

'There's a lot of competition between forces for the most sophisticated courses and trying to get the market. Although it's not entirely geared on money. We would probably be bankrupt overnight if we had to run it as an industry . . . I would like to but unfortunately we have county, and let's be honest . . . when did anything in the county get run at a profit. You're tied by their regulations. If we entered the market place in a freer capacity, without a lot of restraints, we could win. But we're restrained by Home Office protocol, ACPO.'   (inst. 81: 3, 8–9)

Considerations such as the prospect of profit are of some concern to trainers but hardly impinge on the awareness of recruits. However, as this study is concerned with the process of training it takes into account the experience of those who provide formal (and informal) socialization as well as those who receive it. The need to approach training as a process is implicit in the concept of socialization. Further consideration of the concept precedes a look at recruits' first thoughts on joining the police.

2
The socialization process

Organization is a concept which presupposes that people use common-sense schemes of interpretation as powerful resources for organizing their daily activities (Schutz 1967). The properties of organization cannot be indicated without reference to the methodical organizing activities of members themselves (Speier 1971: 16–17). Such a stance was taken by Skolnick (1966) in his analysis of police discretion: the legal context is perceived and modified by the discretionary action of officers, rather than the way in which organizational policies can determine or set these options. There is a dialectic between such policies and processes affecting their achievement by officers, such as the informal reward system, supervisory system, and the agents' view of their work and its imperatives.

A sensitivity to process and change, autonomy and choice, mark this approach. Structure is seen as changing and partial rather than absolute, and members as creative choice-makers assessing meaning within a situated context. The guiding metaphor for the organization's internal cohesion is 'loose coupling', indicating the inexact nature of the relationships between intentions, actions and outcomes.

The strong implication is that one needs to examine both how the organization defines its project and how members construct a vision of the world and act accordingly. Members are hardly free to fashion their world entirely by their own lights. Members idealize and effectively reify their own positions by playing out roles to internal and external audiences (Manning 1980: 20). They also create constraints on these worlds by such efforts. The notion is that of the 'enacted environment' (Weick 1969), a reflexive concept, referring not only to what is 'seen' but to the structure by which such a vision is possible. An emphasis on the 'enacted environment' directs attention to the order-producing elements of the organization, which, being members' conceptions, are not codified like legal rules but whose disregard 'will result in questioning a person's competence or in his or her disqualification as a knowledgeable member' (Knorr-Cetina 1981: 4). The task of a competence theory of action is to find how members' conceptions are organized to produce 'orderly' behaviour patterns. As one traces the novices' attempts to develop adroit handling of the organization's symbol sets, one may learn much about the organization. It is important that the appearance of rationality promoted by the 'enacted environment' idea does not make us lose sight of the 'loose coupling', and the status of the novice, inevitably making mistakes, helps warn us against this.

Van Maanen and Schein (1979: 230) assert that police training is *collective, sequential, fixed, serial, closed* and involves *investiture*. Batches of novices are trained at the same time, and the process follows a series of identifiable stages, e.g. recruit school, probation, and first posting. The closed socialization mode binds together the batch in a process which is oriented to investiture into the new status and 'stripping' away of the old; desocialization precedes socialization. Trainers seek to reduce any diversity among recruits. Manning (1981: 2421) notes that such a pattern 'produces collectively oriented persons with strong cohort ties who are internally separated by slightly differing cohort experiences. They are integrated vertically by shared bases of experience . . . and strongly identify with their on-the-job trainers.' At least initially, training can be, and is intended as, a somewhat trying experience. 'Suffering . . . appears to be a prominent component in the training for all occupations that exhibit strong attention to standards of competence and performance and to identification with the occupation as a collectivity' (Moore 1969: 878). The initiate is put through a series of difficult tasks and duties, some unpleasant. From this arises the salience of peers and informal socialization sources.

> These challenging and painful experiences are shared with others, who thus have a fellowship of suffering. Now if we add the probability that peers and adult role models constitute significant others, and thus that relations with them are marked by some degree of affectivity, we are well on the way to comprehending how an occupational identity gets formed.   (Moore 1969: 879)

At first the organization has a good deal of influence; recruits have to know the system before they can play it.

> Organisational socialisation . . . provides . . . the new member with a set of rules, perspectives, prescriptions, techniques, and/or tools necessary for him to continue as a participant in the organisation. . . . (C)ritical occupational perspectives develop . . . as the new member passes through his initiation rituals.   (Van Maanen 1974: 81)

These career perspectives are not concerned directly with routine, everyday practice, but with long-range, occupationally relevant orientations. They provide an 'operating' *ideology* which assists the constables in developing a conception of who they are and what they are to do.

Anticipatory socialization

In examining the influence on recruits of their experience prior to joining the police two sources of data were used, the 'reason for joining' essays, and interviews. Responses on prior contact with police and attitudes of friends and kin towards the police bear on the views with which they approach police service. This does not imply that the reader will be asked to tolerate a very high level of inference in relation to these replies, as the interest is in their representation of the kinds of accounts which recruits to an occupation feel it appropriate to give to those who may well influence their progress at work. This is particularly so with the reason-for-joining essays. As to the current popularity of policing as a job, the Policy Studies Institute survey found that 19 per cent of Londoners aged 15–44 had considered joining the force. Only 13 per cent of West Indians and 10 per cent of Asians had considered it, compared to 20 per cent of whites. There was no significant variation by age, little difference by sex and there was evidence that policing was 'relatively classless' (Smith 1983: 205).

A number of studies of anticipatory socialization argue that potential recruits prospectively imagine the demands of the occupation and rehearse their practice of it (Thornton and Nardi 1975). Their frame of reference combines their own views with their understanding of those of the occupational reference group(s), which may be known to them by contact. Reference groups embrace imaginary groups such as the presentations of the police by the mass media, or the subject's own daydreams, and actual police contacts. Reference groups transmit such information as perceived status, future role expectations, and police-related self-conceptions (Merton and Rossi 1968). They initiate a process of re-evaluation of self-identity. Facilitators or retardants of the process are the amount of time spent in anticipatory socialization (van Maanen 1975) and the accuracy of the transmitted information (Thornton and Nardi 1975) but one also needs to take into account any prior experience of a similar occupation, such as work as a military policeman or social security investigator. This point should not be put more strongly, as van Maanen's comparable investigation shows that such characteristics are short-lived. This is consistent with the argument that, rather than their background, the chief influence on the recruits was their current experience of work and, particularly, the culture generated by police to cope with it. 'Consequently the police culture can be viewed as moulding the attitudes – with numbing regularity – of virtually all who enter' (van Maanen 1975: 215).

Whether the 'moulding of attitudes' necessarily results in a patterning of all the officer's subsequent actions is another matter. All that the emphasis on work-based culture implies is that priority is given to influences arising from the work setting rather than officer biography. Further, decisions made on individual grounds, those divergent from the occupational culture, are necessarily less visible; they are likely to be taken when the officer is alone. It is relatively easy to document the influence of others on an individual's action but perhaps only from reflexive eye-witness accounts, like those by police turned researchers, that we get a sense of the individual standing against the prevailing norms of the occupational reference group.

These essays are also a source of information on the rehearsal prior to joining the culture of the applicant's imputations regarding the police value system. In these essays, or properly notes, which appear as part of the candidate's application form, one perceives a version of the neophyte's idea of the police organization at its broadest. As discussion of anticipatory socialization suggests, applicants are not quite total outsiders. Some have police-relevant experience or police acquaintances. The range of reasons for joining will first be reviewed and then the images of policing they represent. These may be compared to the reasons given by cadets in Hopper's (1977) American study. Many of them said they liked being outdoors and driving around; a second reason was that police 'do different things every day' and a third was the cadet's yearning for excitement. A fourth reason was wanting to help people, a fifth was job security, and the sixth was that the cadet had held a similar job before and enjoyed it (Hopper 1977: 154–5). Hopper found both those with law enforcement experience and those without equally likely to cite liking to be outdoors and driving around, excitement and variety, and job security. However, those without a background in law enforcement were far more likely to say they wanted to help people.

A total of eighty essays were available. It was noticeable that virtually all the 'reasons' for seeking a police career which arose in the interviews were also offered here; the principal difference was in the emphasis given to particular reasons. It will not surprise those accustomed to conducting admissions or job interviews that the more selfless 'reasons', such as an urge to help people, considerably exceeded the citation of instrumental reasons, like job security and pay, whereas by the time of the initial interview, having been accepted to the force, the balance was redressing itself. The essays represent a strategy by which individuals orient themselves to what they think the police interviewers want to hear. Indeed, even the rather scarce references to job security balance the instrumental image of self by allusion to more 'worthy' goals. Thus, 'I want a varied working life, a secure future, and a job which is useful to the community. The police force also offers job satisfaction and good promotion prospects' (Interview Aid Form

2–9) (IAF). Promotion chances exceeded mention of job security (and certainly pay) as an instrumental attraction thought reasonable to mention, suggesting that keenness and ambition are seen as characteristics recruiters will favour. 'I would like a career which will enable me to work with responsibility, people, and a job which has plenty of promotion chances if you're willing to work hard' (IAF 2–18). More forceful still is the assertion that 'the reason I would like to be a police officer is that I would like to be somebody in this world. The police force gives me excellent prospects for promotion whilst being a very worthwhile occupation' (IAF 2–21). While these reasons seek to present a particular image of the applicant, a large class of others address the applicant's conception of police work. Interestingly, relatively few refer to crime fighting, and even these emphasize either co-operative notions of crime control, such as 'explaining' the law to those uncertain they have committed an offence, or the suggestion that, by the applicants leading an exemplary life, a good model will be held up to those tempted by crime.

Unique, characteristic aspects of the occupation are seen as pertaining to the location of the work – the street and not the station – outside the normal context of work in offices and factories, and the pattern of time on duty, outside business hours. 'I also like working shifts as I consider myself to be better in the afternoon and night. Police work is a job of dedication and commitment, with shiftwork, being on call' (IAF 2–6). Keenness on the shift system is explained by a PC with seven years' service, linking shifts with 'variety'. 'I quite enjoy shift work. . . . The variation between the day shift and the night shift is tremendous. It's the variety that keeps you going' (83: 3,1). The most popular reason cited by recruits was variety. 'The varied duties and responsibilities of a police officer appear attractive compared to the limited content of most posts in industry and government' (IAF 1–21). This was expressed in contrast to more conventional occupations: 'serving as a police officer appeals to me because of the variation of different duties one has throughout the week. I would not enjoy a job where I knew what was going to happen every day' (IAF 2–2). A particular attraction to ex-service people was what some referred to as 'uniformed service'. This differs from expressions of a sense of duty and service; it specifically addresses the satisfaction experienced in being part of a 'disciplined' body, as in this charming combination of two police-relevant meanings of the term. 'I would like to become a member of a disciplinary force having left the Army' (IAF 1–15). They presume that some will have qualms about uniforms, which they have overcome. 'I have a lot to offer the service and the community. I have ten years experience in the army to draw upon and I am used to the discipline and wearing of uniform' (IAF 2–7). One instructor saw 'liking to carry a uniform' as the prime reason for joining, contrasting this and public service motives. 'I don't go along with what everyone puts down that they want to help society and maintain law and order. Basically what attracts a man is the image of seeing himself in uniform' (81: 4,1). However, it is more usual to encounter individuals whom family responsibilities oblige to seek similar but more static work. 'At present I'm serving in the Royal Navy as a Leading Regulator, which is Naval Police work. My family is restricted . . . I want to carry on in a uniformed service. The police is the ideal second career for me' (IAF 2–24).

Apart from uniform, another obvious aspect of police work to which applicants rehearse their orientation is the outdoor life (IAF 1–26). Applicants often equate 'outdoor' with 'exciting'. 'I would like to be a police officer exactly because I get the impression that, as a career, it is exciting, challenging, and very much an outdoor job' (IAF 2–13). The idea of 'excitement' is generally drawn in contrast to other work. 'I want to be a police officer because I feel I need a challenge in life. I feel at the moment I'm in a rut that I want to get out of' (IAF 2–10). The same idea is more pungently expressed in the assertion that 'I am fed up with being a nine-to-five commuter, of having little responsibility, of doing a job that I could do blindfolded standing on my head. I want variety and fresh air, a challenge, a chance to use some initiative, and even some excitement' (IAF 2–25). That catalogue aptly summarizes the 'reasons' which represent prospective notions of the nature of police work. Only two mentioned kin in the police, which the interviews indicate has considerable salience. 'As my father was an officer in the police force I have been bought (sic) up to respect the police, and now feel that I would like to become a part of the force' (IAF 1–19).

Ideas concerning a sense of duty, wishing to be of service to the community, helping people and working with people were the class of reasons most used by applicants. It should be clear enough why making such claims about the self is seen as naming a desirable quality. It may be seen as addressing a quality of the police the organization most wants to put over, and does so through such public relations occasions as school and careers office visits. Some allusions to being of service were more assertive, telling the police what they should be doing is helping people (implying 'rather than just enforcing the law'). At its simplest this class of reasons takes the form of an expressed preference for 'working with people'. Thus, '(i)n the police force I see myself working with and helping people, to help themselves' (IAF 1–1) or 'I want to become a police officer because I like meeting and helping people and like being of service to the community' (IAF 2–1). In these expressions there is an air of naiveté. It seems not to occur to these applicants that one way police 'help' the community is to prosecute its members. But a hint that an awareness of this nasty aspect of the work exists may be discerned in remarks like this, by the same respondent, 'I would make a good police officer because I understand people's problems and am not easily taken in by either friends or people I don't know' (IAF 2–1). Even here the applicant cannot quite mention crime, but broaches the hint by way of her empathetic qualities.

The more elaborate version of this reason involves allusions to the applicant's sense of duty or desire to serve the community. This may make clear that the sense of duty is predicated on an exchange relation where status and respect compensate the officer. 'The main (reasons) are that the police force plays a very vital role in the community and it gains a lot of respect from the community. . . . By joining the police I will perform my duty to the community to the best I can' (IAF 1–15). An intriguing development of this equation of duty and respect occurs where applicants proffer themselves as exemplars of good behaviour and therefore good influences on others whom the police would wish to enlist.

> I see myself helping the community by leadership, gaining the respect of children by setting a good example so that they can base their lives on this example. I firmly believe that policing means more than just arresting a person and placing him in jail, these persons should be given as much help by the police officer when he has done his punishment so as to enable them to become a useful part of the community again.　　　　　　　　　　　　　　　　　　　　　　　　(IAF 2–7)

This was one of the few explicit allusions to crime control and it is noteworthy that it was still couched in terms more redolent of counselling than control. The combination of a good example and a helpful adviser was a consistent component of the duty-to-community reasons.

> As a police officer I see myself as a friendly face to people of a certain locality, someone they can approach if they are having troubles and someone that they can speak to if they think that someone has done wrong, especially if they are not sure that it is an offence.
> 　　　　　　　　　　　　　　　　　　　　　　　　　　　　(IAF 2–9)

This does not imply that being an exemplar of decency is necessarily linked with a community service emphasis. It may be linked to a crime-fighting orientation: 'I see myself being an example of behaviour to the public as a police officer and ideally to assist with the prevention of crime and if necessary the detection of it' (IAF 2–12) or even 'I want to help people in trouble, uphold the law, and Prevent Crime' (IAF 2–5). The idea of helping the community by fighting crime – 'As a police officer

I would be helping to create a trouble-free society in which we could all live' (IAF 2–4) – even invokes speculation on the cause of crime. 'We need a very strong police force in this changing period where there is a lot more spare time for people which seems to be increasing the crime rate' (IAF 2–24). However, the predominant emphasis in this class of reasons suggests that, as this thoughtful 'essay' suggests, most recruits see themselves controlling crime by skills of negotiation and communication.

> Today's modern police officer is no longer looked on as the 'village bobby', he is a skilled man in a very demanding job. He must be able to act and communicate with people in all walks of life from the industrial manager to the perpetual drunk. The reason I want to be a police officer is that I possess many of the qualities that go into making the good officer. Prior to my present job I was training to be a retail manager which demanded close contact with the customer. In many occasions I was able to turn an irate customer into a satisfied one, by carefully chosen words.   (IAF 1–18)

A clear implication of these essays is that successful prospective police recruits regard the occupation, or think that the organization wishes to be regarded, as one oriented more to social service than to crime control. This may be a realistic prospective orientation in light of the substantial component of social service in routine policing, but it is also an allusion to an orientation which, by all accounts, is devalued in the occupational culture.

In addition to asking why the applicant wished to become a police officer the interview aid form asks what applicants see themselves doing as police officers. Often they took this opportunity to indicate preference for specialist duty: 'as a police officer I would be very interested in a special branch such as working with dogs or the CID' (a chastening equation). Some accounts diverge from beat work altogether. 'I would like to be involved with the technical aspects of crime prevention and detection. Whilst I may not be qualified for the forensics department I would be interested to work hand in hand with them' (IAF 2–21). Again there is an emphasis on communication skills. 'I feel I can get on well with people. Working with the county council I got to know a lot of people from all walks of life . . . I am quite a sociable person because I have had no complaints about my Nature and Behaviour '(IAF 1–14). One whose father was a constable wrote, 'I see the role of a police officer as mainly being a law enforcer, but also I think it is important that at the same time an officer should be able to build an understanding with the people of the community in which he works' (IAF 1–19). Some have work experience enabling them to specify what aspect of police work compels their interest. 'I should like to be employed on investigative duties. I have already had some experience of this type of work and I have found that it gives me the kind of job satisfaction I'm looking for' (IAF 1–26). A former cadet referred to the need to get on with colleagues: 'I also enjoy working with other people and find it easy to mix in groups; I like working in a team but I can get on well by myself if I have to' (IAF 2–2). A co-operative spirit must be tempered by qualities of self-reliance, and some applicants stress their dominance quite firmly: 'I have good discipline, I can take charge of most situations that may arise' (IAF 2–3). Few allude to danger but one made reference to it in the context of mastery: 'You need to keep calm and be aware of the danger. I see myself in the police force fighting crime' (IAF 2–16). Another answered the question of what he saw himself doing tersely, 'dealing with the unexpected' (IAF 2–24).

None of these responses are flights of fancy, but they are partial. This is not just because few applicants seem much inclined to practise creative writing (most of the quotations represent the candidate's answer in its entirety) but also reflects the incomplete knowledge they have on which to base an image of the police. However, some applicants, equally terse, did offer a realistic image of the PC's work. One quaint but accurate perception was, 'I see myself as a visual deterrent against petty crimes' (IAF 3–6), which nicely balanced the crime-busting replies. Another apt response was, 'during my initial training and first 6–18 months I would imagine the work I would be doing would be very basic, such as station work, and I would be put on the beat' (IAF 2–6). One whose response earnt a large tick on the application form wrote simply, 'I see myself patrolling by foot or otherwise, enforcing law and order' (IAF 3–9) which was elaborated by another to, 'I can see myself dealing with drunks, answering peoples queries, dealing with football crowds' (IAF 3–7). This last reply illustrates how applicants may marshall their limited experience or observations of police practice.

Some officers conducting selection interviews have thorough analyses of the interview situation available from in-service training. Supporting documents review the purpose of written papers, analyse 'personality and the interview situation' and problems to avoid.

> He will have hopes and fears, have formed attitudes, beliefs and feelings, and acquired habits and mannerisms. His speech – through accent, dialect and vocabulary – and his physical appearance and demeanour will create a facade which may reflect accurately, or exaggerate or hide his true personality.   (Bramshill: 30)

Care is taken to urge the need for 'objective' appraisal and interviewers are warned against being deceived by the candidate's anxiety, their own intuition, or the 'self image or halo effect'. Advised that 'the interview is not an interrogation', interviewers are told to seek 'contact, content and control'. Interview types are explained, including the 'stress' type, where contrived misunderstandings are used to 'probe the candidate's demeanour'. Caution is recommended and attention given to achieving rapport and avoiding ambiguous wording. The 'link question' is discussed as a means to develop fresh enquiries from information revealed. The example chosen is intriguing:

> *Interviewer*: 'The description of your work with the Afrikaan Mining Co. in Cape Town sounds interesting. How did the policy of Apartheid affect the employment position in an English-owned firm?' This provides the candidate with a chance really to show his knowledge on things like personnel problems in a multi-racial situation, management techniques and perhaps an indication of his own attitude on the question of racial discrimination. (Bramshill: 32)

Guidance also dwells on selection criteria with a statement on the 'normal distribution curve' advising that the 'average man' is found in the 'broad middle stream of 40%' of the population (Bramshill: 33). Assessment is scaled using Munro Fraser's Five Point Plan, which covers Impact (dress, appearance, manner, speech, and health); Qualifications and Experience; Brains and Abilities (innate aptitudes); Adjustment and Stability ('attitudes towards discipline, unpleasant conditions, frustration, and disappointment'); and Motivation (drive, determination, and decisiveness).

Availability of such advice to selected officers does not mean interviews always proceed systematically. The very limited research on recruit selections certainly suggests deviations. During our research, recruit interviews were conducted by the chief superintendent in charge of the TE, an assistant chief from HQ and a local divisional commander, the latter as a 'practice' representative to meet complaints that training was beyond the influence of the field. These interviews, which we were not able to observe, were described as being quite demanding if necessary. The chief superintendent said some candidates could be assessed after ten minutes. They would look closer at someone with a lot of background, such as a graduate, since the need to check if they could do the intellectual work could be discounted; this would be more thoroughly explored with ex-military applicants. The extra time with graduates examined motivation. Ten of the nineteen graduate applicants in 1979 were rejected. Several had apparently quite clearly been 'perfect little Hitlers' intent on power – 'I wouldn't touch them with a disinfected barge pole' – and all three interviewers independently picked this up. Another candidate 'who in a sense had everything going for him' –

public school, Oxford, 'good sportsman, into rugby' – wanted to dictate where he could work. It had to be where his wife, a GP, had her practice. The panel thought he would want to tell them how to do their job (field-notes, 7.7.80).

The example of the 'link question' on apartheid appeared to have registered with the panel. As an instance of adroit interviewing techniques, mention was made of white South African and Zimbabwean applicants they had recently seen. The panel questioned them very closely on race. One interviewer said the South African government was based on white racial supremacy and asked for the candidate's views on race. The candidate said he had left South Africa for that reason, to which the interviewer responded by asking why it had taken him so long. He was also asked what would happen if he had to police a coloured area with his 'South African views'. An interviewer pressed him, reportedly stating, 'You're just on a coward's run. You'll be here for a few months and you'll just join the National Front. You have to police West Indians, Asians, they're all British citizens, all equal before the law'. Not all these applicants were accepted (field notes, 7.7.80).

As well as the interview aid forms, selection panels review character references, the results of a medical examination, an educational test, and a check on Special Branch records, and take cognizance of the applicant's domestic situation, deemed particularly important in the case of married women. But in terms of the applicants' understanding of the work they know less about candidates than do, for example, admissions panels for entry to social work training (where prior social work experience is required). The interviews themselves do not seem to improve this (Hanley 1979). They assume, as do recruits, that policing's unique character can only be learnt after entry. One would not expect applicants to possess an elaborate image of policing. What is revealing about the essays is their indication of the range of permissible reasons for seeking a police career, and the concentration of these reasons on notions of duty, social service, public relations, and advice at the expense of crime control. In many ways these assumptions are more realistic than those the occupational culture so vigorously asserts.

Prior life-styles

The recruits' allusions to their prior life-style were particularly oriented to membership of subcultural groups such as 'skinheads', military experience, and unemployment. One of the interviewees who had been a skinhead drew on the experience in arguing that, despite cultural differences, he felt he could get on with blacks.

'I've never had trouble. When I was in Northampton you get a bit of trouble with them, but I reckon it's the same with anybody. . . . It's the same with skinheads when that was a craze. I mean I was a skinhead. We used to go round in a big bunch and used to get the greasers, they were the enemy.'   (4: 5, 3)

Another commented, 'I've got lots of young friends who like the life a bit' (5: 4, 1). But individuals may also be discerned seeking to place their episode of rebellion in a longer perspective, including their arrival in the police, so that former values are not seen as irrelevant but as a necessary stage now superseded.

'(L)ike everybody, you go through the stage that you rebel against everything and they (parents) see you progressing that way. They think 'goodness me' when you do say you've joined (the police), you go back to the beginning again . . . They have a narrow outlook and when you start rebelling against it they become a bit more detached and then, when you go back to that, they can't understand why.'
                                                          (1: 4, 2)

People change, as the recruit knows from his own experience, and can even run full circle in their affiliations. This is a pretty deflating point for attitude models which assume a simple linearity of belief (cause) and action (effect). Individuals who arrive in the police by this route have an appreciation of the values policing represents which requires them to select in some degree of self-consciousness those values they can abide. One must distinguish the values of police from the operating ideology of policing; this young man's values lie at the other extreme to recruits regarding policing from the perspective of military service. Yet both feel only those who have been in the police can know what policing is like.

Experience of unemployment represents a relatively novel route into policing. In the past, desirable employees gained work, and the police did not want those other employers deemed undesirable. Only people who wanted a police career regardless of pay and social drawbacks applied. During the period of the study unemployment forced the hand of many who would not in the past have considered a police career. The police recognized this by stiffening educational standards, and the unemployment situation heightened anxiety about the performance of those lucky enough to have been enlisted.

'I come from Chesterfield and the job situation there, to get a job in an office was very difficult. I kept going to the youth employment place and . . . I never ever got sent to any interviews because there were no vacancies and then I just thought I wanted something different with variety so I thought I'll join the (police) cadets.'   (4: 2, 1)

Asked what his friends thought of his choice of work another commented 'most of them were unemployed' (5: 4, 1).

Military experience provides a conventional route to the police. 'I wanted to leave the army . . . and being in the military police it was the obvious move to make' (2: 2, 1). So obvious a move, perhaps, that there has in the past been a pay-led circulation between the two occupations. One respondent knew people

> 'that have left the army and gone into the police force. Or people that have left the police force and come into the army. Obviously before the police had a pay rise, quite a lot of them went into the armed forces because it was better paid. Now the tables have turned.' (3: 2, 1)

Apparently the enforcement segments of the military particularly feed and are fed by civil police. A respondent whose childhood interest in the police was blocked on medical grounds worked in a magistrates office until joining the navy. 'When I went to . . . the police side of the navy and I worked . . . nearly two years on the drug squad, I decided . . . I've had my wanderings, it's time I settled down and I started thinking about trying for the police again' (4: 4, 1). The attractions of a policing career for the military were exploited in a recruiting drive during our research. In something of a coup they used the army's recruiting network to distribute a blurb on Derbyshire police to bases all over the world. A special weekend was put on for those interested, taking the line that 'Derbyshire take care of you'. The idea was that heavy recruiting of ex-soldiers, especially military police, would be good for the force image because the public would not just see 'a spotty faced young lad', but the co-operating colonel 'got a rocket' from his own authorities for distributing promotional materials (field notes, 10.1.80). This group also had a high wastage rate. A senior officer said the ex-naval recruits were the worst. The ratings were still 'treated like pigs' by naval officers and so were unused to exercising responsibility. Many got heavily into debt, others were used to the 'work hard at sea, when ashore get pissed' ethos, while others came with domestic problems (field notes 7.7.80). Ex-military recruits may well see in the police another disciplined, uniformed outdoor life but what is most significant is that recruits whose prior life-styles indicate quite different backgrounds emphasize the same aspects of the police career.

Prior contact with police

The concept of anticipatory socialization implies differences in the strength of influences and quality of information between the various reference groups. For its immediacy and early significance, contact with police as kin or close friend must have strong potential to influence the applicant's image of the occupation. However that influence may be negative, positive, or simply 'realism-enhancing'; the officer known may be embittered or an enthusiast. The extent of recruit prior contact with police is high. In the United States van Maanen (1974: 88) asserted 'virtually all recruitment occurs via generational or friendship networks involving on-line police officers and potential recruits'. One benefit, confirmed by interviews, is support which helps meet the stress of the long selection process. All the interviews drawn on here were conducted in the first week of training.

One strategy of the prospective recruit is to approach serving police for advice. The salience of such advisers is apparent in a female recruit's decision not to enter the military; she approached two policewomen about the choice.

> 'I really talked to (them) before I decided what I wanted to do. Because I really wanted to go in the armed forces but they said you'd have to wait till you're 21 for a commission because you'd get bored with being just a private . . .'   (1: 1, 1)

More typical was influence in the recruit's background. 'I knew a few policemen in the past and they made an impression on me' (1: 3, 1). He knew three 'quite well' through his parents, and his best friend, whose father was a policeman, joined the month after he did. Another recruit said of his chats with his policeman uncle 'that was one of the things that turned me most onto the police' (2: 1, 1). Salience of close kin is considerable for younger recruits. 'Me Dad knew some, who became friends of the family . . . It was them that prompted me to join the cadets' (5: 1, 1).

This avenue seems direct enough but one must be cautious. In the following, intensity and priority are there but salience turns out to be negative. First the respondent stressed the immediacy of his contact with the telling phrase 'I only had to say'. 'My father-in-law is a policeman, I know a lot of his friends, I come up and play badminton and meet a lot of them. You see, I only had to say' (1: 4, 1). This suggests he only had to express the merest interest and the process would begin, but in fact he ignored what they said because it was negative. 'A policeman like him and his friends, twenty-three years in the force. They said, "Don't join now." 'Cause it's changed that much. They're looking at the different attitudes the public have, and the amount of paperwork' (1: 4, 1–2). This is a particularly pertinent case because the actual reason given for his decision was that he wanted a job out of doors and the complaints by his police contacts were to do with public hostility and paperwork, directly contradicting the chief attraction cited. One might anticipate this man feeling particular resentment to the public and paperwork, and there is a hint of a rueful feeling in his remark that 'once you could get away without forms in quadruplicate. I think everybody wishes it was like that now. Well, I do' (1: 4, 2).

Circulation between police and military means the police the recruit knows are often people formerly known in the military. Acquaintances leave the armed forces, some enter the police and others follow their example (3: 1, 1). One who was originally in the police in 1960 and was then in RAF security knew others who had returned to a police career.

> 'A lot of my friends were in the Manchester police when I (originally) joined. One or two drifted away and then drifted back in again . . . I knew a lot of Ministry of Defence policemen. I applied for there and was turned down. But when I got in the Derbyshire police they all wished me the very best; they just couldn't understand why I didn't get in the MoD police.' (3: 4, 2)

Some recruits participated in a social network which included civil and military police.

> 'I was a supervisor in the military police. I knew what they were able to produce for me, quality of work-wise and personality-wise, but people that I went for a drink with, that I talked to and related to, were civil police officers, mainly CID.' (3: 5, 1)

This suggests an obvious channel of information about the police career; military and civil police co-operate, particularly in garrison towns. A former naval drug squad officer 'got to know people working on the drug squad in Hampshire and I obviously asked them "as a policeman, what do you think of it?"' (4: 4, 1). A similar process occurs with control-related civil occupations.

> 'As an investigator with an unemployment benefit office I met quite a few policemen through going to court on behalf of the department and in investigation and helping the police. Having talked to them, they seemed to enjoy it. With the present situation of the civil service, and the police force, obviously the latest pay rise was an important factor.' (5: 2, 1)

Another source was civilian police employees, in this case augmented by a cousin and brother-in-law in the force. 'What made me decide to do the police, I'd already worked up here as a civilian . . . in the housing department. As well as having two members of the family who told me about the job' (5: 4, 1).

While these prior contacts increased the likelihood of considering a police career they are not sufficient in themselves, so that a police career cannot simply be 'read off' from recruit biography. The recruits still approach the career tentatively, awaiting practice to determine the career's rightness for them. Then too it should be remembered that these are the people from these backgrounds who have in fact entered the police; others similarly influenced may have avoided the career. It may be that those people on whom the influence of police kin and friends is 'successful' may particularly draw this facet out of their biography. This points to the individual as the arbiter of career choice, and to the certainty that a negotiation of the influence of occupational cultures against the individual's own perceptions must take place during training and early experience. At the early stage of recruitment individuals are still quite certain that, whatever the influences, it is they who decide on the basis of the work itself. This is so even when biography seems to have its own inexorable dynamic. 'I joined the cadets first for a year to help make up my mind. Well, my father and his father were both in the police force. I suppose to a certain extent I wanted to follow in their footsteps . . . But I was thinking about the disadvantages' (6: 1, 1).

While these accounts gave an unanticipated bolster to van Maanen's finding on sources of recruitment they are not without negative references to the police. This reinforces the independence of recruit appraisals. This respondent both acknowledges his parents' influence and asserts his own need to have a basis for comparison. 'I thought about joining the police when I was 16 and my parents talked me out of it and said it was an unpleasant job, and I'm glad really because the way I've done it, I've seen some more before I've come in' (4: 3, 1). Having decided to join, another recruit allows his decision was still contingent in asserting that his conversation with a friend in the London police 'clinched' his decision. He also airs the interesting idea that citizens experience a certain dread of the police, a feeling whose expression signals his continuance in the transitional stage during training.

> 'Just before I was coming up to join I met a friend I hadn't seen for two years and he had been in the Metropolitan Police, and that clinched it, talking to him. He was saying, "It's a lot more heavy down there, there's a lot more work in London." I don't know any other policemen. They used to scare me.'   (4: 5, 1)

The esteem in which police are held can vary between kin, so that such influences are split. In this case, the recruit's maternal grandfather was a London policeman while his father was opposed.

> 'A lot of me Mum's side of the family were all for it because of that . . . They was always hoping that someone would do it. I weren't pushed into it or nothing. It came as a bit of a shock when I told them

I was thinking of joining. My dad . . . was proud when I was in the marines (but) . . . they said their attitude to the police is changed by knowing that I've actually come in. Same with me. You're sitting in a pub and they walk in and you feel uncomfortable. That's why it was good I've done a weekend course with the services, they (police) put on, to find out that the policemen are exactly the same as me and you.'

(4: 5, 2)

These reservations about being a member of an occupational group who make people such as oneself feel uncomfortable can conceivably be overcome, but the lingering distrust underlying it continues to be manifest in ideas expressed by some recruits that they could not carry out police work in areas where they have friends. This clearly bespeaks the divergence of the role they will be asked to take on and their conception of self derived from past biography and socialization. It is a strong indication that becoming a police officer has strong consequences for one's self-identity. One recognizes that the new identity created to cope with one's new occupation and status can always be catastrophically deflated by those who know one too well. Those who can recall one's childhood peccadilloes and delinquencies can cause a harrowing penetration of one's new guise; whatever their current status and however assertively one wears the uniform, their mocking cuts through to one's past self.

'I thought of doing it in Northampton, where I was born, but I've got so many friends there that I don't think I'd be able to do the job properly. Where I am now nobody knows me really and I don't know nobody . . . Also, if I ever see one of my mates he's bound to hurl abuse at me anyway. "Look at him standing over there like that."'

(4: 5, 1)

Such pressure is felt notoriously strongly by members of ethnic minorities.

'I've spoken to coloured lads who have said, "I'd love to be a policeman but I couldn't be a policeman in the area where I live." They . . . don't come in the police not because they don't want to but . . . out of fear that they would get cut off from their friends.'(4: 4, 4)

Those with police experience know that such fears are real; one way of coping is to withdraw from all but superficial contact outside work because, in a sense, citizens are the elements in one's work.

'I've been a military policeman for twelve years. There's a saying in Yorkshire, "Do nowt for owt, do it for yourself," and I've learned that it's very true. Nobody wants anything from anybody else unless they want it for a reason. The landlord buys you a drink in the pub and the next night you're telling him he is open after hours. You've got a very guarded way of life as a police officer.'   (3: 5, 1)

The social isolation remarked by many and evident in this response is being rehearsed in these demurrals from work in one's home area. Such feelings are long-lived and long-remembered. A PC with ten years' service spoke of the breakthrough into feeling comfortable with the job he experienced after a year's service due to getting 'to know a little circle of people in the profession' (83: 4, 2).

A final point may be made about anticipatory socialization. Reinforcement for the idea that neither police contact nor military experience nor any other prior influence significantly limit the recruits' resolution of their own version of the police role is provided by Bennett's (1984) finding that recruits with high anticipatory socialization scores did not increase their value similarity once they began working in the police environment. Pre-employment conceptions did not aid their accommodation to the role. Prior information may simply be misleading and, while influential initially, it is of waning importance once the recruit is confronted by the reality of the job itself.

Friends, kin and career

Part of that reality is the social isolation commonly experienced by police and which provides one of the principal underpinnings of the occupational culture. A good deal of information was collected on this, particularly from comments on the reactions of friends and relatives. Strong views were expressed by eighteen of the twenty-one recruits interviewed in their first week of training; the matter was much on their minds. Relatives were more positive than friends. One class of responses is that of the 'hardened trooper', stoically accepting a self-inflicted separation from the community which they see as dictated by the stance of suspicion required by the job. 'That's the only place I will have friends, within the force. Because every time I meet somebody in civvy street I must question their motives for relating to me' (3: 5, 1). In this stance the beleaguered officer gathers his true friends, his kin, around him in protective custody.

> 'I don't think that I've got a person that I can call a friend. There's nobody I need to question why I do anything. My father's as happy as a sandboy now. My wife's pleased that I'm happy and the children are proud. That's the people that matter to me.'   (3: 5, 1)

There is no doubt that many recruits were anxious about their friends' reactions and had their anxiety confirmed. This is one of the first points at which they had to begin renegotiating their sense of self-identity. The sense of self is built up in a continual process of interaction with others; changing the audience who 'receive' one's personality, or performance of it, requires a re-casting of the self. Times such as entry to a new occupation, particularly one in which incumbents virtually represent the state on the street corner, focus attention not only on all the business of learning new skills, language and collegiate relations but inward on what this is doing to one's self. Certain aspects of personality are selected from the welter of contradictory and shifting characteristics present in the self; one is inclined to be touchy and hungry for information about how one's shifting performance is being received. In this quotation not only is a 'reason' for his decision discovered within the respondent's personality – 'autocratic' – but he indicates the value he still places on his former friends and his (rather poignant) gratitude for those who did not openly reject him.

'Do you want a quotation? Somebody said, "You've always been a bastard and now you're going to get paid for it." It was light-hearted but I got a feeling that under it this was perhaps what policemen were. I've been accused of being autocratic in the past . . . Some people said, "We definitely need police, I couldn't do it but I'm glad you are." I was a senior NCO in the air force and in the crew room before I left people were saying, "Don't just disappear, come back and let us know what it's like," so I intend to do that.'   (4: 3, 2)

The question whether friends would be found mainly in the police or outside elicited a number of comments which confirm that the suspicious attitude the officer learns is reciprocated not just by citizens but by friends, and that this denial of routine confidences begins as soon as one decides to join.

'Most people get put off when they find you're a policewoman . . . I was at school for all those years with all the same people. They find you're going to be in the police force and they start watching what they're going to say. They won't admit this and they won't admit that. They're always ready to tell you they're going to get a new tax disc, they won't admit that they're not bothering like they used to.'(1: 1, 1)

The tone indicated the recruit experiences this as a betrayal; a limitation suddenly placed on a relationship where frankness was the norm signals the beginning of the separation of the officer from her normal community in a way as tangible as her new uniform. If she is to remain in the new and disbarring role she has to edit her acquaintance; she cannot continue to let such slights cause pain. She is led to a common response, dismissal of these former friends, and she does so with the idea that these are not the right people for a police constable to know, thus encouraging the hold of her new role. 'It does upset me a bit but then most wanted to keep in touch. But if they haven't done that then they're friends you didn't need in the first place' (1: 1, 1).

Others are less willing to let go, giving rise to a 'have it both ways' class of response which notes the social attractions of the new culture while perhaps naively expecting their friends to make allowances.

> 'You're working with policemen all the time so you're bound to make friends. Old friends probably all are a bit suspicious but you've just got to accept it. I could be with my best friend tonight and tomorrow I could nick him for something. I should hope that he'd take that into consideration. I'd just hope he knows it's because he's done wrong, and probably once I'd met him we'd be friends again.'   (1: 2, 1)

Of course, by 'taking the officer's job into consideration' the officer may be suggesting that his friends keep things from him, but as the readers of romantic novels know that is no basis for a relationship. Nevertheless it is very common for recruits to distinguish their 'real friends' from those who cannot tolerate their new job. 'It's not going to make any difference to me real friends. They know I'm still me' (1: 3, 1). Apart from its novelty, being in the police is an awkward status for many young men.

> 'I can't believe that I'm in really. But I don't think they'll treat me any differently, I mean they're not angels, but they're not trouble-causers. They like a good time like everyone, but my true mates, if they disappear, they're not really my friends.'   (5: 3, 1)

They also respond with the benefit of the doubt to derisive reactions. 'When I told them I'd got the job they (pause) didn't make any comments with malice in it, they made a few jokes really' (5: 3, 1). A further development of the unwanted friend idea has a sophisticated fail-safe mechanism built into it.

> 'It depends on the type of company you've kept before going into the police force. I feel that if you've kept that kind of company who wouldn't be friendly with you, you wouldn't have got into the police force in the first place.'   (5: 2, 2)

This novel idea suggests that in some way the all-seeing police force is able to weed out those whose friends would take it the wrong way.

Of course the issue is not a crisis for all recruits, particularly those whose life is more home-centred, and particularly ex-soldiers whose social life always centred on work. Family members generally seemed positive: 'It's a worthwhile job and they're proud of me' (2: 1, 1). That sense of pride may be sorely tried, however, as public reserve toward police is known to extend to their families. 'The wife wasn't too bothered because we have been in one or two unpleasant places (in the army); it's the same, you still get the insults' (2: 2, 1–2). Another was shaken by his workmates' reaction. 'They were amazed actually . . . at why I should want to leave, and since then a lot of them have never spoken to me . . . And the wife had trouble too' (3: 1, 1–2). Former soldiers are acutely aware of rank, and of their friends feeling that 'as being out of the senior rank in the army (they thought) I was going back down the bottom of the ladder again . . . They really cried down one of the chaps who went out as a policeman and thought he was a right nut case' (3: 1, 2).

Faced with the realization that joining the police means re-casting their life and sense of identity the recruits assume other recruits must in a fundamental way be the same as themselves. 'People who join will, I expect, have a similar frame of mind to myself' (4: 1, 1). Material circumstances reinforce this. 'The house I've moved into is a row of police houses so all the people I've immediately got to know up there are policemen' (4: 5, 1). Recruits begin to perceive an overlap of professional and sociable returns.

> I'm hoping that I don't find them completely within the police because I've noticed policemen I know think they don't have many friends. And my experience already has been that people are extremely friendly (in this area). . . . As long as you don't put up barriers the better feeling there is between the public and the police and not only that, the better you can do your job.' (4: 3, 1)

The officer has discerned an instrumental reason for seeking friendship.

Isolation is a real cost. The impact of personal change is apparent in wistful comments about youthful friends.

> 'I've got lots of young friends who like the life a bit and really I've got to forget them. . . . The police, I suppose I'll have to adapt myself to a lot of police friends, which I don't really mind. My friends outside the police, I'll probably get on with them without a me and them sort of thing. . . . Most of them were unemployed, the rest were labourers, builders, plumbers, they thought it was something else.' (5: 4, 1)

In a rather dazed fashion the recruit tries to get used to his new status. Others acknowledge the organization's interest in their social life. 'It may have an effect on where you go in your own time, which is one of the disadvantages . . . and socially it may give me limitations to the people I mix with' (6: 1, 1).

After a year's training and service the same sub-samples were re-interviewed; as might be expected the concentration of social life around work had now taken hold. For some the police were providing what they deemed affable colleagues and a stable social life, drawn mainly from officers on the same shift. 'You tend to go about with your people off your shift, because you finish at the same time. You get to know them. If he's married like you, then you get invited out for a meal' (6: 1, 2). Being on the same shift is not just a source of friends because of the hours but also identity of experience, the building up of a stock of events in common.

Problems over friendship included social isolates in the station. 'We don't talk to everybody, we stay with about our normal five, we go out together at night-time, just us five, because some of them, they just don't seem to want to have anybody else with them, they like to be left alone' (6: 1, 4–5). Those who report they still have their former friends admit they see them only rarely.

> 'I've still got all my friends who I had before I joined the force but, shift work again, I hardly ever see them now. I hardly ever see my mother, I'm hardly ever at home, and you get no chance to see your old friends. We all go out from work for a drink after . . . These are things people would want to think about when considering the police as a career.'   (10: 1, 1–2)

For locals there is compensation in beat work.

> 'I've found I've lost a lot of friends since I've been in the police force. . . . They seem to distrust you. Then I've also found I've gained a lot of friends that I knew from the old days, when I was at school. . . . I've walked around in the streets and I've re-met these people years later.'   (11: 1, 2)

For the young single recruit parents are also important. 'It's taken me away from my family; I've moved into digs. You miss out quite a lot on the social life; you finish at half past ten at night and you don't have any chance to see anybody, if you've got a girl friend, and on nights of course' (11: 1, 2). While the police can help some employees, for example a young woman PC stationed near her parental home because her mother was ill, other cases provide a sharp contrast. 'They've posted me to a strange town, so all my friends are in the police. I don't know many other people' (8: 3, 1).

That this may support an occupational culture which helps officers in other ways is not the only reason a police-centred social life is welcomed by some officers. Ambitious officers may deliberately limit their social life to advance themselves. One cannot simply dismiss the isolated as 'isolates'. A recruit was earlier noted who declared he had no friends, was self-sufficient, though affable. After a year his stance had become a strategy. Getting too friendly could endanger his career by being beholden to others to help theirs.

'I known I'm a strange man but I have no friends. . . . I've got my world inside my house and people that I pass the time of day with, but no friends. . . . Although I've got . . . an outgoing personality . . . I don't go out of my way to get on with people. . . . When I'm down here two prisoners escaped at C and . . . one of my mates (there) is in the crap, and if it's a really close friend you might just find yourself wondering how you can help him out. Whereas if you haven't formed that deep a relationship you haven't got that problem. I know it's avoiding relationships but I've got a very good relationship with my wife.'   (9: 1, 3)

He was seeking to regain the status he had as an army sergeant by keeping his contacts 'professional'. It was a temporary reward-led strategy.

'These two years are very intense. Once I've got the job cracked, or I decide that I'm giving up in the promotion stakes and I'll become a rather obese village bobby who hasn't got a lot to think about except keeping in with the governors and everybody else gets a clip in the ear and told to go home, I might start looking for friendships. But at the moment I haven't got time for it. It would be an inconvenience quite honestly.'   (9:1, 3)

Police work involves frequent changes in postings, shifts and accommodation. This heightens one's reliance on the police for a social life. When one hears that 'we all seem to stick together . . . and work together and play together' (12: 2, 1) one must reflect on why this apparently inoffensive and normal drawing on work for social life has been regarded as a problem. The argument is that the police are turned inward on their own company, with their own mores, becoming remote from the customs and mores of the community they police.

Job security, job satisfaction and status

It was noted that idealistic reasons featured in early attractions of the job. But policing has also been an ill-paid occupation, whatever its current favour, and the study was conducted during worsening unemployment and recession. Under these conditions and with this background no one is safe, and this formed a theme of rising emphasis in the data. Five questions relevant to instrumentalism were put to our sample (see Appendix III). At induction, 34 per cent did not agree to any of the instrumental views, 30 per cent agreed to one and 34 per cent agreed to two. By year one, 20 per cent agreed with none, 34 per cent with one, 25 per cent with two and 15 per cent with three. At year two, only 14 per cent agreed with none, 36 per cent with one, 44 per cent with two, 4 per cent with three and 3 per cent with four. Instrumentalism plainly grows in importance over time.

The ex-soldiers' choice of civilian career is especially constrained by material circumstances. Few own their own homes: 'Being in an army house all the time, this was the only job I could really take' (1: 2, 1). They are not the only ones with an eye to the future. As councils increasingly 'privatize' refuse collection not even dustmen can count on secure employment. 'I was a dustman before this and I enjoyed that for two years, but there's no future in being a dustman. No security, that was one of the main points' (1: 4, 1). A police career also offers prospects for re-training: 'For someone of my age it was a great opportunity to start a new career. I couldn't start in a job at 27 on the salary that I started on, or even get in as a trainee' (10: 2, 1). Some put a money value on job security. 'Probably at 23 years old you're not aware that job security is worth an extra £2000 a year so you just have a normal labouring job where you can get sacked anytime' (5: 2, 1). These respondents were clearly becoming more mindful that you've-never-had-it-so-good was finally giving way to you-may-never-have-it-again. 'If you had asked me twelve months ago I would say nothing (about job security). I wouldn't rate it at all. However, with the upsurge of insecurity I rate it reasonably highly' (11: 2, 1).

Under the Conservative government of 1979 police pay improved dramatically, sustaining 'special case' increases that looked particularly favourable to public sector workers. Yet there was a strong consciousness of the meanness of the past.

> 'There's a bloke on the course now, he did three years and packed it up because the pay was about £18 a week in the sixties. . . . Now he's coming back again. That shows that the money's a bit of a factor. The nurses have proved it, people like that.' (1:4, 3–4)

The allusion is to the reluctance to strike of workers in 'sensitive' occupations, and how it breaks down in recession. Another respondent had gone through this process. 'I was in the police originally in 1959–60. I enjoyed the job but the pay was very bad so I went back in the forces. . . . Money, it's not everything but for £25 a week . . . the pay overrules the job satisfaction' (3: 4, 1).

Some made their decision look decidedly pay-led.

> 'Obviously the latest pay rise was an important factor. It increases my pay by £40 a week. I'm a strong believer that we all want to work for

money. I think that's 85 per cent of the reason why we work. It (joining) was for personal gain. With the government cutbacks I couldn't see myself getting a promotion . . . and the civil service pay, I couldn't afford to live on it, what with being married just over a year.'

(5: 2, 1)

It must have been a galling situation for a dole fraud investigator. A direct trade-off was often noted between high pay and the job's demands.

'There is a good reason for paying us a good wage to keep us satisfied, to keep us happy in what we are doing. It is sometimes an obnoxious job and it can get a little bit dangerous, and I'm a firm believer in paying the wages for the job.' (11: 2, 1)

This was elaborated in a final response. Seeking to explain why a second pay rise was made within a year of joining,

'I've spoken to senior officers and I think there's a different reason (to keeping the pay ahead of inflation) . . . We're being prepared for something, liked the armed forces. Probably the winter of discontent didn't happen like they was expecting it to. So they paid us for what probably they were expecting to pay for. It might come this winter. We don't know.' (12: 3, 1–2)

This foreboding (and accurate) analysis would not be possible within the simple confines of an unalloyed duty/service ideology. It represents an instrumental orientation the police management increasingly encounter and which the strength of the occupational culture may harbour as effectively as the more adaptive mechanisms which help people cope with police work.

Good pay was seen as one of the three most important factors in job choice by 60 per cent initially, increasing to 64 per cent after two years. There are interesting rank variations in pay. Above the rank of sergeant effective pay (taking into account travel time, loss of overtime pay and increased hours) can be reduced by promotion. This suggests that the incentive for seeking advancement is as much status as pay related. Analysis of motivation in joining the police has often emphasized the importance of status mobility (Box 1981). This perspective is well known to officers; a chief superintendent stressed the importance of status rise in entering the police, describing it as a job for working-class people. Raised in a Yorkshire mining village, his father was a railwayman and his mother was from a mining family (field notes, 26.9.80). Based on father's occupation when known, 19 per cent of our recruits came from a middle-class and 56 per cent from a working-class background.

Policing has an appeal as a worthwhile occupation, even when the person has done highly skilled manual work.

> 'I was going to take up police work when I left school at 15 but when I applied they encouraged me to a trade first, give me the background of people and life. . . . The money was about the same figure. So for job satisfaction it wasn't worth sticking with the old job.' (3: 1, 1)

As well as duty and service the chief allusions by ex-soldiers are to varied, outdoor work and to 'industrial relations'; many felt more comfortable in a non-unionized occupation.

> 'Job satisfaction and being in the services for twenty-two years, I got a job in a warehouse, thinking I wanted a complete change. It didn't suit me, working indoors and also . . . I couldn't take being told what to do by the unions. . . . It was good pay, hours were good but as far as job satisfaction went it was rock bottom.' (3: 2, 1)

In choosing a police career 63 per cent put interest and variety as their first choice, 27 per cent picked sense of performing a public service. Good pay was first choice for 7 per cent, while good workmates was most important for only 3 per cent. After a year there was only a slight increase in those picking good pay as first choice (10 per cent) and a small decline in those picking public service (22 per cent). Similarly, at year two there was no appreciable change in the overall first choice distribution.

Reduced income particularly affected ex-soldiers. Pay is clearly placed lower than intrinsic sources of job satisfaction here because the recruit wanted work with variety and sporting activities. 'I took a drop in wages. I was a sergeant in the army . . . The pay isn't really all that important. It's just satisfaction in the job I'll be doing' (1: 2, 1). One of the respondents whose choice of careers out of the military was constrained, he might in any case belittle the importance of pay.

> 'It was a big step. I didn't know you could fail on the interview and I thought, I come out of the army after nine years, and if I get turned down I've had it. The only thing to do is to sign back on 'cause really I could not do anything else.' (1: 2, 2)

Many ex-soldiers were highly sensitive to rank. 'When I had an interview in Germany . . . there were people of different ranks up to majors. . . . They didn't want to give up the rank. You're throwing a hell of a lot of rank away, after twenty years of telling someone what to do' (1: 2, 3). Faced with these points about pay and rank the chief virtue of the police for ex-soldiers is that it is a career with some similarities to the military based in England. 'Job security was (a factor) plus housing. Pay didn't really come into it, because I've taken a drop now and I applied last year when it was even lower' (2: 2, 1). Some 41 per cent of the recruit sample had a military background.

After the first year's service a more reasoned and realistic assessment of other important factors like autonomy and job security was possible. 'You're your own boss when you're outside, as opposed to being constantly under supervision. You can make your own decisions. . . . You're meeting different people and doing different jobs all the time' (8: 1, 1). On joining the respondent had put prime stress on a job with variety and on a sense of worthwhile service; he now stressed security.

> 'It (job security) is important, especially in today's age, no job in industry is safe, whereas in the police after you've done your two years, your job's fairly safe unless you do something stupid. I would say that it probably is more important than the pay.'   (8: 1, 1)

Others who felt the importance of job security displayed discomfort in occupying probationer status.

> 'Obviously job security has (changed in importance) because of the present situation with jobs. Being so much more difficult to come by you obviously have to put a lot more into your work to look after your job. . . . At the present time it was job security that was more important than money.'   (8: 2, 1)

Doubts about job security appear intense even for those defining their satisfactions as intrinsic rather than instrumental. One who specifically said job security and pay were less important than that 'it's a way of life and you get a great deal of satisfaction to deal with crime' said,

> 'You've got to have security to be able to do your job because the majority of any police force is made up of men and women in the first two years, and sitting in the parade room they're all consciously sweating and letting everybody know that they are worried about their job. When men are worried to that degree their motivation and their course of action is mainly impaired.'   (9: 1, 1)

Policing is work which requires identity change. 'The day the new recruit walks through the doors of the police academy he leaves society behind to enter a profession that does more than give him a job, it defines who he is' (Ahern 1972: 3). Having invested in such change, having withdrawn from certain relationships and activities, one may well be most concerned that the new self be nurtured rather than having to start again. The sophistication of the recruit's comment on sweating in the parade room is his use of the police manager's value system, to make a critique of police personnel policy. This can lead to the officer doing or not doing things in the interest of his maintaining a good employee image rather than in the interests of justice, he concluded.

These materials have enabled a determination of the several sorts of reasons thought to offer plausible accounts of the attractions and demerits of police work. Our data gave information on the range of qualities applicants and first year officers respond to and which they offer to outsiders, and an impression of the focal concerns applied to the job. The reasons are not highly disparate, mixing instrumental and idealistic reasons, and showing a trend to cite, if not emphasize, instrumental over idealistic reasons with increasing experience. The trend to instrumental over idealistic reasons is borne out by attitude shift measures, as is the increase in ideas attributable to the occupational culture. An element in this is the lead given by more experienced officers.

The responses of training school instructors, both concerning recruits' and their own motivations, matched those of recruits. They were particularly inclined to stress the preference for active work as opposed to 'sitting behind a desk' (81: 1, 1) and thought the ex-soldiers were most likely to cite instrumental motives and to have few qualifications for other work.

> 'I was equipped to navigate a ship anywhere in the world by naval college. After that I had no trade and . . . no qualifications. . . . I saw a lot of my contemporaries going away for considerable lengths of time, and I thought . . . "I've got to make a break" . . . I am someone who seeks security in employment and I wanted something which would offer me a chance to progress.'   (81: 5, 1)

Pay was poor but there were rewards for long service, an immediate house and 'security was my factor'. Younger recruits were seen as most likely to take an idealistic stance: 'they might think, "Oh, I'd like to uphold law and order and I like the sound of the good guys"' (81: 2, 1); whereas security would be important to older recruits: 'to put it bluntly, provided you keep your nose clean you've got a job' (81: 2, 1).

Images of the job

Danger and excitement comprise a major set of ideas used to exemplify police work, and distinguish it from other work. In such statements novices express in condensed form the particular character of police work as they perceive it. Danger and excitement are interwoven in stories which define differences to other work. The constable's attitude to danger is not just of a threat to personal safety, as a miner might have to the pit. Danger is a source of excitement, and the successful resolution of dangerous situations holds high salience in the officer's role concept. Further, it is a big part of the officer's distinction between themselves and the public.

'The danger inherent in police work is part of the centripetal force pulling patrolmen together as well as contributing to their role as strangers to the general public. . . . The risks of policing also provide real psychological satisfaction to men who spend most of their time performing activities of the more mundane or routine variety.'

(van Maanen 1974: 102)

There is a further dimension to the officer's refined conception of excitement and danger. The forms of 'easing behaviour' are well known, but less so is 'making work', converting boredom to excitement by generating one's own activity. Car stops on the pretext of faulty lights are one such means; their concern with lights is secondary to their hope to discover a more serious offence. 'Chasing cars is a means of punctuating the boredom; it exercises the skill and judgement of the driver and serves to remind the officer that he is really working' (Norris 1983: 58). In this way excitement becomes not only an integral source of job satisfaction but one which is somewhat within the control of the officer. 'When policing seems slow and dull and there is little action on the ground, stories stressing speed and action serve to remind officers of what they believe policing is really like' (Holdaway 1983: 56). As stories they can be elaborated and embellished, but all celebrate police action in an arena open to any motorist. Indeed, the 'rat-race' or road duel is a commonplace activity for aggressive drivers, but police need an excuse to engage in them.

The same applies to physical action.

'Many potentially dangerous situations in which officers can be involved in a fight have their hedonistic aspect. The very masculine character of police work, emphasizing aggression and bravado, combines with the generally hedonistic perspective of the lower ranks to magnify the importance (almost the pleasure) of fights.'

(Holdaway 1983: 130–1)

Holdaway describes officers racing down the stairs from the canteen 'shouting as if they are playing cowboys' when a call to a club for young blacks is received, and when car chases which end in the use of force are described 'excitement, action and fun are fundamental to the telling' (p. 131). Such scenes cannot be lost on probationers, providing an early lesson why training school 'isn't any use'. Again, the excitement officers experience in such cases is self-generated, largely within their own control. Elements of risky situations having potential for 'fun' are played on, even while sensible fear is experienced at the danger. Cain (1973: 72) notes that constables fall back on crime work as their defining task because it legitimates their work. The benefits are clear enough but so is the fact that beat PCs simply do not have much crime work; consequently 'the feeling that something in police work had eluded them was compensated for by action'.

Of course this particular, complex approach to danger is not present in the early stages; it must be nurtured and sustained by the model of those more experienced. That taking on a sophisticated conception of danger involves a process of learning that impinges on self-identity is most evident in statements suggesting a contrast in what significant others attached to one's old self make of the new role.

> 'My mother . . . thought I was in a job where I was likely to get thumped round the ear, which is true. My mother never ever thinks of her offspring as ever being able to stand on their own two feet. My wife was quite happy. But every now and then she has her doubts . . . because you've only got to pick up a newspaper to see the gun offences in this area.'   (4: 3, 2)

The recruit's response to a question about job security related it to personal safety.

> 'The security is quite important, but there's no fantastic security with this job for a start. You could be out of a job because you're injured very quickly, with very little to cover your expenses, so it's got less security than the air force.'   (4: 3, 1)

The attitude of significant others to danger in a police career is also based on their general feeling about its desirability.

> 'Me Mum . . . She really persuaded me. She did say, "Don't worry too much because of all the trouble, because you get yourself as much chance of trouble now in the police as if you're not." Especially violence, you're always prone to get trouble.'   (5: 3, 2)

Nor do the police want recruits to entertain any illusions.

> 'I've found that they don't wrap you up in cotton wool, so to speak. They hit you from the start. . . . The second day we was shown a film on demonstrations which highlights the problems of policemen getting injured on duty, and that's only the second day. If you didn't want to be a policeman you would have got your coat on there and then.'
>   (5: 2, 2)

Of course such warnings encourage those who relish the prospect of risk-taking and robust physical exercise. 'I think our police support unit is sufficient at the moment to deal with anything violent. . . . I think I'd like to go into PSU training. Maybe it's because of the heroics. It appeals to me' (6: 1, 4). Danger represents a source of both stress and satisfaction, and recruits begin to distinguish the non-police from the police perspective on it. There are plenty of other less glamorous sources of stress where such compensation does not exist. After a year this example was given of the worst part of the work.

> 'Going round to somebody's door and saying, "Can I have a word with you?", and, although you consciously try to get it across by your attitude and your presence, you've got to tell them that they have lost their kiddie or their husband. It is still very hard to hold back that lump in your throat until you get outside that door.' (9: 1, 1)

The fascinating thing about this is the way the officer gradually distances himself from the emotion of the example even as he tells it. In what follows he does so by, first, alluding to the detachment with which police at accidents insulate themselves (in contrast to when they bear bad news), second, by illustrating a distancing device police use in this latter event and, third, by an ironic aside.

> 'At a traffic accident the body can be there dead and its only one of the many problems you've got to deal with. But where you go round to somebody's house, before you go there you've knocked the neighbour up . . . and you're not certain the neighbour's a friend but you've got to have somebody there for her to lay off on so you, as a policeman, can stay detached and move out if necessary. . . . They can always stick the knife in and say, "I'm sorry but my husband hasn't gone to work."' (9: 1, 1)

The last, ironic, point is straight from the police culture, a device which deflates the emotionalism of the anecdote, enabling one to resolve the possibly damning story about the dehumanizing demands of the role by a cynical laugh. It also indicates that the officer has to be alert to every contingency of a highly contingent world, for that sort of thing happens and he must be protected from feeling foolish as well as tragic.

Danger is one organizing theme by which the work's essence is captured. Its difference to other work is another; the outdoor life, variety, excitement and autonomy are each discriminants. Drawing a contrast between work outside and indoors addresses not simply the sense of place but the organization of the work. People enjoying outdoor work are probably referring to differences in autonomy, supervisory relationships and the sequence of events in work, as well as to the pleasures of pounding the pavement. Outdoors work is case-based, autonomous and discretionary. 'I wanted a job in the great outdoors, and I've had jobs in factories and offices but they got me down. I find I'm a lot happier outside' (1: 4, 1). Similarly, 'I know too many people who have worked in offices and they feel that they're in their little pigeonhole. I wanted to be out and about, moving, and . . . in contact with people' (4: 1, 1).

There is a strong orientation to activity in such responses: 'We're all ready to get stuck into it. They're all ex-servicemen and we don't like hanging about doing nothing' (3: 4, 2). Such keenness can eventually provoke stress. Since there is no effective means of deferring response to routine matters despatchers tend to treat all messages with similar urgency and this vain attempt to deal immediately with every incoming demand also means they send patrols to find out details instead of getting them themselves. This results in a sense of intense and continual pressure. Yet this initially appeals to those who see a negative trait of conventional work as the monotonous uniformity of its product or sequence of activities; the expectation that one may at any time face the unexpected is one of the work's sustaining features.

> 'I didn't fancy an office job because I've worked in an office before. . . . I've also worked in a factory for six months . . . and I enjoyed it mainly because the blokes I worked with were good but . . . the police simply was more what I wanted, a job . . . that was really interesting and what had no routine to it.'   (5: 3, 1)

Distinctions between other work and policing index the person's perception of their essential self; they are presented as unifying threads running through their work career.

Contrast with other occupations is more plausible as a *post hoc* motive, but when it is cited by the experienced, as in this tutor constable's comments on joining, it identifies key elements of occupational imagery.

> 'It's a job I wanted to do from a little boy, but when I left school I don't think I was tall enough. I entered into factory life and they said, "Go through routine shop floor and then you can apply to various jobs." . . . By the time I'd done my apprenticeship . . . they wouldn't let us get off the floor, they were short of skilled men and they'd trained us and wanted to keep us there. . . . We don't see ourselves doing this for the next forty-odd years, same place, same faces.'
>   (TC 83: 1, 1)

His work experience 'launched' themes of the unreliability of managers and the stultifying nature of work indoors into his ideas about occupations.

Further, recruits learn the 'variety' of duties and potential 'excitements' are the province of constables but not of those higher up.

> 'Once you get promoted you tend to be more in the office, and lose

touch with what goes on on the ground. . . . I was a military policeman and became the station sergeant. . . . In Germany . . . the military policeman does very much the same job – he's out on patrol, he does breathalyzers and goes to break-ins. He is a normal bobby . . . and you're back in the station, you're twiddling your thumbs, they have the fun. They're out on the streets, they're having to sort out a fight. Let's face it, these things are what gets you going.' (3: 2, 3)

It is difficult to imagine other occupations which would fulfil the same needs. Autonomy, from the constable's perspective, is actually reduced as one rises in rank. The opportunities for 'autonomy' and 'variety' of work inhere not just in the police role but in the constable's role. As a PC 'you're allowed to work on your own initiative. . . . I didn't want a job where you've got somebody climbing on your back all the time' (3: 4, 1). Job satisfaction and variety are bound up with autonomy.

A summary of these qualities would probably read like this final response.

'My father and his father were both in the police force. To a certain extent I wanted to follow in their footsteps, creating a service for the public. A lot of variety in it. You can specialize. Shift work and you don't get bored with life. Good pay. I like a disciplined job, to be respected, and do something useful.' (6: 1, 1)

Although few cited such a range of attractions, these points tell us much about recent images of policing.

Among these statements may be found components of the perspective police apply to their work. Such components are seen as the vocabulary on which police selectively draw when they think about the occupation. The essential thing many recruits emphasize about the police is the idea of discipline. Discipline may be directed inward or outward. The police are disciplined by an administrative and behavioural code as an hierarchical organization, and they apply discipline as a check on disorder and infraction. They earn public respect by maintaining their constitutional role but more tangibly by a visible presence on the street. 'Everybody respects the police . . . and everybody knows that the police will look after them by keeping the villains and all that locked up. You can walk along those streets and more or less the police are in control' (1: 2, 1). The control of crime is emphasized in conceptions based on respect; respect is for good work and the essential criterion of good work is crime control, as measured by public safety. This is generally not conceived as a team effort with other agencies but as a lonely mission. The police 'make law and order. If you didn't have law and order you just have anarchy and chaos. People doing what they wanted' (1: 3, 1).

The image is of a Hobbesian social contract; the police are its enforcers and moreover are the effective part of Leviathan. Without the police the state could only turn to the military. The police can draw on respect, and out of that, citizens voluntarily surrender their potential to do 'what they wanted'.

This respect is not just awe of the powerful. Recruits recognize the role is not just enforcement but extends to 'public relations'. The meaning of 'public relations' is complex and not literal. When they cite public relations, as often happens, they do not mean they literally do what 'PR men' do. (It is doubtful if they know what PR men do.) They refer to verbalized skills of negotiation which, by a variety of rhetorical devices, secure citizens' compliance with suggested courses of action. The role requires consent, and consent is implicitly subject to an exchange of respect for effectiveness.

> 'The main contribution is law and order. (The control of crime?) Well, the control of the structure of society, otherwise you've got anarchy. But as well as that, of course, you're a friend. . . . So it's a public relations job . . . more than anything, a social worker in a small way, and you've a variety of roles really. If people will let you.'(1: 4, 1)

There is an awareness that one not only represents the police but the whole edifice of the state; officers see their responsibilities include a symbolic dimension. 'It's probably the only contact people have with the authorities, the government if you like. And it plays the most important part in keeping society together, some kind of rule of law' (2: 1, 1). A component of the constable's imagery of the police and society is that in a special way the police are constitutive of the state. Even if it is as tersely put as the assertion that the police contribution to society is 'making it work' (3: 1, 1) there is a recognition of the burden such a task represents. The recruits' imagery of police holding potential chaos in check is a prescient anticipation of a core value. A world requiring tough control is a world which 'sustains the rank and file rhapsody of crime-fighting, search, chase and capture, of action and hedonism' (Holdaway 1983: 37). Unlike American police, who perceive a world of present, continual danger, the constable's image is of a world potentially erupting, always on the brink, saved from sliding over by the force. Faced with the calm of the average division, the warrant for tough policing is found in the assertion.

This burden extends to feeling that the role has consequences for personal, off-duty behaviour. At year one 67 per cent agreed that a PC's behaviour must be exemplary at all times and at year two 84 per cent agreed. At induction 95 per cent agreed that one's duty should come before one's private life. By year one agreement fell to 83 per cent but by year two it rose to 92 per cent.

'They basically make the society. Without the police force, without law and order, you haven't got society. Full stop. In the military police I wasn't on a par with them (civil police) experience-wise or work-wise but I had the same responsibility in the way I conducted my life.'

(3: 5, 1)

Because the logic is that the police create the conditions under which the state can function by representing its overarching authority, the respect the police expect arises from their symbolic role rather than their effectiveness in controlling crime, keeping order or managing traffic. People should respect the police implicitly, because the police role in creating order is predicated on citizens granting authority to the police.

'Primarily they're the defender of the peace, they're there to keep law and order. We have got to have authority to keep law and order. In some states around the world without that authority it just gets ridiculous, so you've got to have someone to keep the peace and law.'

(3: 2, 1)

This conception of authority is based on a rather negative image of human nature, as one might expect from its basis in a Hobbesian version of social control. Without control anarchy is not just inevitable but immediate; chaos is always waiting at the door. Traffic as well as people in other settings must be controlled. Few sociologists have been interested in this area of police work, but behaviour in cars is one of the best indices of the propensity to deviate present in us all and there may be merit in the idea that driving styles express much of a person's character. Cars themselves can be analysed as fantasy objects putting to the world an image of self one hopes to nurture. No one is better placed to perceive them as vehicles for the lusts as well as transportation than the traffic cop, and it is not surprising that this recruit sees such work in the same dour vein as human nature in general. The main police contribution is

'obviously a control of society. Without police it would be a more and more violent world to live in, and without police it would have snowballed into a free-for-all. . . . Also the growth of traffic is an immense problem the police face, and the control of the motorist. Basically just making the country a decent place to live in.'   (5: 2, 1)

The symbolic 'respect' idea does not deny that an equally well-grounded component of the essential nature of the police is the pragmatic version which places emphasis on crime control *per se*. Here the police mission is summarized as 'protecting the public and property' (3: 3, 1). This version is intolerant of 'social service' work and at induction 35 per cent agreed there was too much social service work, with 41 per cent at year one and 40 per cent at year two. Some expressions of a sense of mission suggest a social pathology model.

> 'It's fairly obvious with the modern-day society, the increasing violence. I was living in Mosside in Manchester for three weeks. There's a lot of coloureds there, out of work, that are bored. They're hanging around all day getting into a lot of mischief. Only things like fights outside bookies' shops, but it could be quite serious if somebody didn't step in and stop it. It will be needed more and more. This has got to be stamped out and you're getting the same way as America now, parts of the country where you daren't walk out.'   (3: 4, 1)

Instrumental 'employee's perspective' elements of the vocabulary are mobilized as experience increases, with a reduced attention to the more 'idealistic' elements. The 'idealistic' recruits in Hopper's study were first to have trouble in adjusting. They were bothered by the restrictions and changes in their personal lives the discipline code entailed and upset that rules set forth in class were not uniformly followed on the street (Hopper 1977: 160). The instrumental approach to police employment trades neither on a sense of vocation nor crusading mission. Police rhetoric holds on deposit a number of component elements. These may be deployed in a particular balance by individuals which varies by time and experience, although some clusters of the elements may form a conceptual apparatus applied with some consistency by one officer, and a particular cluster of elements may achieve widespread currency at some time in response to a compelling event such as a riot or murder of a police officer.

After a year, then, the essential things about the job receive a different emphasis because what is uppermost in the recruit's mind changes. What becomes of immediate importance is not what the job is for but how it is and ought to be done. Police work involves a much deeper identity transformation than recruits anticipate. That is, at least, a way to interpret the frequent assertion that those who have not experienced the work cannot know what it is like. It is an assertion that this practice and the beliefs upon which it is based cannot be appreciated from the outside. This recruit rejects his earlier view. 'Variety' came glibly as a recruit, but only after a year of the work could he grasp what adjustments of self, what knowledge and skills, are necessary to the pursuit of an occupation where any moment can bring a new demand.

> 'There's never a day the same. (That's what you thought it would be like when you joined isn't it?) You do, yes, but you don't realize. Nobody else can, until you've actually done the job, nobody can begin to tell you what it's going to be like. You don't appreciate any of the situations till you're actually working.'   (12: 3, 1)

3

The structure and process of training

The discipline and loyalty so important to the architects of the Metropolitan Police, Charles Rowan and Richard Mayne, were to be achieved by recruitment practices and harsh punishment for violations of rules. Recruiting is to a single standard but hiring is local except at the highest levels; training and allocation are regionally controlled. The present system of training dates from a Home Office Working Party set up in 1970, whose recommendations were approved by the Police Training Council and sent to chief constables in 1973. The stages of probationer training were fixed as Induction/Initial/Local Procedure/'On the Job' and further instruction/Continuation/Attachments. Its core is the ten-week course at one of the six Home Office police training centres (the Initial Course), with a local procedure course, short tutor constable attachment ('to act as the recruit's mentor'), short attachments to CID and traffic and a return to the centre at eighteen months for a two-week 'Continuation Course'. A syllabus at force level was recommended to reinforce the Initial Course.

The objectives of training are to: (1) provide basic knowledge of law and practice in normal police duty; (2) provide instruction in legal, procedural, and practical developments; (3) develop potential; (4) prepare selected personnel for work in specialist fields; and (5) prepare selected personnel for supervisory duties (Bramshill: 42). Trainers are charged to consider the unique responsibility and constitutional status of constables, their role in society and the effect of 'attitude, environment and climate' on their work, particularly their dependence on the co-operation of the public in achieving 'effective policing by consent'. The scope and objective of probationer training is to produce an 'efficient' constable within the two years' probation. There is no statutory definition of this, nor a generally applied job description. Whether a constable is efficient is decided by default, under disciplinary regulations.

The one-week induction course in local training establishments varies but generally covers basic administration, conditions of service, and operating procedures. The ten weeks in the regional centre (Dishforth for Derbyshire probationers) emphasize legal and practical aspects. The local procedure course gives individual forces scope for interpretation. The 1973 circular recommended topics on 'dealing with the public' to ensure that 'constables can approach all members of the public with confidence and establish rapport'. Courses were to include 'public relations' lessons to give an 'understanding of the role of the police service . . . whether enforcing the law or dealing with a minor domestic problem'. Divisional community affairs officers usually take the several periods on community relations, reviewing press relations, social services, juvenile liaison, road safety, exhibitions, and race relations. The periodic returns to local training interspersed with patrol/specialist attachments reinforce initial law and procedure lessons. Eighteen months from joining probationers return to the regional centre for a two-week continuation course; to reinforce initial material by incorporating field experience; about 20 per cent of time is spent on lectures, slightly more on discussion. Small group discussion is followed by longer discussion led by instructors; topics include accidents, race relations, juveniles, drugs, domestic disputes.

Home Office District Training Centres

The centres provide training to a common syllabus and standard for all recruits outside the Metropolitan, which has its own training school. Under the 1964 Police Act the Home Secretary has a duty to maintain the centres and promote the 'efficiency of the police service'. He is advised on the running of each centre by chief constables and local authority representatives. There is a history of friction between training centres and local government representatives, centring on finance, including Dishforth, the district centre for Derbyshire, with 300 on average on courses and a £3 million budget.

Each day at the district centre is divided into seven periods. Seventeen are presently devoted to social studies/public relations, including 'rights of the individual', 'police and the demonstrator' and 'police and social problems'. There is a period on 'individual and public prejudice' and two on 'community relations'. The 1973 recommendations were that these sessions be taken by outside speakers from community relations departments, colleges, and elsewhere but under the new 'associated police studies' training centre staff became responsible and the showing of films replaced the lecture format. Force instructors and immediate supervisors have been less than satisfied with the Initial Course, finding recruits not well-versed in aspects such as report-writing, statement-taking and 'attitudinal' matters. The two-week Continuation Course was to revise subjects, introduce new topics and involve recruits in research, presentations, practical exercises, and discussion. In practice it gives chief officers an assessment by training centre staff at the stage when appointments have to be confirmed.

The two-tier training structure leads to some understandable rivalries. Force trainers felt they had a tighter group of staff over whom 'hierarchy and martinetry' did not prevail. Another merit of the TE was its ethos of no sexual dalliance, whereas at the DTC there were numerous PTIs who 'can't keep their hands off the backsides of female recruits' (field notes, 17.12.80), a comment also made by some recruits. A high-ranking PTI stated that in the TE the rationale was that discipline was an aspect of management, whereas in the DTC it was that management was an aspect of discipline. In the TE, one was party to decisions made about one's employment whereas at DTC you were 'pushed around as required' by the hierarchy.

To recruits the DTC seems forbidding early in training, preserving the anonymity of distance and regional, not local, focus. 'This week hasn't been so strict but I should think when I do me proper training in Yorkshire it will be very strict and I'll probably find adjusting to that hard' (5: 3, 2). The TE was a friendlier, local institution. 'It will be a lot harder when we go to the training centre. I'm expecting that, we're sort of built up to it' (5: 4, 1). It was perceived as one of the principal sources of assessment and as having an influential effect on subsequent career. 'They take the training at Dishforth into account quite a lot and your conduct record' (5: 5, 2). In retrospect some found it too demanding.

> 'There is too much pressure in the initial training. There is an awful lot crammed into it. It ought to be in two parts to give you a rest because by the end you've got that much inside your brain that's just brand new. . . . Although they only teach you the basics you need to know such a lot, that it's hard to get over.' (8: 3, 2)

His solution was to reduce drill to allow the same material to be gone over twice. Opinions of the DTC were less charitable among TE staff than probationers. Apart from the rigid discipline and alleged 'sexual harassment', the DTC was too reliant on external academic lecturers. These did not turn out 'if the weather's wet' and had 'a chip on their shoulder against police'. They were less competent lecturers than relatively untrained PTIs (field notes, 17.12.80). There were also problems in the DTC 'practicals' which were reported as close to being a form of 'one-upmanship' or retailing 'tricks of the trade' which were actually non-generalizable. This eroded recruits' confidence rather than building it up.

Attitudes to formal training

Just as formal processes do not account for all the legal and administrative knowledge gathered by novices, neither is informal socialization the only source of knowledge about practice. Indeed orientation to, and investment of value in, the occupational culture, is partly accomplished by the training school. When reviews of training's effectiveness are urged it is sometimes presumed that poor training is to blame for bad practice. Data are then produced which declare the extremely limited influence of training institutions. These inquiries miss the point that what goes on in the training school is much more than formal socialization. Novices are here for the first time in continuous contact with police, many of whom have greater experience, but also with many of their peers as well. The latter enable a rehearsal of how occupational culture can nurture and protect its members, with exam-swotting syndicates, a social life involving those in the same groups and some of the forms of collaboration and collusion that any body of students use to survive the student role. At the same time contact with police instructors and other experienced offices is a source of knowledge about the essential tenets of police culture. These *may* be imparted formally, that is, by explicit reference, but are much more likely to emanate from the couching of ideas, the examples given and the style of filling-in talk, back-chat, and corridor conversation. One must, then, be alert to the informal and implicit aspects of the formal socialization agency, recognizing that, when people want to know, they are learning all the time. Neither informal nor formal knowledge is the exclusive domain of a given agency.

Recruits do not pass through training like automatons but reflect on their experience and evaluate the programme according to practical use on the street. The occupational culture, functioning as a repository for the collective wisdom of police, is an intervening source of evaluation. Because social scientists too long neglected the occupational culture, reading the ranks as though they were a cipher for the police organization or their own socio-demographic background, much recent effort has sought the origin of police practices in the culture and status of the ranks. But one must not forget that entry to the police is not automatically entry to the culture, that some officers will not and never will wish to fit into that culture, that there is more than one police culture, and that individual decisions are always an expression of the individual's perspective at the time as he or she uniquely makes sense of all perceived influences.

As one has seen there are a variety of degrees of familiarity with police work among different recruits. Thus it is not possible to associate the bearing of certain components of occupational ideology with the outset of either training or service *per se*. This is not just because of anticipatory socialization or the informal undercurrents of the formal agency. It is also a result of the differing exposure of recruits to the police prior to joining. Some are related to police (4 per cent had fathers in the police), some have served as military police or been cadets. Others have had no direct contact. The disparity of background means that for some recruits, such as single women, the assumptions of training seem rather irrelevant. 'Tuesday we fill in two lines on a form. Didn't do anything else all day 'cause it was forms for married men' (1: 1, 2). It is a measure of the keenness of people to make a sense of their work with which they can be familiar and comfortable, rather than a measure of the potency of occupational culture, that the recruits acquire a common perspective on training emphasizing their points of similarity rather than differences.

To be impressed by the congruences and common relevances arising from shared experience is not to deny the existence of distinctions by recruits of recruits, nor is it to belittle the project and achievements of the force TE. The latter is the recruit's home base during training, but is only intermittently visited and for brief periods. Becker (1964: 43) suggests that if we look at professional training from the perspective of the profession rather than its clients we will encounter the view universal in 'any occupation towards the institutions which train people for entrance into them' that the training is too idealistic and not 'practical'. Some 30 per cent of respondents in one police division felt training only prepared them for street duty to the most limited extent and too little time was spent on dealing with people (73 per cent), working a beat (70 per cent), crime prevention (58 per cent), law and the court system (58 per cent), and dealing with racial problems (51 per cent) (Police Foundation 1982).

Before attending the DTC recruits are unaware how much material will be covered and in what depth, and the pressure of daily and weekly tests provokes anxiety that they will not learn or retain all that is necessary. Asked if he found any subjects irrelevant a recruit at the one year stage replied, 'No, it was the opposite actually. Some of them I wondered why the hell they didn't put more emphasis on them' (9: 1, 4). He was also uneasy about the assessments, which he felt should not just test knowledge but personality.

> 'Virtually everybody has gone over to this subjective "Weller Loop" system: slip tests, weekly tests. But there was no real objective test of personality, and whether there was any weakness in your personality that caused you to be a policeman. There's one thing you can't afford in this job and that's a chip on your shoulder.'   (9: 1, 4)

Other criticisms were more readily anticipated. 'I have to really study at night and as soon as the day's finished at five o'clock I go back over to the block and press me uniform and then I'm just revising, I don't go out or anything' (10: 1, 2). As in any educational institution the pace of work and mode of assessment are controversial. However, a year's experience helped to confirm the value of knowledge which may earlier have been doubtful. This recruit did not find law instruction tedious: 'Not really, now, because I can relate it to what we've done.' However, he questioned the rigid criteria used to judge test answers. There is a daily test of the previous day's teaching, a weekly exam, and at the end of the third week an overall test; each recruit must also present a fifteen-minute talk on a specific topic, such as powers of entry and search with regard to poaching. These were 'good for bringing yourself out' but the test required 'the actual words that they use on the typed student lesson notes. So it's a play on those actual words rather than, generally speaking, the knowledge' (12: 1, 7–8).

Yet like the apocryphal New York kids with straight F's in mathematics and total recall of baseball team batting averages, if a knowledge is valued it can be learned.

> 'I don't like studying and I don't like just sitting down and reading. But if it's for a cause like this I don't mind. . . . I've been learning definitions every night this week (but) . . . if at school I had to sit down and learn a chapter in a book I couldn't do it.' (5: 3, 2)

As well as daily tests at the TE recruits submit a file for assessment.

> 'This week was making off without payment. That's where a person takes a taxi ride and when they get to the destination they leave the taxi without paying. You submit a file which outlines the circumstances of the offence, the statement from the taxi-driver and a statement from us when we interview the offender.' (8: 1, 2)

The TE generally amplifies material presented at the training centre, including basic topics like damage and theft.

Training has been criticized for its heavy emphasis on legal knowledge (Alderson 1979, Punch 1979a). In the recruit and probationer curriculum 'much of the legal material covered is esoteric and of little immediate value to the newly qualified constable' (Taylor 1982: 4). This emphasis is essentially defensive, based on the fear that novices may encounter situations whose legality they cannot judge. It is another prop to the view of policing as law enforcement. Further, it suggests that constables operate without support or advice (see McClure 1980). Recruit training is based on an initial experience emphasizing discipline and *esprit de corps*, continuing into a form of apprenticeship training with brief formal inputs interspersed. Brown accurately summarized the curriculum being designed with the image of an 'athletic lawyer' in mind (Brown 1983: 123). In the recommended Initial Course syllabus, 'General Police Duties' includes the wide range of routine matters not fitting into crime or road traffic. The 35 classroom and 59 practical sessions here, on topics such as patrolling a beat, pocket notebooks, domestic disputes, lost and found property, and vagrants, were increased by 20 sessions in 1983, including more on children and youths, licensed premises, and firearms. The 42 criminal law periods, 28 classroom, 14 practical, were also expanded, with the introduction of shoplifting and further sessions on sexual offences, criminal damage, burglary, and criminal deception. Also increased were the 56 periods, 26 classroom and 30 practical, on Road Traffic, with 9 more classes. Only 2 classes on crime prevention are featured and Home Office recognition that this is one of the few credible means to reduce crime still has not paid off because of the 1983 Working Party's limp recommendation that 'it should permeate the whole of probationer training' (Police Training Council 1983).

For their part, instructors see their personal approach having an influence on recruits, with some attributing a major role to it.

> 'The attitudes of kids who go to training school and come away . . .
> you will have noticed probably a huge change, and that's because of
> the sergeant instructors. Tremendous power. They don't know they've
> got that power but they have. I'm conscious of the slightest slip of the
> tongue, the way they take it.' (81: 1, 10)

For recruits the training centre and TE presented two problems. First, they represented an educational setting associated with school. Some expressed diffidence or frustration about further 'book learning'. This has an obvious connection with the action orientation frequently expressed by recruits and endorsed by the occupational culture. Second, the amount of instruction crammed into brief periods in the training centre/school was a strain. Some also found law instruction repetitious due to previous knowledge, a perennial complaint teachers encounter. This recruit had been in the military police. 'For me it's a bit too long 'cause I'm already halfway there. But for people who know nothing about the law it's probably two years. And then you're only scratching the surface really' (2: 2, 2). His last comment deflates his point in a manner also familiar to teachers.

As social work teachers have found, it is very difficult to get the right sequence of core knowledge in training with both a practical and theoretical emphasis.

> 'I didn't like the local procedure one. All this hanging about, then they
> were just showing us what we were going to do at the station, had to
> fill in a crime report and of course we didn't know what we were
> doing. All these different forms, it was just a waste of time. We spent
> a week doing that. These courses are a bit tough for the ones who
> aren't so bright, but I prefer them. Because there are times when

you're out on the street and you just don't know, so you have to grovel, and hope people think you know what you're doing. You need to learn it.'   (7: 2, 2)

Probationers' feelings about training are relatively enduring. Indeed tutor constables reflect similar views in speaking of their own probationary training, as did this TC with ten years' service.

'I'd done a limited amount of studying after leaving school. So to start all that again, concentrated like it is, left me in a little bit of a mess. . . . I struggled with regard to knowing the law because I'd not been used to pressurized learning.'   (83: 4, 1)

Like current recruits, the material did not slip into place until experience was gained.

'After about twelve months, I was finding, "Oh, I understand that bit now," and I could put that into practice, but such compact learning just gets things into your mind and confuses what little bit you did know. Through seeing a certain thing happen I could say "I remember a little bit about that," read it up later and say, "I know all the way now." Whereas after thirteen weeks training school I came out confused. . . . I was doing things and I didn't know why or much about it at all.'   (83: 4, 1–2)

Police culture does not highly value 'book learning' or academic ability as a skill for police officers. In the US there is evidence that educated officers get lower performance ratings *because* they are educated (Sherman 1978: 186–7). Evidence on the impact of education on performance is 'scant, conflicting and ambiguous' (Bennett and Haen 1979: 149). Certainly many cadets are crestfallen when they find that joining the police at 16 entails two years of classroom instruction in subjects they thought they had left behind at school. 'You can't really say you're looking forward to getting down there and swotting' (1: 4, 2). It is not unusual to encounter reservations about academic ability and examinations were often cited as the only part of training the recruit worried about.

'The problem I'm worried about is the studying, because I'm not really all that good at academic work, and I've not done it for such a long time. I know I'm going to really have to work hard and study on my own, but I'm determined to study hard.'   (4: 2, 2)

This was often in strong contrast to the favourable anticipation of the practical work; the same recruit continued, 'I'm just looking forward to all the attachments . . . and to the job itself' (4: 2, 2). Being reconciled to study also elicits claims about the *overall* feeling of the group.

> 'The only thing I'm not looking forward to is the classroom work. I'm willing to learn it because I know I can do the job. But you ask anybody on the course and they will all say, "I'm not looking forward to this," that's how the others would be, exactly the same.'(4: 5, 2)

The difference between this and school is the evident utility of what is taught and thus the recruit is 'willing to learn', but no one in this occupation, he feels, would relish study. After a year recruits grasped that the justification for learning technical matters for immediate recall was the avoidance of trouble in the encounter. Earlier distinctions between essential and 'technical' knowledge were collapsed.

> 'The class *is* very technical but there's always something else, that it's too technical to look up on the spot. There's technical offences that are committed on motorcars, you have to get it right. You have to have specialist knowledge of the various regulations.' (8: 1, 2)

Police are not entirely immune from the law of the land in their tort or criminal liability. However, the legal position of the office of constable and its resultant powers is hardly a matter of clarity (Hogarth 1982; Marshall 1965). Ambiguity of statute is a familiar complaint to police researchers, but experience teaches the imaginative that law is no hindrance but a resource.

> General, loosely-worded, ambiguous statutes and sections did not create problems for the practical police officer. . . . The interpretational latitude provided by such legal instruments enabled the police officer . . . not only to refrain from making arrests but to make an arrest and then invoke the *resource charge* to provide legal legitimation. (Chatterton 1983: 26)

The experienced appreciate the latitude it offers.

The instruction in law and 'police subjects' has an observably practical emphasis, and does not seek to give more than guidance for probationers' action and the limits of the law. There is little real depth on issues that are particularly problematic for police, such as race relations. Asked if there was attention to race relations a one year officer replied, 'there is a certain amount done, which I feel is adequate for where I'm stationed because I've only got a very very small number of immigrants' (8: 3, 2). However, there was a common emphasis on more law instruction. This became marked after a year, and one recruit's views display the criterion police apply to knowledge once they know the work. He invoked a key distinction between 'bread and butter' and inessential subjects.

'This course particularly, War-duties. Now I just can't see any point. If there's going to be a war I can't see it being conventional. Some looney's going to push a button before long and then it's all going to be over. . . . When we could be learning bread and butter stuff, robbery, theft. The things we've got to know out on the streets. Not that if someone presses a button a great bomb is going to come down and blow us all up. Oblivion.'   (11: 1, 2)

Asked if it was the 'psychology' of robbery, or law relating to it, he wanted more on, he continued,

'the legal side, because that's all this training is for as far as I can see. You just don't get enough of it. . . . We've just had two lessons, Law Relating to Animals! They could have had something on theft or robbery or blackmail or something bread and butter. . . . What we call bread and butter offences, they're what we work on. All day, every day.'   (11: 1, 2–3)

Technical knowledge has another function from a socialization perspective. 'Aside from facilitating precise technical communication, esoteric language serves to identify and exclude and thus to confirm occupational identity. It appears also to serve a psychological function: "now I am thinking technically"' (Moore 1969: 879).

It seems self-evident that police should know the law, and the pragmatism of their comments illustrates the basis on which classroom training is received by recruits. It also seems self-evident that police should be fit. Some 25 per cent of Initial Course lessons are physical activity: games, physical training, self-defence, swimming, life-saving, first-aid and drill. In the revised fifteen-week programme, there is a proportionate increase in this area (77 to 110 lessons). The teaching of aikido (a defensive martial art) is to be doubled to twenty periods, using instructors trained in minimum use of force. While no 'scholars' who professed joy at the chance to learn law were encountered, there were a number for whom sports were highly esteemed. Some had joined partly for the sport: 'I wanted to carry on doing a lot of sport because I'm an athlete' (1: 2, 1). Physical exercise draws on assertions of the value in building character of tough outdoor work. 'The majority of (cadet training), especially the Peak courses, the character-building courses as they call them, helped a lot. You're bound to find your character traipsing through the Peak country' (6: 1, 2). Emphasis on stamina, calm determination and tolerance of physical discomfort are promoted in hiking. Hikers will know the experience of awesome loneliness, and how one's isolation from society when 'lost' is tempered by the bond to one's companions.

However, outdoor pursuits include drill as well as sport, and drill was the subject of little enthusiasm.

> 'The discipline of course, if you've not been in the army it's a bit strange. The boy scouts is a bit different from drilling about and keep your boots polished . . . But you've got to look forward to it. Can't really start off on the wrong foot.'   (1: 4, 2)

The recruit's search for analogies – army, boy scouts – fails; there is nothing like it in his experience. But he takes drill to be relevant because at this stage he cannot rightly judge, and knows his attitude *is* being judged. Initiating the recruits into the mysteries of the organization, the police have a fund of willing compliance to draw on. Later it may not be so – the work and their colleagues will have intervened – but presently the recruits are game to do as ordered.

> 'I'll be honest. At 34 years of age I'm not looking forward to running four miles across country, and I smoke. But I've been doing three-mile runs every day to practise for it. But I'm not going to enjoy it but I'm going to do it because it's required.'   (3: 5, 2)

The two 'buts' in the last sentence nicely express that the recruit is true enough to himself that he will not like this stiff medicine and yet is a disciplined enough fellow to follow orders.

Drill stands for obedience, regimentation, uniformity, submission but pride in station.

> 'A certain part of the intake had never marched before, me included. . . . I'd never ironed a pair of trousers in my life. I'd polished my shoes but I hadn't "balled" them to a mirror-like finish. And the discipline is there to start with, you must do as you're told. And I think that's a good thing because you can't just be doing as you want when you're a policeman. You've got to carry the orders out. From the beginning they've made it quite clear who is the boss.'   (5: 2, 2)

Through attitudes to physical standards of dress and deportment the recruit learns the most basic aspect of the organization, its notions of compliance. It is the framework in which their practice and mental set evolves but the culture soon tempers it.

> 'It comes as a shock to me, 'cause . . . I'm not used to the discipline. And cleaning me boots. I haven't cleaned me shoes for about two years, so it was pretty hard. But what I've found, the blokes who have been training me, sort of strict out on the parade ground, where I suppose they've got to be strict, but once you get talking to them, they're very nice.'   (5: 3, 2)

It would be wrong to say the value of drill was evident to all.

> 'There was far too much emphasis on drill. I like the subject but I think it has little relevance to the job. We have parades (at TE), which are very acceptable for standards of smartness, but up there (DTC) it was a lot of drill, it was totally unnecessary. There's going to be very few occasions in my working career when I'm going to be called on to use that.'
> (8: 3, 2)

From the manager's perspective, drill imparts a sense of camaraderie; from the PC's perspective it smacks of regimentation and belittles their independent decision-making, which they must use and expect their colleagues to use, on the street. But drill serves the common cause of the manager's and worker's perspective, if it builds a group awareness. 'Camaraderie' is just the manager's version of the PC's 'all in the same boat' consciousness. Drill bears lessons salient to both formal and informal components of police culture.

As unfamiliar a device as drill was the use of role play 'games' to bring alive situations which seem abstruse or dull. This is done in both the TE and DTC. 'If you are reading about vehicle tax, I don't think its the most interesting thing. On the course the role playing is the most interesting' (1: 3, 2). However, such simulations take preparation and need to be realistic. If they are not the session can break down into giggles. At the DTC

> 'the sergeants tended to exaggerate things. Looking back, some of them were really stupid. People climbing out of the windows of the car and all you've done is ask them for their insurance certificate. They just say it is the worst situation that they've ever experienced, that they're trying to show us how we'd deal with their worst.'
> (7: 2, 2)

Even here the recruit is willing to perceive a logic but the sergeants might just have been having fun, or regard role playing as not educationally serious. The point was taken up by another recruit with a year's experience.

> 'It does simulate in a way but when there's the classroom standing round looking at you, you can't really say what you feel. You think it might be wrong what you say. . . . .. Everybody's laughing. It would be far better to go out with a PC first for a period and then come back in and while they're teaching you, you can say, "Well, this bobby did it that way."'
> (12: 1, 7)

It is a commonplace of police training that a stronger value is placed on field experience than classroom instruction. Cadets are obliged to stomach a greater dose of class work and more restricted field experience, and had no doubt what they derive most satisfaction from.

'It wasn't the thing I expected when I joined the cadets. I think people are under an illusion that you start being a policeman, and you generally get to know about the police, but you don't. It's just like going back to school. But after that the next one and a half years were very good. They gave me a chance to go into a division, which gave me a chance to see police life from the inside and also work up here (at HQ). It was the first chance I ever got of dealing with the public. I was able to go out with the police officers on the beat.' (5: 1, 2)

Cadets are subject to the influence of formal organizational values without the concomitant influence of the occupational culture for a much longer time than recruits but share their stress on 'the proper job'.

'As a cadet I was lucky enough to get out on division for eight months of that time, so I had a fair insight into the job. 'Cause I'd rather be out there, I'd rather get on with the proper job. The cadet training scheme was really going to the various departments in the police station and our own attachment. I was attached to a Cheshire Home, getting to know different types of people. Fairly good on the whole. Some of it I found a bit degrading, when you had to go out snow-clearing paths; you're chosen for small, mean tasks.' (6: 1, 2)

In both the above responses classroom instruction receives no positive references. Proponents of the view that 'common sense' is the essential ingredient of good policing would concur; there are many in the occupational culture. They feel the interval between learning a procedure and trying it out should be brief.

'It's the best training you'll ever get up at (district) training school but when you come back you think you know it all and when it comes to practice you don't. You lose all confidence in yourself until you're taken out with your tutor bobby. . . . If somebody shows you what to do, you'll do it, but read it from a book, it's hard. (7: 1, 4)

Rotation between teaching and practice with a tight turn-around is the ideal, but practice is too unpredictable to yield examples on call of what one has recently learnt. The recruits' assessment of the practical relevance of formal training is no criticism of the staff. The difficulty lies in the recalcitrance and contingency of real-life examples, an early source of the operating ideology's emphasis on the emergent properties of interaction. Confirming that he learnt more from his tutor constable than training school this recruit continued, 'they're all policemen down here, they know what to do themselves, but it's very difficult to understand sitting in a classroom. . . . It's completely different when you're out there' (7: 2, 2). Another continued, 'you're just given an area to work, so you can't say, "I'll deal with accidents today," it's whatever happens on your area' (8: 1, 4). This gives recruits and experienced officers a near-fatalist notion that the job is inherently unteachable without contact with the public, and that there is nothing the training agencies can do about it unless the recruit is fortunate to encounter by chance the situation in practice.

Learning from practice is 'easier'. Its immediacy and qualitative basis of assessment accounts for recruits' preference for practice.

> 'It's much easier to learn than training school (DTC). There you learn your basic powers of arrest . . . then go onto the beat for a year and learn from practical demonstrations, which are nothing like your prac-ticals at training school. . . . Then you come here (TE) and it's much easier to learn the work. You can apply it to the practice you've done on the beat.'   (8: 2, 3)

Only experience supports the interrelation of training and practice.

> 'Before, I knew this stuff but it was all just words, and when you actually do the job it becomes understandable. Early in my service I was trying to relate theory to practice, which doesn't quite mix, but after a while you get the hang of the situations.'   (8: 3, 6)

Hall *et al.* (1978) suggest pragmatism and belief in common sense is central to working-class ideology. 'There's only one thing police work's based on. That's common sense . . . But it breeds common sense because you come unstuck if you don't have it. . . . You've got to get out there and in amongst it. That's where the knowledge comes – out there, not in this place' (9: 1, 7). This exceptional statement of the posi-tion praises common sense even more highly by equating it with police practice – the job actually 'breeds' a quality assumed to be innate and therefore unlearnable. Thus conceived, training is limited to a sensitizing (initial) and an amplifying (intermittent) task.

> 'After you've been out for a year . . . the actual theory of the stuff I can now relate to what I've already done. Before we couldn't relate it to anything, we had to just learn the words and when you went out, you almost forgot it because you couldn't relate the words to the action. But now we can relate the picture of what's happening to what they're teaching us and I seem to know a lot more than I did.'
>   (12: 1, 6)

After six months of training Brown asked 101 recruits whether they found any disparity between the 'role oriented demands of training and on-the-beat patrol work'. She found

> a definite discrepancy between the training school expectations of the police role, with over half believing the training school expected the police officer to act as a legal agent compared to less than a third believing this role was expected from the other role-related audiences.
>
> (Brown 1983: 123)

About 65 per cent thought initial training was limited in length, depth and scope.

Attitudes to probationer status

As a probationer the sensitive interest displayed by recruiters gives way dramatically to a sense that one is continually on trial. The knowledge one was under scrutiny for two years, allied with the menace of unemployment, gave recruits a continual feeling that one foot wrong and they were out. The 'formal, mechanical and arbitrary' bureaucratic features of the career become apparent (van Maanen 1974: 88–9). Yet this is not a point when the occupational culture can much help recruits. Since they are novices they are not yet to be trusted. Nor can they count on the support of other recruits. In this light eagerness to get training done and hit the beat is not surprising. 'Just get the training over with and get out on the street, that's all I want' (2: 2, 2). This is not just a desire to slough off the uncomfortable transitional status by gaining a familiarity with the work on which basis one can claim membership. It indicates that, during transition, one cannot derive satisfaction from the intrinsic merits of the job. One is held back by limits on what one is competent to do. Indeed, novices relish the prospect of getting the work right themselves, without peers or supervisor. 'Everybody will say its going to be going on the beat on your own. That's going to be the thing to look forward to' (5: 1, 2).

Thus the recruits insist that real police work is on the beat, not specialist duties and certainly not training. Training keeps getting in the way of the natural laboratory of the streets, where practice is really learnt. 'We've had a week in divisional headquarters, prosecutions, communications room, three probationary courses in between and five weeks driving course. Your period on the beat is interrupted all the time, so I liked it when I was on the beat' (7: 2, 3). The recruits' emphasis in their first week matched their preference after a year. This valuation of the beat diverges from the occupational culture of the experienced, for whom specialist duties hold greater attractions. The street is a great teacher but its lessons can be learnt; it is only as a novice that it is a mystery and has a mystique. Those who have abundant experience of it and still remain have learnt what it has that fulfils their needs, and why they cannot leave. Theirs is not the enthusiasm of the untried.

Interpersonal skills are learnt on the beat, not in the academy. Training is like school study, imparted by rote and assessed by tests. The danger is that the same hostility and anxiety many recruits apparently felt towards school is felt towards the police classroom. 'People don't understand the law . . . and you've just got to learn it all. It really is hard. You've got to go back at night-time 'cause you haven't taken it in during that day' (7: 1, 2). Law, it seems, is not 'common sense' but an arcane mystery which cannot be apprehended by reason, so must be memorized (Fielding 1984). This encourages established procedures to remain fixed. 'At first you think, "How is that working? Why do you do this? That doesn't make any sense." But by the time you've finished it all comes into one set pattern and you know what to do. If you don't they'll show you what to do' (7: 1, 2). Learning law is not only a way of coping on the street but of protecting oneself from other professional groups.

> 'I was quite surprised we got as little instruction (in law) as we get, and a lot of it is self-help. It's you as stands in the box and has those, what I can only describe as "fly-boys", some of them are bloody good – these solicitors – but some of them are absolutely, well! If you want to stand there and take abuse from them, then you've got to know what you're at, and the best thing is for you to find out.'   (9: 1, 3)

The experience of training confirms the recruits' feeling that they must survive by their own efforts, and this self-help perspective matches the demands of the beat. 'A lot of it boils down to you. Admittedly you do get work given to you, but the policeman on the street has to find his own work and that way you get experience' (10: 2, 4). Independence and self-help is reinforced by training. 'If you're getting a low mark every day then you're either not taking the knowledge in or you're not doing any work on your own at night' (12: 3, 5). This contradicts the line that each officer relies on all others. A dialectic between individualist and solidaristic approaches is set up which marks the officer's ensuing career. As Reiner (1978) shows, these orientations influence choices to pursue promotion or not break ranks.

While these influences are beginning to impinge on their awareness recruits also have the trouble of bearing the transitional status. They are, at least, spared a visibly stigmatizing mark which might alert the public to their inexperience. Small subterfuge is used to manage the public and negotiate this status without trauma.

> 'People come up to you when you first go on your own and say,

"You're new, where have you been?" You just say, "I've been at another station," or something like this. If you tell them you've just come from training school then they do have a go at you and see what you're made of.'   (7: 1, 5)

It is a sensible device for handling a situation he rightly senses could be dangerous, but his experience with the public also occurs with colleagues, who he cannot handle by such a device. Van Maanen (1977: 21) notes that novices try to shed the stigmatized 'rookie' label by various means of transcending their station. Tactics including 'taking on more responsibility than permissible, ingratiating oneself with superiors, making pretentious use of local argot or even behaving vituperatively toward other newcomers'.

Fortunately the present 'inexperience' (in years of service) of UK police forces means peers have recently been in the same situation and there is less humiliation and more sharing with established officers than might be predicted from American findings. The ragging that goes on has a tentative base. 'My (tutor constable) had only just gone over two years when he took me out. . . . When I'd finished my attachment (other PCs) used to say, "How do you fill this in? You learned this at Dishforth." "Well, I've forgotten." But they'll show you. They're very helpful' (7: 1, 6). Likewise, 'if they could help you they would, if they didn't know they'd say, "Go and see the sergeant." They all have to start from the beginning, don't they?' (8: 2, 4). Yet there were exceptions. 'They've gone through it . . . so generally speaking are OK. You get the odd one who looks down on you because you are a probationer' (12: 3, 10). The 'go ask the sergeant' syndrome becomes burdensome for supervisors where very high proportions of a shift are probationers, as happens frequently.

'On our shift it is mainly probationers. There's one with five years and you think, "He's the man who knows it all," and there's six of us who are probationers. The older ones tend to moan a bit. From the sergeant you get the view that you should know something because its full of probationers and you're trying to think, "Should I know it before I ask him."'   (12: 1, 12)

Recruits do not escape the initiation problems common in disciplined hierarchical organizations. This indicates several processes which delineate status transition. First, the more experienced officers are celebrating one of the few privileges of their slightly higher standing on the organization. Second, they can do so in the knowledge that their action is a safety barrier for selecting out those who are over-sensitive. These may need 'bringing down' to the hard realities of police work and of their place in the scheme of things. Those that cannot endure a little barracking may be unreliable colleagues. Third, they do so in the awareness that superior officers also value experience and therefore seniority; their assessment only affirms the wisdom of management's judgement. Entry to the occupation *should* be a trial, because whatever the police organization dishes out the public can exceed.

Recruits express the increasing realism of their image of the work in terms of formal instruction versus experience. Asked if his original image of policing was changed by training one replied,

> 'I found out policemen's work isn't what everybody thinks it is but I wouldn't think the training's got anything to do with it. At training school they're officers who have had a lot of experience and they often convey less than all of it by relating their experiences to you in that subject. Quite often it's like mnemonics, something will trigger. You'll be out and think, "I remember him saying something like this." You may not remember it verbatim but from relating to it as his experience.'   (10: 2, 4–5)

The recruit suggests what they learn about actual practice from formal training is from the offhand digressions of instructors. Further, it only acquires significance by being 'triggered' by an event occurring in practice. Another complained that training had not prepared him for the criteria assessing practice – 'no matter how well you get on with the public and how much property you check you only get gauged on the offences which you bring in, self-initiated work' (12: 1, 9).

A final respondent did feel training had changed him, does identify formal instruction as somewhat effective, but insists it is 'seeing how the job works' which leads to revision of one's perception.

> 'When you're outside looking in you think of the police as a highly efficient body. Then you come in and see how it works in practice, mistakes are made just like every walk of life. But . . . a lot of people are ignorant of the law. They don't know whether you're doing a good or a bad job.'   (12: 3, 5–6)

Matters such as law were amenable to tuition, whereas others, equally relevant, were not. 'They can't teach you community relations. It's down to your opinion when it comes to dealing with social classes' (12: 3, 6). The training school's philosophy was to treat all members of society with equanimity.

> 'When I worked in the unemployment benefit I dealt with the low class or the less fortunate. I'm dealing with a lot of the same people because I'm afraid to say a lot of criminals are unemployed. But not all criminals are unemployed, not all unemployed are criminals, so you've got to be sensible about it.'   (12: 3, 6)

This officer's attitudes changed considerably. Although he consistently saw public relations officer as most like policing, 'lawyer' rose from fifth to second most like policing. Despite having been a benefits officer, social work was seen as least like policing after a year of training and this continued. There was a shift from strong agreement to disagreement that criminals are sick people and that most people are deterred by threat of heavy penalties. He shifted from disagreement to agreement that policing involves too much social service work, that the police administration is out of touch with the ranks and that there was too much paperwork. He spoke of 'the things they try to do in training' to affect attitudes.

'The emphasis is on treat everyone as an equal. It's not up to you to decide what's right. It is, but it's not, y'know, everybody's innocent until proved guilty. Doesn't matter what he does in life, colour or his background, treat everybody the same. If you see them breaking the law . . . you report them and let the court decide whether they're right or wrong. But self-opinion always crops up every time.'(12: 3, 6–7)

The notion of the officer as the law's impartial forward edge is contradicted by the acknowledgement that officers must exercise discretion – 'it's not up to you to decide what's right. It is, but . . .'. The 'impartial agent' idea is further deflated by the assertion that 'self-opinion always crops up'. The insight is there to recognize that the patrol situation insulates discretion and individual choice.

Instructors and their work

Instructors are the recruits' first clear role models. They may be people with specialist expertise, or a wide experience of policing for whom this is a brief assignment. One instructor joined as a cadet, worked a car posting in a mining town before being assigned to a prosperous area of Derby (81: 1, 7). An eighteen-month posting to CID administration followed ('it's an essential part of a career to see how paper moves, because it jumps hurdles if you know what happens'), which led to his getting a CID course 'as a reward'. Three years as a detective was followed by Special Branch on immigration cases – 'fascinating work' – before promotion to section sergeant in a nearby town, a transfer in the same role and his present assignment to training, which arose out of his expressing interest at a staff appraisal in the topic he now taught. Another had been a sergeant police duties instructor (81: 5, 3) and 'then I was a one man band . . . as a careers and recruiting officer' because 'I had got an instructor's background, also I had a service background which I made a play for, thinking they are a good source of recruits' (81: 5, 3).

There is no standard route to the training establishment, operational service figures greatly in the instructor's career, and both senior officers and instructors recognize in training a route for advancement. However,

'instructors for the recruits are chosen not necessarily because . . . they've got high quality as instructors but very often length of service. . . . In my case they said they were looking for a father figure, somebody who had a long experience outside who could teach by example. If somebody hinges the point he's making on a little anecdote you are far more likely to learn it.'   (81: 2, 4)

Police instructors clearly pick up the homilies and devices of the teaching profession, but it is a matter of caprice whether they come to the job with teaching experience. Their teaching duties are eclectic: 'I was employed to take over the community relations course but I'm also involved in special constabulary training, traffic wardens, Peak Park wardens, induction courses for new sergeants . . . Special Operations Unit courses' (81: 1, 2). He was chosen

'because on a staff appraisal the superintendent said, "What courses would you like to go on?" I'd been on quite a few. I said, "I'll have one of these drugs courses, one of these community liaison courses, that looks quite interesting." Then (officer i/c training) said, "You're interested in community relations?" and I said, "Yeah, yeah." I am and even more so now I've been doing it for two years'(81: 1, 2–3).

It is not unusual to teach twenty-four different subjects (81: 2, 2). Even an officer who had been a recruit/probationer instructor elsewhere had not been brought in to carry on teaching but in response to an advertisement for patrol inspectors (81: 5, 3). The exception was a highly specialised sergeant. 'After attending the Central Planning Unit Instructors course I went to the CPU itself with responsibility for the visual aids section, and taught student instructors the use of visual aids.' Yet his greatest satisfaction was recruit training.

'That is probably the best and most rewarding job in the police service. . . . You got people from every conceivable background. You got your degree man right next to the lad that had given up his milk round. It was interesting to see how they formed in groups and how you got your isolate who wouldn't fit.'   (81: 4, 2–3)

A 'generalist' expectation applies at recruit training level. 'There you teach all subjects . . . There isn't a subject I couldn't go in and teach initial recruits on' (81: 3, 3). There is a measure of interchangeability in subjects instructors handle. 'They stay on one subject but if I said, "Tomorrow I want you to teach sexual offences to probationers," then he would do so' (81: 3, 6).

Instructors do receive training, and the 'syllabus' is tightly specified and explicit. 'They have you on a course for eight weeks to teach you how to teach objectively. The lessons (for recruit training) are structured so that you have specific objectives, which at the end of the fifty-minute period, those students should know' (81: 2, 3). The instructors' initial course has a reputation for toughness, and some have to be counselled out.

> 'As a student instructor you didn't know what you was expecting . . . And we had a couple of failures. We got people who suddenly thought, "It's a very difficult course," or "It's bullshit here." Because it's recognized that it's the hardest course in the police service.'(81: 4, 3)

To save resources it was decided to try candidate instructors out in front of a class at the TE before training. The force did not want to accept 'weeding out' at the CPU course. 'That's saved us some money and the embarrassment of the kid having to go to a commandant up there' (81: 4, 3–4). Other problems will sound familiar to academics: too much administration ('our own form of paperwork'), too little course preparation time.

Police instructors are assessed observationally by 'the amount of involvement with the class and the amount of feedback' (81: 2, 3). A pass level mark is also specified and it is expected that each participant will achieve it; instructor performance is assessed on this basis. This may seem rigid; in practice choices by those assigning particular subjects to individuals are mediated by their knowledge of aptitude, personality, time 'left' for the incumbent in that posting, retirement, and other exigencies (81: 3, 6). 'We have *continuity* with Inspector A. He's been here quite some time and this is his second spell in training, but he's due for retirement very soon. If he's happy they're going to leave him here' (81: 3, 6). The chief instructor would prefer another regime. 'The ideal situation is that we bring in an instructor for two to three years, then he goes out to grass and he might come back later. This is why academics in other fields don't often make good teachers.'

Rote learning is still prevalent in recruit training, but for the experienced provision is increasingly seminar-based and interactive. This is both a consequence of pedagogical philosophy and the insistence of participants. An example was the discussion of the Scarman Report in a series of seminars on community policing which enable interactive teaching (field notes, 16.5.83). The discussion was keen; debate was vigorous, and there was opportunity to compare notes with colleagues. The more specialized the subject, the less likely the syllabus is to be closely set externally, and the more 'interactive' the mode of teaching. The subjects described as 'very basic' are on the Initial Course, including topics like theft and burglary, where the content is mainly legal definitions (81: 1, 2). Examples of specialist subjects, drawn from one instructor's brief, include 'breathalyzer law, betting, gaming and lotteries, young persons, sexual offences and licensing laws' (81: 1, 2). The development and exploitation of specialist interests, tailoring assignments to an instructor's strengths, is attempted (81: 3, 3). Instructors can develop a more discursive and thoughtful treatment for higher level courses; subtleties can be drawn out. The central service package for the inspector's Initial Course involved 'the psychology of management, then mixing into that the theory of management, professionalism' (81: 5, 3).

The instructors emphasized the worth of 'interactive' teaching, securing class involvement. They saw practice applications as a leaven for the generally dry legal input. In recruit training this meant the frequent use of examples, which served to provoke questions and answers in relation to a point of law, followed by a formal statement from the lecturer. This was preferred to more elaborate exercises such as role-play simulations. 'Not the role play but, yes, class involvement is essential for learning, and putting theory into practice by giving examples.' He avoided 'straight' lecturing. 'Because lecturing is just telling them. I work on the principle that its all there and all I've got to do is get it out and then they understand it. I involve the class as much as I can' (81: 1, 3). The rhetoric of common sense is here; the instructor suggests they already have the basis of understanding, which he marshals. Another instructor insisted the stereotype of rote learning of the law was wrong as he used a 'question and answer technique' (81: 2, 3). He suggested a 'police method of teaching' which worked from the level of participants' comprehension: 'the objective method of teaching . . . means you aim for as high a level of involvement with the students as you can get'. Nevertheless, the recruit sessions were observably stiff and formal compared to those for experienced people who might have more service than instructors. Nor do the recruit interviews suggest the distinction from rote learning is grasped.

A flavour of the 'practical' examples can be given from two instances. One was described as 'a simple thing just to illustrate common sense'. A recruit is given a sealed envelope, with £5 written on the outside and told the bearer has just found it and wants to report it. The recruit is shown how to proceed by making a note in the pocket book with details of the finder and issuing a receipt. The instructor then opens the envelope and reveals that it contains only £2. Invariably the recruit issues the receipt without opening the envelope; the constable would be liable for the difference. 'The crunch comes when he gets him to sign for it without opening it. It's an ordinary routine thing and yet it's the kind of situation where you could find yourself' (81: 2, 5). A similar trick happens in firearms lessons. The class is told never to point a gun at anyone, to check it is unloaded whenever one is handed to them, shown the range of police weapons and how to 'break' them, and advised if they are unsure to leave the gun alone and get someone who knows. As the group waits for the next session the instructor is absent and a gun is on the front desk. The instructor waits outside for the inevitable sound of a gun being fired – 'you can guarantee there's a bang before you walk in and there's a guy standing there looking for the hole' (81: 3, 16). The gun is 'loaded' with play 'caps'. An instructor remarked, 'That sort of training and reaction we can perhaps do sufficient in that practical situation to make them never do it again. I can guarantee *that* guy will never do it again.'

More clearly tailored role plays were mentioned. The courtroom example is highly amenable to this.

'Take the experience of going into a court for the first time with the nerves. If you can put it over in such a way in training by role playing and practical exercise that when the time comes for him actually to go in court, he can say, "This is like we did at training," that is absolutely super. In the inspector's courses we get people to stand up in front of their peer group and discuss, brief men on what they will do. At the beginning they're very hesitant, they repeat themselves, they hang onto the lectern for grim death.'   (81: 5, 7)

The acknowledged advantage is the opportunity for rehearsal where poor performance is inconsequential, but the method is seen as most appropriate above recruit training.

A further illustration establishes the place of such exercises in recruit training. In a high percentage of breathalyzer cases 'the non-criminal side of the public are much more likely to come into contact with police officers in a situation where they might be arrested', and it is a very sensitive area for recruits to grasp (81: 2, 4–5). Role plays simulate actual behaviour met in such cases, where drink makes the driver belligerent or incompetent in complying with the required procedure. This explicitly addresses the interrelation of law, its interpretation and application in practice, crucial matters in training. It was offered as *indicative* of the practical orientation of training by the instructor. But it emerged that such attention to a practical contingency is exceptional. At the DTC mock trials and other simulations are done 'a fair bit' (as recruits noted above), but, as the chief instructor said, 'We don't here, we lecture.' DTC worked on 'virgin recruits, as it were, who haven't seen the police and police work, don't really know what they're doing yet, and (are) acting out situations when they don't know the context' (81: 3, 9). On return to the TE 'we give them a couple of practicals on local procedure if we have time. Go over breathalyzer and show them the Derbyshire forms.' The place of simulations in this stage of recruit training was subordinate to the 'administrative' matters emphasized on the local procedure course.

The critique of simulation is that one cannot anticipate the whole range of variation that police encounter.

> 'The only way that you can really learn police work . . . any work dealing with people, (is to get) more experience dealing with people in the different situations you find them. There's a limit to which you can teach. You cannot effectively play roles because it's acting and they know it's acting and they act back. You don't put them under the same pressure that the real-life situation will do. . . . We do on-the-job training.'
> (81: 3, 9)

Senior officers had chosen to abandon the former training sequence (Appendix II) to get recruits on the beat early, so reinforcement of law-learning could be developed from the contingencies of real-life situations instead of having 'course after course during the first two years'. There is another critical point to make about simulations. Those observed were clearly 'played for laughs'. An instructor who pointed out the lack of recreation in recruit training made this understandable, and incidentally provided an account of why simulations may be made ineffective as training devices.

> 'If we've had a lesson, instead of going back to class we'll do driving licences, insurance, test certificates, we'll go outside and let a student take over the role and do a mock-up of that situation. It lets in a bit of humour into the situation, and as you know, humour relieves any tension in a classroom atmosphere. It gives a breath of fresh air, and they object to coming back here (TE) because it's like school, so we're really taking them back halfway into their natural environment.'
> (81: 4, 8)

Simulations are an excursion, a time 'away' from training.

Instructors appear to feel that a 'practical' orientation is good to espouse, but they commend a use of it which is either undermined by their jokey couching of the performance (which may indeed have latent functions) or which is seldom pursued with recruits. Teaching methods *are* an issue – 'if you find your students aren't absorbing what you're trying to put over, your methods are wrong (and) you've therefore got to change' (81: 5, 4). An aside that was made as an instructor contrasted recruit and senior officer teaching methods confirms the status of 'interactive' methods.

> 'Unlike the recruit side where it's point-blank lecturing. You tell them and they learn. (Do you ever try the seminar with recruits?) (Pause.)

I don't think you can. For a learning situation of the very basic level it has got to be "I am the teacher, you are the student, I am going to give you the benefit of my vast knowledge."' (81: 5, 5)

Simulations and exercises had to be carefully set:

'This is a sliding scale on the experience of your student: if you pitch it too low, you're insulting their intelligence, if you pitch it too high it just goes over their heads and they won't be able to participate.' (81: 5, 7)

Further, although one had to 'put it over like there's nothing rehearsed' it took a lot of preparation and the instructor would have rehearsed it and 'catered for every contingency that may arise'. Such effort is not cost-effective in large teaching groups because it relies on participation; students must not feel they are merely an audience.

That theme underlies the contrast between recruit and experienced-officer training, as it does the debate between instructors about the advantages of a system which has sought lately to focus more on practical police work than regurgitating legal definitions. Certainly in rote learning the lack of student participation outside stereotyped classroom roles made for problems of motivation and commitment.

'When I did the (old) thirteen-week course . . . an instructor came in with a big wad of notes and read them to you. Of an evening, you went back to your room and wrote out all these notes in longhand. You was thinking, "Crikey, I've got all this to write up, I've uniform to press, and the bar opens at nine o'clock." So there was very little attention paid to the actual note-making. Very little communications from the class. One-way traffic, and the learning curve came in. You used to get definitions pumped into you, ninety-three of them, which you had to learn parrot fashion.' (81: 4, 5)

Rote learning was not just a poor teaching method but inappropriate for police work.

'Somebody comes up to the recruit. "The bloke living down the street, I've not seen him for two days. His milk's still on the step." What definition did that cover? Know a lot about law . . . but law is a very minute part of our daily happening. We're dealing with the people in the street. That was never taught so the lad had to radio, "Hello, Sergeant, a woman has reported . . . " "Well, deal with it." "Well, I've not been told how to deal with it."' (81, 4, 5–6)

This indicates a live contrast between rote and inductive learning. One instructor learnt much from a visit to a French police academy. Sessions for raw recruits were typified by the use of a road accident video. The clip shows the unfolding course of events. The students are involved by being asked what information they have from the video. 'That's listed on the board, it's within their knowledge, and they've participated' (81: 4, 4–5). Such methods draw on resources, and are partly matters of class size. Recruit intakes are now lower than the groups of forty seen at the start of research. An overall figure of fifteen per class was given in 1981 (81: 1, 3). Class sizes are also amenable to a more interactive teaching style at DTCs, where even class sizes considered 'large' by instructors seldom exceed twenty-six (81: 4, 3). The video equipment is already in this force as in others, for training senior officers in media presentations. It is under-utilized for lack of staff knowledgeable and imaginative about how to use it. As with computers there is a shortage of skilled staff. 'There'll definitely be a growing need for people who know how to program. We're stuck in this force at the moment as we haven't got the money' (81: 2, 13). Applications of computing and video technology remain at the margin of the training expertise, and barely touch recruits.

It is easy to collect expressions of job satisfaction from PTIs. Some even place the work more highly than operational service: 'If I could kick everything out of the window and just do community relations courses I would have tremendous fun' (81: 1, 8). The work demands flexibility, the TE having to be responsive to a fluctuating market – 'we sometimes get little courses to put on from traffic wardens to civilian instruction'. Recourse to professional pride assuages frustration.

'There is no organisation in this country that can get courses over quicker and more effectively than we can. We've got some men who are natural teachers . . . The ability they've got is to a professional level which in the two years that they work here, it's quite formidable. When you think of the variety of things they have to do.'(81: 3, 5–6)

It was a demanding role with intrinsic satisfactions.

'I've got fairly dedicated men that are dedicated trainers. Occasionally one slips through who wants an easy life but I can assure you that he would soon go because there's just not an easy life here. You often hear the cry, "Let me go out to have a rest on Division," whereas Division always reckons the other way round.'   (81: 3, 10–11)

Another instructor related his own index of satisfaction to a minority but significant version of the police task, a neat instance of the acquisition of a (deviant) organizational criterion of value.

'Police training centre initial ten-week course, most rewarding job. I never went for good "results". If my class shook hands at the end and said, "Thanks for all you've done," I thought, "That's given them something to go on, some good advice from the past." I'm not bothered about the lad with the 92 per cent in the back row. . . . Some still write to me and that's the success I measure. . . . We've got too much round examinations and results instead of moulding a person to go out into the community.' (81: 4, 11)

For the instructors, training is a way they can put forward their own interpretation of police work. But this is subject to the powerful constraint of the centrally dictated syllabus. The syllabus is set by the Central Planning Unit (CPU). Their emphasis is 'uniformity of aim'. The scope for interpretation at force level was mainly within teaching methods and not syllabus but variations occur in examples and exercises, not least because the syllabus dates. 'The CPU can't foresee every new change . . . and they expect us to use common sense. Some of the exercises aren't geared to modern-day policing. I would like to see more emphasis on all courses on the community aspect' (81: 3, 7).

As noted, classmarks are used as an index of instructor performance. This 'principle' leads them to stress more than straight lecturing. 'You are geared to not only teach the subject but by asking questions and exchanging views you can test whether they are learning.' The emphasis on effective communication justifies a tough pass level.

'This is why they ask for a 70 per cent pass mark. . . . Compared with other academic levels that's rather a high standard . . . but bearing in mind the limited objectives you can expect that kind of response. It's not uncommon to get a class average of 80 per cent plus.'(81: 2, 4)

Yet instructors look beyond this to gauge the impact of their work. Like other teachers they see a certain tyranny in the marking system; the following remark is informed by the vagaries of the promotion system (itself overtly based on 'formal' criteria) as well as the grading system.

'Everything depends on the examination, and I'm afraid that measures the success of an individual in training and is looked upon right from chief constable down. If somebody has . . . hit the right day and right questions and got 91 per cent and been presented with a baton of honour he is a huge success and it's noted on his personal file. However, if the instructor has not detected that a lad has got problems at home that's never looked into. The girl at a certain time in the month will not perform adequately. You can ask them questions and suddenly they will run out of the class crying. A lot of officers have no idea about that at all. In promotion examinations it's the same. If somebody can

go into promotion exam, hit it right on the day, he's the right man.'
(81: 4, 10–11)

However clearly defined the 'objective' teaching system, then, instructors take account of more than marks.

Instructors are concerned with the character and disposition of students.

> 'On a normal appraisal file, the things we measure here are the endeavour they put into their work, their appearance, their ability to talk amongst, and acceptance of, their colleagues, the way they are themselves accepted. Their amenability to discipline, their common-sense general approach to everyday things they meet here, and their academic standpoint.'
> (81: 3, 15–16)

Matters of deportment and 'attitude' assume importance in the absence of a means for trainers to gauge interaction with the public. 'How they operate when they meet Mrs Bloggs on the street there's no way we can tell, even on simulated practicals, because they are acting a role. We can show them a few . . . little pointers. I don't like role play, I hate it and I hate to see it done' (81: 3, 16). Believing this, assessment relies on manifest, surface matters which have, at best, an implicit relation to practical competence.

> 'We can yell and scream at them as far as deportment and dress. I take particular note of their appearance when they arrive here and, if they're bad, that's reported. We can bully them whilst they're here to get themselves up to standard. We can do something but it's very limited.'
> (81: 3, 16–17)

The instructors widely profess to see a contrast to the raw recruit after training, and use manifest physical signs to measure its impact. 'Certainly you notice the difference between initial recruits on a local procedure course and when they come back. The ones that were ex-cadets suddenly don't look like ex-cadets any more. They've matured' (81: 1, 4). One can press further for what these apparent changes suggest to the instructors. They argue that the essential change is an increasingly realistic appreciation of the role, particularly its constraints and contingencies. The mechanism is the corollary and contextual features of formal training, not learning the law.

> 'Some recruits quite clearly have misconceptions about police and in some cases . . . the misconceptions are definitely anti-police. They are the kind of conceptions which are, shall we say, inherited in certain strata of society. After their basic training, when they're beginning to get a better insight of what police work is all about – the restrictions,

the framework you have to work in – they begin to learn about the problems that a police officer has to face. Although we have a lot of lessons on police powers, the emphasis is on how these powers are limited. They realize police haven't as much power as they thought they had. They also learn that because of this you've got to be very careful in current society not to go beyond the pale. Not only because it's likely to bring criticism upon them but because it's not the best way to do the job. Play it by the rules, and always but always make it clearly understood that you're playing by the rules. It's no good playing by the rules if the bloke that you're dealing with thinks it's unfair.' (81: 2, 5–6)

The instructor gave an example. While out of uniform he arrested two boys in his neighbourhood and he had to invest considerable effort convincing them this was legitimate. The theme of the anecdote was exercising control by achieving consent: recruits had to become sensitive to the negotiated character of resolutions.

Change is not apparent from pass rates on tests. The instructors gauge the impact of their work from the response achieved in classes. They are avid for indications of the utility of their work. 'You can, talking to them, know they've changed. Probationers, I can tell their attitudes by the reaction when I say, "This is essential, you've got to do it" . . . and they're quiet. They're taking this in and not arguing' (81: 1, 5). These are the same marks of comprehension any teacher uses. The remoteness of a final index shows how hard it is to assess the impact of any teaching. 'You've got to wait until twenty years' time, when they are in an executive position and say, 'That was one of my old boys. He's doing something we were advocating twenty years ago''' (81: 1, 5).

Despite the problem of identifying the impact of their work, instructors are generally confident and enthusiastic. They are plainly aware of its limited (or obscure) effect. They accept that, in the contrast between formal agencies of socialization and occupational culture, the latter has a big part to play (81: 4, 9). Most accept that in the long term, the prime influence is working practices on shift, rather than anything in training (81: 2, 8). They are humble about their own influence.

'I must admit I can't see that we in the training department have the . . . necessary contact. You've got to be with them all the time. . . . The first day I always tell them, "I don't give a damn what you do whilst you're out on Division. You're here for a three-week course and all I'm concerned about is that whilst you're here . . . you will obtain as much benefit from this course as we can. Providing you perform satisfactorily, do a reasonable amount of work . . . you will get a reasonable report from me. If you don't co-operate you will be reported on accordingly." It's very very rare that they fail to respond.

It's as if for three weeks they think ''I've got other things I'd rather be doing but I'm here, I'll muck in.'' The only way . . . we could have more influence to be honest, is above my level. At inspector level, sergeant training . . . perhaps we could influence their attitudes and they reflect it in their control once they get outside.'   (81: 2, 8–9)

The instructors recognize the influence of training is limited by the way it is regarded 'outside'. Other influences on performance are named, centring on the working situation.

'The biggest effect on the probationer is the sergeant. Although his peers have something to do with it, you will find they already have been affected by this particular sergeant. . . . If you've got a sergeant who is violent, you will get a shift of violent police officers. If you've got a good professional sergeant, you get a shift of good effective professionals. The sergeant is with them all the time and as recruits he's their immediate supervisor. They look up to him immediately and what he says is the gospel. I've seen normal recruits turned by the attitudes of the sergeant and they become sergeants in that same mould'.   (81: 1, 6)

Neither formal training nor the tutor constable are stressed; close contact and daily control rather than the mode of socialization make for this influence. Experience of the work (and key incidents) is added to the occupational culture.

'What affected me was that nice little old lady that I wanted to care for (who) suddenly turned round and smacked me in the teeth. I learnt a valuable lesson I've never forgotten. . . . The police learn about people: when they're lying and how you can tell. You learn about people lying when that very nice little old dear, who swears blind she's never stolen anything in her life . . . you found the pantry bulging and she eventually admits she's stolen the lot. ''The lying rat.'' That teaches you. You're told a 101 times on your probationer courses . . . if there's any doubt about a prisoner you handcuff him. The only time you learn that is when you forget and walk ahead of your prisoner and look round and he's running like hell and you're having to do a bit of a run and might have lost him. That's what teaches them.'
(81: 3, 14–15)

Yet while experience is a great teacher, it is not reliable.

Instructors were critical of the programme of recruit training, touching on deficiencies of police training in general. There were several sources of dissatisfaction. First, the time available was too short. 'I don't think the courses as they stand are long enough. . . . The police are the beggars at it, trying to put a gallon in a pint pot' (81: 4, 6). This haste was less understandable now recruitment was healthy.

'I can see a reason for it a few years ago, to get a man standing on the street. Everybody that joined was a blessing. But now I feel if we are to go forward professionally we must improve. . . . I don't think there's many apprenticeships that are served with as little basic training.' (81: 4, 6–7)

The constraints of time dictated a pace that was not conducive to learning.

'They were on the go all the time, ruled from 7 a.m. till 11 p.m. In reality a policeman's life doesn't move at that rate when he's outside. So why give him this bashing initially? From breakfast onto the drill square, then into classroom, then swimming, then first aid, then back into classroom, then they change for PT and on it went.' (81: 4, 7)

Time was needed for recruits to relax and synthesize material. 'In this three-week package there's not even a recreation period. Even at the DTC every Wednesday afternoon's for sport where one can go and let off steam. It's got to be longer and there's got to be more practical applications' (81: 4, 8). It was not simply a matter of too much drill but of what priorities were seen within the tight package; practical exercises or role play applications were neglected.

The tight regime affected the degree of care taken over each individual. The lack of a means of counselling made for problems of 'quality control'; something like a 'personal tutor' system was needed. Counselling had never been managed well, and present provision was only token.

'It never occurs in the police force other than the remedial centres, supplementary training units on initial courses. All they have here is a tutorial at the end of his three-week course. Surely that's not right. At the end of the course nothing can be rectified and he's probably too embarrassed to tell you in the classroom what his problems are. He'll think, "If I say what my problems are they're probably going to laugh." But if we could get them in on second day, "You've been out in the sticks for a year, what are your personal problems? It's confidential between us, what do you see?" the course could be run in light of the faults of those particular students. But at the moment, you will have on Monday courts of law, law relating to dogs on Thursday, bonk, bonk, bonk. There's no variation at all.' (81: 4, 9)

Worryingly, the area most frequently named as neglected was community relations. In addition to DTC sessions community relations amounts to two one-hour periods on the three-week TE course. This was too little to get through the recruits' heavy misconceptions.

> 'We're not doing it. We get the chief inspector whose responsible for community liaison 'cause he must be the expert in the county. He's meeting the Sikhs and West Indians and getting involved. But people think this aspect is just the policeman with blacks. The word ''community'' is far wider than that, and a lot of people don't appreciate this but the community is old people, kids at school, women going into shops during the menopause and stealing. This is our community. How are we going to get round it? We've got to have a big re-think or else we're going to have big trouble.'   (81: 4, 14)

An entrenched conflict had grown up over the move from a thirteen-week to a ten-week block of initial training. The dispute revealed a division between advocates of a thorough legal grounding and proponents of the approach which seeks to relate law to practice. 'I don't like the present system of initial training because I don't think it is deep enough. . . . The theory (is) we rely to a greater extent on on-the-job training: the more experienced men imparting it to the inferior' (81: 5, 7–8). He had learnt about murder, manslaughter, coinage offences, forgeries.

> 'We had to learn ''definitions'' parrot fashion, and eighteen years ago I learnt it and I can tell you now. I found it a great help as a recruit being able in the back of my mind to go through the parrot fashion definition of what my powers were. If you ask some recruits today why they would do it, ''I am doing it under the Ways and Means Act, I'll do it and sort it out later,'' which is wrong.'   (81: 5, 8)

Those on the 'liberal' side also see their system as crucial in the enforcement encounter. Where the instructor spoke of the comfort from mentally reciting his powers prior to intervention, this instructor spoke of precisely that mental process as irrelevant and misleading. A sergeant, asked over the radio how to deal with a case, could expect to hear,

> ' ''I've done the definition of circumstantial evidence and forgery but I've never been taught this.'' This brought the ten-week course in, and a blend of practical policing and theory. . . . We get a lot of people, even in this department, who say, ''But the thirteen-week lot know these definitions, very good.'' It was good, for passing examinations, but it was not good for practical police work.'   (81: 4, 6)

The grounds for debate are set within the boundaries of routine practice, but the rhetoric can be deployed to support contrasting positions.

A good deal of identification with educational purposes, with putting the 'training point of view', was manifest in these debates. Instructors feel many frustrations with 'the operational side', despite their own circulation between training and other duties. The hypocritical stance taken by operational officers toward training was resented.

> 'If you asked all the chief inspectors that hadn't been in training they'd tell you it's a waste of time, we don't train anybody. Yet if you asked them their commitment to training, then it would be *our* job, because most of them don't see their role. When sergeants first come here you say, "Who does the training?" and I've yet to have someone say, "We do". It's you. I would say we train the trainers.
>
> (81: 3, 21–2)

Instructors are aware their work is a much-disvalued enterprise whose links to 'real' police work are suspiciously remote. In these circumstances the tutor constables could be something of a life-line. Taken from the essential operational role as 'experienced' constables their role as field trainers could be expected to instil in them a respect for training, and to give trainers a way to disperse new ideas directly among other constables.

It seems this is anything but the case. Many instructors are sergeants and have, when operational, actually chosen constables to act as tutors. They do not regard the TCs as a group but as individuals, and consequently cannot assess the current TCs. 'I can't answer that, I don't know who they are now' (81: 1, 6). Their ignorance of the present TCs shows that the integration of instructors and TCs is remote. They still see the TCs as important, but emphasize the danger in relying on one individual for such a crucial part of training.

> 'The brand-new, keen young police officer who is busting full of knowledge from the training school will go back and, if he has the misfortune to be put up with, and I use the term in parenthesis, "tutor constable", who has run out of steam or is fed up, there is a danger that he will lapse from that keenness, and not keep up his training and his enthusiasm.'
>
> (81: 5, 10)

Those that did assess the current TCs had a low regard for them. Some even challenged their worth on the grounds that the system encourages dependency. 'It's a protected environment. They've got a shoulder to lean on when they're in trouble, they know they're not on their own and that they can make mistakes and get away with it because he's there to bail them out' (81: 3, 12). As to quality, 'a lot of our TCs are not of the standard I would like to see. We've got the wrong people doing it.' It is vital to realize that this is one of the problems resulting from the organization's promotional and specialization system.

'If you're any good, after two or three years you start being looked at. If you want to get on as quickly as you can you start channelling yourself where you can get the most good for your future. So the better constables after three or four years end up in CID or traffic or the specialist squads. The other guys get promoted, the ones with supervisory qualities. . . . You are not left with the best man to use as a TC. You're usually stuck with that man you think, "I would rather he didn't do it but I've no one else." The only way to do it is to stop all the other processes so some of the best men are left.'

(81: 3, 12)

The system was unfair to senior constables who do not want promotion.

'Too many people on staff appraisal interviews write "non-ambitious" and, for it, put "failure" in brackets. . . . These men are ambitious within their sphere. They don't want promotion, they don't want the added responsibility of heavy supervision. They like the job they do and want to continue it. But they end up with chips on their shoulder because everybody else thinks they're "plodders" and "wooden tops".'   (81: 3, 14)

An instructor involved in training TCs initially approached several existing TCs. One told him their attitude was that most probationers were 'not much good anyway, I take them back to the police station and dump them' and another expressed particular hostility to ex-military recruits – 'they think they're the Queen's bees' (81: 4, 10). The instructor concluded that 'their senior officers haven't been very very selective'. In the TC training, the candidates were particularly loath to assess and report on their probationers. Instructors felt this was more a sign of resistance to the role than a practical difficulty to which a solution was being sought.

'It's very very difficult asking a constable to report on a constable. It's very very hard to get over to them that they must report. (They would) frequently ask, "What's your advice if there's a clash of personality? Or you get somebody who comes along and will not be advised. He's a man of 38, I am 22. He's old enough to be my father." I say you still have more to offer him about the job. But some of them won't be told. Is he the right man if he can't get over this minor problem?'

(81: 4, 10)

The constraint imposed on training by the organizational reward and management structure is apparent. Two things recurred in discussing the 'local organization' – consultation, and the correct role of management. Instructors felt 'we could have better management techniques here'

(81: 1, 9), citing the need for meetings to determine priorities and anticipate developments. The prevailing line was, 'we've taken a lot of the management ideas on board and we're not any better managed than before' (81: 4, 2). As to consultation, 'I can't remember the last meeting here, a staff meeting on training involving everybody' (81: 4, 12). With most instructors in the rank of sergeant, consultation between them and the highest ranking officers in the TE offered most benefit but was reported as least frequent. Management was seen as inflexible, unduly bureaucratic and lacking an appreciation of training (81: 2, 12–13). Key instructors with major responsibilities spoke of a lack of clarity about their responsibilities, and about decisions whose rationale was unclear. 'I've been off four months and my role's been changed while I've been off. I've been back six weeks and still don't know what I'm supposed to be doing now in detail' (81: 3, 20). Staff were afflicted with the feeling they were responsible in the event of mishap without being involved in decision-making, and by an impression that bureaucratic forms were more closely attended than functional content. 'I see myself very much as a general dogsbody. As someone who should know everything but only when things are going badly.' Criticism of senior officers is sharper when they are unacquainted with the work of the 'troops'. 'This one doesn't know about teaching. He's not a teacher, to my mind he just can't' (81: 3, 20). Some instructors seemed beleaguered.

> 'I feel as if the person in charge just looks on me as part of the furniture. I'd like to change my job. But for my men it would be disaster because I'm the only link that's got sanity at the moment. . . . Some of us have to try and get the job done but they keep giving us more work and telling us we're not working and can't see why we're pressured. He should be taking that flak from us so we can get on with the job but he puts it onto us as well.'   (81: 3, 21)

Officers under pressure in this way divert their frustration onto the 'organization'. The rank structure is seen as interposing obstructive distinctions instead of recognizing achievement or encouraging positive innovation. 'When they become promoted from sergeant to inspector they're told, "Now you're somewhere above the rest and you've not to be on Christian-name terms" . . . That's starting it off, a chief superintendent telling a newly promoted inspector. He's saying, "You must be a little more isolated." That happens here' (81: 4, 12). Feeling shunned, the basic grade trainers conclude, 'the only people that do any training are the sergeants, *they* are the junior management here'. They return stubbornly to the idea that no one who has not done the job can possibly 'understand' it. The people into the higher positions in training, the commandants and deputies, haven't had the benefit that we have of teaching and understanding the recruits on the ten-week course (81: 4, 13). Where inter-rank consultation over objectives and policy is a novelty there is scope for such scepticism to thrive.

Training could be a highly co-operative across-rank operation, if only because those with specialist knowledge will know more about that specialism than those of superior rank. It is also a vehicle for the imposition (or facilitation) of change in force policy.

> 'We're dealing with people (in recruit training) up to 40 because we've allowed some senior people in to age the force up a little bit. At one stage I had a probationer course whose average age was older than the initial sergeants' course. That was for a specific purpose.'
>
> (81: 3, 11)

Training is one of the few means available for senior officers to institute new policy and see that it is disseminated in such a way that innovation is seen as something more than a brief enthusiasm born of one individual's ambition, something which will fade away if one does nothing for a while. Training was used during the research not only to get a higher average age for constables but to explain new approaches to community relations. But training suffers the same as does routine patrol from an advancement and promotion system that instils a dedication to genericism among those who profit from it and disaffiliation among those whose orientation is prompted by the intrinsic qualities of the work.

Instructors and recruits

With some of these divisive problems inevitably being conveyed to probationers, the shift is not the only place novices pick up embittered sentiments about the organization. As we have seen, instructors regard recruits as having different abilities and needs to their other students.

> 'There is a technique to teaching your peer group of status, whereby I'm an inspector and I'm putting over certain things to fellow inspectors. Unlike a recruit constables class, where you teach them and they learn from you. In the senior officer training, you may well find some of your students have vaster (sic) professional knowledge than you. . . . So you have got to draw the knowledge from them for the benefit of all as well as guide them.'   (81: 5, 5)

Implicitly the recruits' own experience is seen as less relevant. The problem is that drawing on experience secures participation. Also, with more lecturing and less participation there is less opportunity to check whether the illustrations one has chosen are comprehensible in the students' experience. This pertains not only to whether a 'policing' example has been understood but to assumptions instructors make about recruits' experience and interests.

While they share several bases of evaluation with operational officers, trainers do maintain a somewhat independent perspective within the force. Any working group related by functional interdependence can generate closed-group qualities based on shared experience. But trainers are also somewhat set apart by the 'rest' of the force, and have enough knowledge of policy, proposed changes, and practice in other forces to adopt a somewhat detached stance. Even a system oriented to training rather than education, and with a largely pre-determined syllabus, can pose a challenge to existing values. Educators must assess, and this cannot be done without specifying what is 'good' or 'bad'. Their perception of the subjects, teaching modes and other aspects of the training programme which meet with most resistance reveals further differences from operational perspectives.

Instructors are plainly aware of recruits' complaints, but the crucial point is that instead of endorsing them they challenge them. Asked why recruits drop out in training, an instructor immediately named 'paperwork', but asserted this was no proof that paperwork was irrelevant or excessive.

> 'That's *the* major reason. It's so easy to say paperwork . . . Usually if they can't do the paperwork, they cannot adequately police either. I can never understand how he's a good practical bobby but he's no good on paperwork, because if he's a good bobby he's got to be able to prove whatever he's trying to.' (81: 1, 5)

The instructors' task of assessment and their declared orientation to 'attitudes', i.e. character assessment, encourages an evaluative perspective; their business is to rank and differentiate police rather than to assert all police are 'good' because they are on 'the same' side. '(Paperwork) is the main problem, and sometimes attitude. Sometimes aggressiveness' (81: 1, 6).

The instructor's perspective is also supported by the reaction of police officers to being in an education setting. The instructors certainly react to this. They are prepared to seek ways of making the experience more palatable, as noted. They recognize that if this is done, participation improves as do their indices of effective teaching, 'objective' or otherwise. However, they also remain loyal to the education enterprise, and assert their own perspective if pressed.

> 'They don't like being made to work at books. They find it very difficult to understand why it's important they learn their powers

accurately instead of adopting the Ways and Means Act and hoping. After the first week the majority get extremely involved and they appreciate what we're doing. If they don't then I'll look at them as being a problem.' (81: 3, 11)

The instructors are also aware what subjects are difficult for recruits and have their own idea why. Like the comments on paperwork, this instructor recognizes the complaint, is prepared to consider why it arises but asserts the worth of the problematic topic. 'On the whole they dislike traffic because it's not as practical that a vehicle weighs 3.5 tons. If you say a person is guilty of robbery they can visualize a robbery, but they can't "see" 3.5 tons. That's more difficult to teach. You couldn't cut it out of the training programme. They need to know it but if they were here they would say, "that traffic practice, ugh!"' (81: 1, 4). Instructors are given an 'objective' index with which to assess students and their own performance, but they also adopt a separate standard, that of educational criteria. 'The kid's in classroom from Monday to Friday every week. Nobody in an educational environment can say it's good for teaching or the individual. He's being pumped in a continuous source of knowledge from different instructors' (81: 4, 7).

The role of trainer therefore encourages adoption of a perspective which distinguishes different ways of tackling problems and different adaptations to the police role. The police organization does not encourage inter-rank dependence. There is great functional interdependence amongst constables in urban settings (or at least a great noise about it) but the different ranks are largely divided by the organizational structure. Incumbents strive to keep themselves from the purview of supervisors, and inter-rank relations are marked by stiffness and formality. Despite the constraints noted above, trainers may get closer to the way different probationers address practical problems than their future supervisors will.

'Some of them are clearly much more orientated to the non-academic side of police work and some do extremely well in class and when it comes to handling the public, are not so good. . . . The classes' reaction as a whole will often reflect this. If you've got a preponderance of practical people they'll hang on your anecdotes; if you've got a preponderance of academics you'll find yourself answering queries.'
(81: 2, 5)

As well as differing orientations to law and procedure, instructors are in a position to assess personal adjustment.

The assessment of probationers by instructors draws on qualities beyond those assessed by test scores. The idea of 'maturity' was emphasized.

'A lot of youngsters just get homesick. It sounds ridiculous but it's quite true. I sometimes wonder if we don't coddle youngsters too much. When I left home there was no argument, you were called up for National Service and you went.' (81: 2, 7–8)

The experience taught him 'to make decisions' but 'for a lot of the young recruits, ex-cadets particularly, it comes as an awful shock that suddenly they've got to be a policeman. It's a big wide world out there and they've got to stand on their own two feet' (81: 5, 10–11). Another mark of immaturity was rebelliousness,

'the general resentment of authority. We had one on induction (who) came in on the Monday and on the Tuesday morning decided this wasn't for him. Too regimented, he said.' (81: 2, 7)

They relate the selection criteria to qualities associated with training.

'Frequently you find people that are very poor academically lack basic self-confidence. A police officer who hasn't got a certain degree of self-confidence, he's dangerous . . . and ineffective. . . . They'll be diffident in their contact with the public, their reports are inconclusive, lacking relevant details.' (81: 2, 7–8)

There are other reasons than feeling homesick, being rebellious, and lacking confidence that trainers are obliged to keep a sceptical eye on commitment. The chief suspect motive is the job market. 'At the moment people are entrenching themselves, saying, 'I don't like it but I've got to stick it until things get better' (81: 2, 8). Economic decline makes it hard to distinguish 'true' commitment and whether improvements in the training programme act as dependent or independent variables.

'The recruits are responding to this (new training sequence) and we're getting far better recruits now than we've ever had. We'll never know if it's the system or that we have the opportunity with the economic climate to get better recruits.' (81: 3, 10)

Contact does not have to be intimate to give trainers a sensitive appreciation of the many influences on commitment; they see people at their first moments in the force, and the stages of contact with recruits not only give them a sense of the variation in 'maturity' and money motives but a sensitivity to the process of change.

'I've just read a file of a guy who was immature, who I didn't think would make it. He was a grand lad but he just hadn't got enough ''umph'' behind him. I could see him being walked all over. They put him at a busy division. He's come out of his shell.' (81: 3, 12)

Organization members generate rhetorics which justify and enable their work. Such rhetorics comprise a resource, not a constraint. Few rhetorical systems express an ideology so resolved that it does not preserve adages that contradict each other. They are available for use by either party to some disputed point. The police organization lays emphasis on common sense and practical reasoning. Instructors have a vantage point from which to strike an independent perspective and put views at odds with those used by recruits, operational and senior officers. Yet they adroitly reference, ground and justify their independent perception by drawing on the preferred terms of the rhetoric. Like their field colleagues, they endorse 'practical' knowledge and are dubious of 'theory'. This is so even as they appear 'theoretical' to those from the field. As the chief instructor said, looking forward to returning to operational duty, 'all the people here are natural teachers but there is no such thing as anybody not going back to practice' because 'police work is all about real people and real things and you can get to Cloud Cuckoo Land if you stick to the theory' (81: 3, 6).

Instructors are well aware of the limits of formal education, particularly where a syllabus is centrally set. They recognize what it misses by their efforts to bring more 'real' examples and anecdotes into training.

> 'If he is being posted to North Derbyshire I always tell them, "What do you know about horse-racing?" "Nothing, Sergeant." "What do you know about pigeons?" "Nothing, Sergeant." "What do you know about bookmakers' shops?" "Nothing, Sergeant." "Have you ever had an allotment?" "No, Sergeant." "Well, they're the four things you ought to be considering before leaving here as a policeman." Because you've got a common factor there to talk to these people on. You'll be an alien otherwise. That's not in the syllabus at the training centre. It's not in the syllabus here. Its not in the one for tutor constables. It's something you can pass from experience of working in a mining area.'   (81: 4, 11)

By these anecdotes instructors seek to demonstrate their practical wisdom to recruits, and bring home the value of training.

The appeal to practice is an element in the rhetoric that smooths the structure of the organization. Asserting the commitment to practice is a way of joining ranks. Drawing on the rhetoric of the field is a way of asserting the solidarity of police; expressing the primacy of practical skills claims that in the end trainers, recruits and operational officers are all police together. An instructor relates this assertion of common identity to another 'democratizing' technique, that of managing while appearing not to manage.

'It's down to the manager, the instructor, to engender the enthusiasm in the student to want to experiment. Everyone is going to make mistakes in this job but as a manager and a supervisor you've got to say, "I'm pleased you had a go yourself. However, next time don't you think you might do it this way?" With the police service you've got to learn how to do it, how to get your hands dirty. Because when all's said and done, we are all constables. No matter how high a professional status you hold you have got to be prepared to get off your horse and do the job with the chaps.'   (81: 5, 6)

It is a sensitive statement of a delicate skill. What is significant is that, for these educators, the claim to professional value is made not on the grounds of special expertise but by reference to those qualities the operational ethos endorses.

Tutor constables and their work

Officially TCs should 'instruct the probationer in the wise use of discretion in a non-discriminatory way, promote the doctrine of the use of minimum force and provide guidance on the correct approach to the public to avoid complaints and enhance relations' (Brown and Cochrane 1984: 13). Although TCs are 'teachers' with high salience to recruits they are not ciphers for the organization. 'The newcomer must be more concerned with satisfying the expectations of the coach than . . . of the organisation – although such expectations are often congruent' (van Maanen 1975: 226). From watching the TC, recruits learn that organizational demands are always strained through the biography, perception, and situated knowledge of the officer on the ground. TCs provide guidance at the most critical period in recruit careers. Wycoff and Susmilch (1979: 41) often encountered the statement 'tell me who the man's field training officer was and I'll tell you what kind of officer he is'. The Police Training Council (1983: 7) maintains that attitudes are as much 'caught' as they are taught. Brown found that recruits tended to 'mirror' instructors' conceptions of the role and 'attitudes to police work were the product of a good deal of informal advice from police tutors who . . . firmly maintained they directly influenced attitudinal development' (Brown 1983).

With the general de-emphasis of formal training and corresponding stress on linked notions of 'common sense' and practical experience, the TC occupies a crucial position. In that training relies on early patrol experience to impart the skills and techniques of policing the TC may have primary salience as a readily available and officially endorsed model. While recruits come to them after initial classroom instruction,

TCs are their first intensive contact with a police officer. Others on the shift also play a part in this but are confined by the informal tenet that one does not interfere with another's recruit. The recruit's first lesson tempers, if not destroys, their valuation of formal training. Recruits find how great their ignorance of practice is in their first encounters with police who have a detailed knowledge of local terrain and public. 'By watching and mimicking, the neophyte learns characteristic ways to deal with the objects of his occupation: the rowdy bar, the "brass" in the department . . . and the criminal justice complex itself' (van Maanen 1974: 92). Much of this situated knowledge could not form an overt part of training because it is a 'subversive' knowledge. It includes the details of practices generated by the ranks for coping with the work, and their operating ideology justifying these practices, which may well diverge from approved procedure.

Informal socialization exerts strong influence in a way seldom attempted in training. It emphatically suggests how to interpret street events and, furthermore, the interpretation is underlined by the recruit's continual discovery of new-to-him, familiar-to-them experience. The reinforcement of their ready-to-hand interpretation is by engagement in practice, whereas the reinforcement of formal knowledge is only by the indirect means of tests. 'Events are normally interpreted to him by his FTO and other veteran squad members. Thus the "reality shock" . . . is absorbed and defined by the recruit's fellow officers' (van Maanen 1977: 28). But it is not just forming a conceptual apparatus which affords an inroad to the occupational culture. The more tangible prod impelling the recruit to investment in the meanings of the occupational culture is the routine demands of the organization for paperwork and procedure. Surrounded by those who are adept at handling matters, the recruit would have to be confident indeed, if not actually suicidal, to reject the model at hand. It is not at this stage that one would expect to encounter recruits with their own adaptations.

The first patrol is invariably emphasized as exerting strong influence on recruits. Many suffer stage fright. Anxiety heightens the acceptance of candidate procedural models.

> 'When I first went out I had forgotten everything. The first day I was frightened somebody was going to say, "He's got this and he's been to that," and expect me to know what to do; and I went with a tutor bobby and he shows you everything what to do.'   (7: 1, 4)

By this time a contrast with formal, by-the-book, procedure was established. The distinction did not reduce recruits' assessment of formal training but signalled its limitations. The TC is not a better teacher but a more strategically located one.

'It's the best training you'll ever get up at the training school but you think you know it all and when it comes to practice you don't. You lose all confidence until you're taken out with your tutor bobby and he does it all, you watch him and then he says, "Right, you can do one now." If you're doing it wrong he'll say, "Right, let's stop," and he will carry on. If somebody shows you what to do, you'll do it, but read it from a book, it's hard.'

(7: 1, 4)

Clearly the invitation to model one's practice on the TC is strong if he 'does it all' and even takes over the handling of some incident at strategic moments for learning. Rapport is of great importance to the recruits. '(We got on) like a house on fire. He was a good lad and he helped me no end. He'd done a tutor constable course, but he was a good lad and he nursed me all the way through it' (11: 1, 6). Here there is emphasis on personality in preference to either the experience (the recruit was vague about this) or the TC's training (he had been on a course *'but* he was a good lad').

Despite the dramatic assertion that 'if you went out straight on your own you just wouldn't stand a chance', recruits discern different approaches to practice. 'He was the old-fashioned sort. He did still believe that if you saw something (where) you could use your discretion, use it. He's right of course' (7: 2, 4). This also identifies a danger for the TC in undertaking such work; they are opening themselves to scrutiny by supervisors. Their practice, style and attitudes become more highly visible.

'The first fortnight (the TC) didn't talk a lot, and I was trying to weigh up whether he was a reasonable man and I think he was trying to weigh me up to see if I was a clown. . . . As you get on in this job you get more and more guarded and keep yourself more and more to yourself. You keep your opinions and your attitudes to yourself. He was a great bloke but he never ever expressed an opinion on anything or made a statement unless somebody asked him. That's how senior bobbies get, and he had seven years' service.'

(9: 1, 6)

In a 'young' force, the organization is hard-pressed to produce appropriate tutors, as recruits are aware. 'If I got my two years in today there's nothing stopping me going on a tutor bobby's course and taking someone out' (7: 1, 6). Scarman (1981) argued that 'practical training and supervision in the handling of people in situations of potential conflict' was best handled in recruit training by a TC scheme, while the Superintendents' Association urged 'experienced constables should be encouraged to remain on the beat as tutor constables' (letter to the Scarman Inquiry, 28.7.81). As Jones and Winkler (1982) note, there is no shortage of experienced officers, with over half with at least seven years in. The problem is their removal from the beat, leaving tutoring to be done *ad hoc*. The criterion was the negative one of identifying those who some damning trait prevented from tutoring and using everyone else. 'You don't talk in terms of attributes, you talk in terms of disqualifications' (Jones and Winkler 1982: 108). A detective constable returned to the beat as a punishment acknowledged that he would be 'afraid of putting somebody on the wrong footing' because of his disenchantment; in Jones and Winkler's assessment, the *ad hoc* allocation of TCs taught 'little but a contempt for beat work' (p. 108).

As noted, recruits are aware of these pressures. This recruit accounted for the sequence of his TC attachment as one of assessment, eagerness to impress, and growing confidence.

> 'You didn't quite know what to expect. It was the shock from coming out of training school. You're out on the beat with a bobby, trying to impress him, and don't want to make too many mistakes and see how the job goes as well. After about the third week you're starting to look for things and saying, ''What are we going to do about that?'''
>
> (12: 1, 13)

He actually sees eagerness to impress as impeding acquaintance with the job – alert to censure one tries to 'see how the job goes as well'. The initial relationship is reserved and the initial experience of wielding power on the street daunting.

> 'I'm getting on better with him now because I know him better. Before you go on the job you're not used to talking to people openly and to asking somebody for something, say a driving licence. It's a bit nerve-racking actually, stopping a vehicle, but as he brings you into it you get a bit closer and towards the end of the six weeks you've got your character over to him and you know him as well.'   (12: 2, 5)

Increasing realism and confidence means slavish modelling is seen as declining to the end of the tutored time. One begins to build one's own style. Asked if he tried to copy the TC's style he replied, 'Yeah, sure. I followed him and then I got me own style now and it works. I've had no complaints' (12: 2, 5). The initial experience the recruit draws on is a selective one based on the TC's own style and predilections, as well as variations of locality. 'Your first impression on the streets is with your TC. This is the first time you've been out so what he does, you do. You have to' (12: 3, 10). The TC's influence, despite its importance, is also temporally located and limited.

As will be recalled, police instructors express a jaded view of TCs, complaining that little thought other than availability goes into their selection. None of the TCs interviewed had put themselves forward. There were often no alternative choices. '(Do they ever give you any grounds?) They don't have to when you're in a station with only three on a shift. One's on annual leave . . . the other lad was the probationer' (83: 4–5). When there were numerous recruits choice was indeed *ad hoc*. 'I can remember thinking "tremendous, probationers joining the shift". Now it's more through lack of choice that we were picked' (83: 3, 4). Along with randomness goes uncertainty about whether they have performed well. '(I) said, "I've all on looking after me, never mind looking after a tender-aged kid." But it were pointed out that I didn't have any choice. I don't know whether I'm any good at it or not' (83: 4, 3).

Nor were all TCs chosen for the TC course.

> 'The sergeant asks, "How would you like to be considered for the tutor constables' course? We feel that you're good enough to show somebody else what to do." It's no reflection on those that weren't chosen. It's just that the ones that were were felt to be superior to the others.'
> (83: 1, 5)

With assignment rather capricious it is unlikely that selection would engender an orientation to oneself as a 'teacher'. However one WPC's favourable experience of training encouraged this perspective.

> 'Obviously it's more detailed (as an instructor) and it's a very hard training you go through, but I would (wish to serve as an instructor) because I'd have good opportunity then of getting them prepared for going out on the street. Rather than showing them how to do it I've got some say in preparing them. You've got to be that enthusiastic about it so that they are prepared when they get out on the street.'
> (83: 3, 3–4)

Such a strong interest in training was unusual among TCs. This is unsurprising when the training for the role is considered. Tutor constable training has evolved in an *ad hoc* way. A required form of assessment was introduced before training was given. The new two-day TC course was to discuss aims of TC attachments: 'what problems you'll encounter, how to get round them and general instructions of what to do with them' (83: 1, 5). Course content varies, with differing sites and course instructors. 'An inspector came down for the training, and we discussed what we did, what we should do' (83: 3, 4). Another reported a one-day course: 'Talking about what you should do, points you should bring to the attention of your senior officers, your report' (83: 2, 4).

It is said to be difficult to make a constable assess another, but this and the evident commitment of probationers stood for the importance of the role. 'Your report is important and I always say, "If you're no good I'm going to say you're no good, because if you're not someone else will say, so why waste everybody's time." After six weeks they've worked hard, I've always found' (83: 2, 4). Most acknowledge that for a time the tutor is a strong role model. 'Certainly in my case you base a lot of your style and the way you do the job on the person you're attached to' (83: 1, 4). The most justifiable modelling is of routine procedures, where the TC 'knows the ropes'. One who did not expect modelling said it did apply 'when it comes to paper' (83: 2, 5). Probationers are seen as avid for practical knowledge and likely to borrow from anyone with expertise. 'If I'm not there they probably talk to him and say, "If you do it like that you'll be all right"' (83: 2, 6). Jealous remarks reveal an awareness of different styles.

'What I ask is, "If I have taught you a certain way and you're not quite sure, don't go to another police officer, because he will tell you something different." Obviously if that person needs immediate help from one of the experienced bobbies I don't say totally ignore him, but just on things that I try and teach. Because there is set patterns and it's much easier if you do a certain set system.' (83: 5, 6)

The TCs also perceive different degrees of modelling.

'They pick up your techniques for wording particular parts of statements, and follow the way you talk to people. It does all depend on whether it's an 18-year-old or a 35-year-old. A 35-year-old I don't expect to have to say, "This is how we talk to people in Staveley."' (83: 4, 7–8)

They were also aware of the risk in such reliance.

'If you get somebody who has not dealt with much or isn't really bothered, and all he can do is show you the various tea spots and places to hide from the gaffers, that might be hard for some people but it doesn't give them any education in the job.' (83: 1, 4–5)

It is implicit in this assessment that the probationer is not simply being brought into the role but into the culture which grows up around practice of it.

'A beat attachment is your start. It gives you a practical start on the beat that you will work, the area or the station. Come from training school, you don't know anyone from the station, we all look after him for six weeks. You take him round, make him known to practically everybody that you know, pointing out who the criminals are and who are the reasonable people who will help you out.' (83: 2, 3)

Also implicit was the contrast of formal training to beat attachment; the latter is really 'your start'. Further, a 'buddy' system is most appropriate because of the effectiveness of learning by example, the unreality of simulations, and because supervisors are overburdened.

> 'You cannot expect somebody who's just come straight out of training school to walk out on t'street and to do the job right. They can't do the job honour! . . . I'm not saying what I show them is 100 per cent right. But they're shown how to do a certain task practically, as opposed to their mates watching, making fun, whereby they might be a little inhibited. If they don't have a TC it throws all that burden against the sergeant. He'd never get out of his desk.' (83: 4, 5).

TCs grasp that their job is to bring alive law and procedures.

> 'All they think now is, "Litter: it is an offence to deposit litter into a public place from a private." . . . When you see somebody chuck a chip carton down we know that if we say, "I've just seen you drop that, pick it up," we can caution, if we want. If the situation gets out of hand we can take it further. But they're not sure. They think, "There's litter. If they do that it's an offence." It's no good being an apprehensive policeman, thinking, "Oh Christ, do I? Ooh, ah, I think I'll come back tomorrow." It's an on the spot job, so you show 'em "make a decision." ' (83: 4, 5)

TCs also see advantage in exposing more strong-headed recruits to other ideas.

> 'I still need more service before I forget how green and naive we were. Faults I felt in my attachment I want to make sure they don't encounter. Because even if they've got some ideas of their own, you've given them more ideas and if they've got anything about them they will consider them.' (83: 3, 11)

TCs perceived another important but unarticulated function. This was the opportunity to instil in probationers a sense that their work involved work alongside others. It was not simply a sense of collective endeavour but of exactly how one co-operated, e.g. the etiquette of information-seeking.

> 'I can still remember that (beat attachment) was the start of my police career as such: day one when I was out on the streets with someone. It was security in numbers for a few weeks. It's made clear they're not on their own. They're now a member of the shift, another pair of hands to get the work done. There's plenty of helping hands for when they get in deep water. I've been encouraged by my sergeant to do my

role as TC. If I didn't get any feedback off the sergeant, I'd lose interest. Like this problem: he was talking down to the public. I had to talk to the sergeant, "Is it me? Do I just not like the lad? Or is it coming over to you that way?" Once you can get that good relationship it's tremendous because you work together as a shift. There isn't a probationer out there on his own.'   (83: 3, 12)

Building a sense of team makes for less reliance on the TC, and incorporates probationers into what can be a powerful network of expertise, a pooling of specialized knowledge.

'The lads on our shift will come to me because I've recently been on a CID course and say . . . "What would you charge?" and "Can we do this?" On the same basis I will go to Dick who was a road traffic man and say, "Would you go for failing to stop or for failing to report an accident?" . . . and I'll get a bit of noise from him. That's where your probationers pick up a lot of information and good tips. Because it ain't always the sergeant out there with 'em. . . . Provided they come to you and don't go for a second, third, fourth opinion.'
(83: 4, 10–11)

A sensitivity about who and how to ask for advice is one element of a refined working etiquette. The TC found a recruit had been for a second opinion 'and I just clammed up on her'. Later she told him what she had decided 'and that was the bloody one I had told her first and I thought, "That's it from me, I'm not having that again."' Novices have to learn what is locally acceptable and who is jealous of their expertise. It is not just experience of the work but of the workers which is important.

These sensitivities meld back into the work, giving novices an indication of when to go by the book and under what circumstances this particular shift decides to take informal action. For example, in an assault the TC told an uncertain female probationer what his colleagues did. 'Look, even if she isn't complaining of assault it is up to you, looking after number one, to record it. If she wants to withdraw it later because it's her boyfriend, fair enough, but for Christ's sake let it be seen that you know what you're doing'. Her inexperience showed in that she was looking only at the fact that the victim had not been badly hurt – 'she's only got a reddening'. The probationer had not realized it constituted a crime because 'someone else had told her that domestics, it isn't proper assault'. Where law is ambiguous, novices have to learn how to use it as a resource. What the probationer also neglected was that, with disciplinary proceedings always in mind, she should avoid the prospect of complaint because there is no second chance if the required procedure is not done. The probationer had been reluctant because recording it meant a long journey to see the victim again; the TC's advice was to tell the sergeant as he would probably drive her there. 'They can't criticize you for wanting to do the job right, only trying to cover up for doing it wrong . . . 'Cause I fell foul the other way' (83: 4, 12).

The 'teamwork' emphasis is not simply a matter of network loyalty. It is expedient where it insulates from supervision working practices evolved over a period of time or enables an understaffed segment of the organization to carry on functioning. Supervision and constables co-operate in the furtherance of their preferred working style. At one station there were only three sergeants for four shifts, and no supervision at night. The subdivisional base was 14 miles away. Senior constables were acting in a supervisory role; they had a clear idea of their supervisors' concerns and acted accordingly, and it had drawn probationers more tightly to the working group (83: 5, 8). Some also felt that working with probationers benefited their work. It brought new knowledge from training, and revived enthusiasm.

> 'It helps me personally because I put that extra effort in during those six weeks. I stop more cars, to get him used to talking to people and dealing with different offences and I certainly put more enthusiasm into it. For their benefit rather than my own, but I do gain from it. They've just learnt the new rules that I've perhaps heard about but don't understand. It is a two-way thing.' (83: 3, 2)

It is a rarely admitted benefit worth capitalizing on.

Not every posting offers the full range of activities trainers would hope novices experience. It is a dilemma the TCs cannot resolve. 'At a quiet station . . . you're not going to deal with a lot of the jobs but at a busy station you deal with a lot of repetition work' (83: 1, 6–7). A posting to Derby city might promote expertise in dealing with shoplifters but the probationer would deal with few accidents, whereas a country beat would be the converse. The TCs see a need for balance in types of work and in the amount. The form they complete reinforces this.

> 'The important thing is that you attend at least one injury accident, one detected crime, you'd be very unlucky if you got neither. I look to deal with at least one of everything. . . . I'm not saying you can do that throughout the county.' (83: 2, 4)

Pace is an issue. 'Not too busy but enough to keep you going. If you went to Derby you would deal with everything in six months and come out of it all inferior in work standard' (83: 2, 5). Sensible ideas of the desirable mix exist, but too few such postings exist.

'Wouldn't it be nice if for every probationer you could say, "We're going to put you into Perfect Land, where you've got rural, the town, the work but also the public contact. Time to sit down and explain everything, time to get the process done." That never happens.'(83: 5, 5)

The pedagogical skills and techniques used by TCs are neither systematic nor specified. TCs tend to assess appropriate technique on the grounds of the probationer's 'personality'. They first insist on the need to explain procedures very thoroughly and several times.

'If you don't do that you're wasting your time. Because they don't know anything when they come to you. So you've either got the choice of telling them, and getting it sorted out, or telling them they don't know anything right at the very end.'   (83: 5, 5)

It is notable how early the paper record of the officer's actions receives emphasis.

'You've (a) got to explain before (acting). Then (b), afterwards you've got to explain the fact that you've dealt with it. Of course that *always* starts with your pocketbook entry. Your pocketbook entry is more or less your statement, practically your report on it. So if you get that right then it's an experience.'   (83: 2, 5)

Repetition is necessary before novices can lead interventions, but the number of repeats reflects the complexity of the case.

'I would say two or three "knock-offs". Let them watch how you're doing it and then let them do an offence right round. When the offender's gone it's (necessary) to discuss the difference between you and how he's just gone about it. Not in a nasty way, but say, "That's perhaps how I would have done it." If he disagrees, fair enough, might have a good reason. It depends on what work you're doing.'
                    (83: 2, 6)

Such statements indicate the thought TCs give to how to teach, as well as how to defend their conduct of the tutor role.

With TC training neither systematic nor directive, they have to make fine judgements. "You've got to weigh up your probationer. You get some that are very confident, deal with things from the beginning, whereas with someone else you would show them all the way' (83: 3, 4). Variation in approaches also occurs where there is no clear procedure. 'The way we deal with a lot of things is quite logical, like when you get a sudden death. It's things like domestics that you've got to be there, seeing and getting the knowledge at first hand. There's no set of rules' (83: 3, 5). The tutors make a plausible case for these variations – in novices, the case at hand, the law and requirements to document action – increasing the need to explain and check understanding. Further, errors have consequence for other officers.

> 'If you think you only want his (motorist's) insurance and he lives in bloody Wrexham and you actually want his licence as well then filling in that form can be very very important. If you omit one some poor sod has to go to Wrexham, knock on his door and say, "Er, can I have details of your driving licence please." '   (83: 4, 6)

Because the training episode is also a piece of real police work TCs break the convention by which each officer's work is their own and will carry out most of an intervention, or examine the novice's work.

> 'Before you give it to him I make sure. Before they put a fixed penalty on a car I look at it. "Fill that in, yes, right . . ." Show 'em, teach 'em through one, then let them do one on their own and check it before it goes on t'car.'   (83: 4, 6)

This TC has the novice 'do' the first case of a given type of work in a surrogate, guided role.

> 'The first accident that crops up, they will deal with. They will be the reporting officer. But the statement they take from a witness is dictated by me because otherwise you don't get any content. I sometimes do that even now with (colleagues). If me and a less senior bobby go to a job and he wants to do the statement I might find myself dictating it. You take a leading role through seniority. . . . I wouldn't sit there perturbed if the inspector said to me, "I want you to write this statement but I'm going to dictate it." '   (83: 4, 7)

From these ways of imparting procedure the novice learns not only how to provide a technically adequate performance but one which fulfils etiquette.

These points pertain to the tutorial relationship, but the skills TCs impart can also be specified. A particular interest lies in skills of talk, which somewhat unusually have not only received academic attention but are seen as important by constables. In police work as in childhood, skills of talk are first learned by mimicry. The novice is to pick up how the TC does it, because 'you've got to give them that little bit of a wean' (83: 2, 6). Re-learning such seemingly innate skills challenges the novice's self-concept.

> 'Some can talk straight away. But this fellow, absolutely full of confidence but it was unfortunate, . . . it was quite annoying to the public and I could see it, he'd really talk down to them. It's not easy to stop a car and go through the routine as if you've been doing it for

years. You never like to admit that you've just started. But I couldn't let him go on being like that because (a) he might stay like it and (b) he were offending people.'   (83: 3, 6)

It takes tact to teach skills of talk.

'You don't like to show the lad up and I'm sure he appreciates your advice really. Depends how you put it, it's really just as you have discussions with the public. . . . He's not a fully fledged policeman as such, it's just discussions.'   (83: 3, 6)

Because it challenges a skill most of us feel we already have it is also hard to assess if one's 'discussions' have had any impact.

'I did tell him how to talk to people as well. He can take the advice or not. After nine years' service it's nice to think you've got some rapport. I don't know how much sinks in. It's not a question of having said, "Has it sunk in?" You take it for granted that perhaps they are listening to you.'   (83: 5, 6)

Even in the inner city only a fraction of interventions hinge on physical force. The officer's ends are mostly pursued verbally. This lesson is grasped once the novice learns that the manner of talk and the inter-actant's displayed attitude are related. The TC tries to make this recognition painless and avoid gross interference in the novices' first steps. This cannot always be achieved.

'We stopped this car and I'd made up my mind it was only a simple light offence, we'd just tell them to get it repaired. I said to the lad, "We'll just talk to them and see how it goes and play it by ear." He says, "What determines whether you report them or not?" "Basically on the attitude . . . If they take that attitude that you're picking on them and they're really bolshie with you, you can deal with it accor-dingly." This chap was a bit angry and I sort of stood back . . . and he must have taken that as his cue to get his pocketbook out and report this person. It was only a petty lighter. He starts reporting this bloke, gets all het up about it and there was a fair old argument going on and I had to step in. "Just wait there a minute." I explained to the bloke, "I don't know what job you're doing, it's like any job, you first start from the bottom and work up. Unfortunately this lad has only been out two or three days, he's got to start somewhere, he's got to get the prac-tical experience." So straight away he starts picking on me. "Why doesn't he get the experience arresting burglars?" You always get this, but I had to explain what we were doing and that it was for his own good and it would probably be a caution anyway for the pettiness of the offence.'   (83: 1, 7)

What is important is not only the intervention (and its hesitant nature, a sign of the non-interference taboo) but the *posto facto* counselling.

'We explained things over to him and he accepted that he'd been reported. . . . Then I took the lad back and he said he'd dealt with two or three people and they'd all taken this attitude towards him. "Is it me? Why do these people get upset, is it the way I'm doing the job?" I said, "Partly, yes, your approach is a bit wrong." So you go on to tell him not how he should have done it but how he could have done it. If you tell them, "You could have done it this way," they accept that what they've done isn't quite correct.'   (83: 1, 8)

Talk is a route to the skill of assessing citizen compliance/resistance and matters relevant to demeanour.

'If you're the sort of person to say, "You'll be reported for this, I'll make a note," without using any cautions the probationer is going to pick that up. One day he might be dealing with a barrister and if he doesn't use his cautions he's going to be over to the court about it. If you're dealing with a bank manager you've got to remember who you're talking to and deal with him more by the book than you would an old tramp.'   (83: 1, 10)

These various emphases imply that in the experienced constable's view talk is a technique that can be refined. One's use of it can make the difference between success and failure.

'If you sit in on a dozen interviews for crime . . . you would pick up what questions to ask and how to ask them. Not so much, "What shall I say to him?" but "How shall I say it, to get the answer I want?" If you walk into somebody and say, "What about this theft then?" (he'll reply) "I don't know what you're talking about." How are you going to go from there? You've got to work to get it out of them. I don't mean hit them. We're all intelligent enough to detect whether or not somebody's done something just by interview technique, talking to him, questions.'   (83: 2, 3)

Probationers' poor skills of talk were seen as resulting from inexperience by older constables. One needed 'long-term experience of work and life in, say, a factory, see who's nicking and learn about people that way' (field notes, 16.5.83). The TCs are well-placed to observe faults, and to have doubts and 'inappropriate' attitudes revealed.

'A probationer (is) . . . a workhorse. If their interest goes, start walking round miserable, before you know where you are they have to go. Obviously if he's not putting any work in we won't keep him, not with three million unemployed.'   (83: 2, 6)

The role requires a good deal of intervention, and ensuring the probationer is getting enough practice while seeing enough of the TC's practice to learn routines. Simple copying is not enough.

> 'Whoever you're dealing with you try and swing it round so that he is taking the lead. Then you watch him and make sure what he's doing is correct, and if it's starting to slip you can always come back so he can realize . . . he's made a mistake there. He'll pick up the strings again and carry on.'   (83: 1, 6)

At first TCs must help probationers negotiate stage-fright.

> 'You've got an 18-year-old, he doesn't really like going into a shop and saying good morning, somebody's got to coax him along. He doesn't walk up to somebody and say, "Here, you're doing something wrong." Somebody's got to edge him in. Like feeding a baby. I've had six and they've all got through their probation. . . . If I'd had one drop out I would have been disappointed.'   (83: 2, 3)

TCs do assess their own effectiveness in tutoring. In paperwork as on the street, TCs provide a first audience and help probationers avoid too much rejection.

The art of such teaching is to give novices a feeling of agency and direct experience while protecting them from making lasting errors.

> 'They stop a car, you give them the form to produce the documents, which is a real to-do because it's the first task you've given them. And you have to butt in because the tax is out of date and they haven't noticed. It's things like that, where you can't let the offence go missed . . . when they feel, "Oh, no, I thought I was doing great"; it takes the wind out of their sails.'   (83: 3, 6–7)

Managing these delicate situations calls on tact.

> 'I never say, "Oh, this is Constable So-and-so, he's just started." That's one of the worst things you can do. There are some that haven't got the confidence, can't go into the middle of the road and stick their hand up in the air and expect the car to stop.'   (83: 3, 7)

One extra dimension is tuition in the consolidation and advancement of one's career.

> 'If someone asked me, "Which is the best way to get on?" certainly they've got to make themselves known . . . and the best way is by things that get put forward with their name on. But this view about getting more arrests or knock-offs is a bit false. The routine work, paperwork, adds to your file, your name's gone forward. . . . You do have to get some initiated work to show you can identify an offence

. . . but as a probationer the emphasis is too much on getting arrests and knock-offs. They tend to lose the discretion they are first instructed to have.'   (83: 1, 9)

TCs can play a key role in moulding the probationers conception of what activities are organizationally and professionally mandated. The TCs shared this turn against the 'arrest criterion' of activity. At one station a list had lately come out of every constable –

'How many reported for crime, traffic, miscellaneous: one bloke had twenty-six knock-offs on his traffic. It doesn't really bother me, he had a lot more than I had . . . But I was intrigued as to what he's knocked them off for. When he told me he'd knocked one off for failing to sign his driving licence I asked myself whether it was worth it. A member of the public would have thought a lot of it if he'd just said, ''Borrow my pen and sign it,'' and entered it in the caution book.'
                                                          (83: 2, 7)

Similar advice is given regarding the discretion available within the law.

'You go by the book as far as the paperwork is concerned and when you're dealing with the public you try to. You make sure they use the caution. You can deal with something, afterward say, ''You saw the way I dealt with that, now that's one way of dealing with it but the correct way . . .'' and explain the way you should have done as per the book.'   (83: 1, 9)

Such lessons are valuable in a situation of uncertainty.

'I don't put anything on for their benefit because it just defeats the object. They're there to see how we do the job and pick up how to put the theory into practice. There's got to be odd things that are different. One thing that stands out, when you're arresting somebody, saying the caution. They're nervous about doing it. If I'm arresting somebody, say a shoplifter, I would say, ''I am arresting you for the theft of these goods,'' and just say it like that (neutrally) but it's, ''I am arresting you . . .'' (harsh tone). It's not bending the book but showing them how its done. As soon as you start talking with that attitude and a visciousness really, everybody looks at you. The other way you get on with the person better.'   (83: 3, 8)

These are sensible points. Yet whatever the priority assigned by TCs the criteria are only visible to managers if they appear in reports.

In fact the interactional, procedural and legal subtleties seen by TCs have no clear place in recorded assessment. This is not to say they are irrelevant, only invisible. The forms to be completed on probationers do not leave space for detail on interactive tactics, nor for examples of the level of practice achieved. They list several 'standard' incidents, requiring a statement whether they have been experienced.

> 'Everything that probationer dealt with you had to tick off saying that he'd done this – a road accident, a crime, a theft, a sudden death, a courtesy message, delivering a message of death to a relative – and put a remark how he fared with it. And (you) lost a lot of the cases.'
>
> (83: 1, 4)

Nor did TCs feel they were given an idea of what standard probationers should attain (83: 5, 5).

Tutors are acutely aware that they are required to assess the work of a fellow constable. They were keen to comment on their problems in assessment. 'I don't like to compare them with other probationers I've had. I just take them on the value of what they've shown me. (You) show the fault but if it's been corrected, show that it's worked. If it hasn't worked, put it down' (83: 3, 8–9). Probationers can present challenges to the tutor's vision of correct practice.

> 'He thought he could do it from the start and he couldn't. For all I explained he couldn't be expected to do it straight away to the end he was still striving to do the job on his own and doing it wrongly, causing a lot of problems. My role is to guide him in the right direction. If I've tried and haven't achieved it, it goes down on paper so that the sergeant, who is the next one to report, can look for that.'
>
> (83: 3, 9)

There is emphasis on ensuring good colleagues.

> 'At the end of the day you want policemen on your shift that are going to be good bobbies. If he's joining our shift I want to train him right, so he fits in with what is a good team. I'm wary because he is so "I-can-do-the-job" he's going to walk into a situation and get beaten up.'
>
> (83: 3, 9)

A constable who had tutored six probationers was at pains to assert that one who resigned had been 'collectively' assessed.

> 'Right along the chain everybody spotted he wasn't suitable. They did come down to me though and I had to be honest. That's when I thought, "Is it up to me to get a bloke sacked?" It weren't just me. I said, "I don't think he meets requirements on this, that and whatever." Then it went up from sergeant, inspector to superintendent. I was asked again by the inspector, "Do you think if we give him another chance?" I said what I thought and from then on he said,

"I agree with you. I just wanted a second opinion but I had my mind made up first." ' (83: 4, 3)

The TC goes to some lengths to present the decision as not just his.

Taking responsibility for assessing someone on the same rank gives tutors pause.

'"I'm a PC, he's a PC, have I any right to determine what happens to him? If I'm wrong could that lad lose his job through an error of mine? If he does, I don't want to make an assessment." The sergeant replied, "Put down what you think." I saw an "out" in the lack of space on the form. So if I think they're well turned-out I'll say that. If they're enthusiastic and show a lot of vigour I'll put that. Then I'll put if I think they are a sensible person, mature for 19 and I'm sure that in the next two or three years they will develop into a very good officer. If I don't I have to have a re-think. "Is it up to me to put down that I don't think this lad's gonna make it?" Then I just shy away from being exact. Put yourself in the position them poor sods are in. How good were you after six weeks? And were you given a chance? I wasn't very good at all. We can still be honest but we've got to be fair. If they're absolutely rubbish, and scruffy, they've made no effort at all to look any better or show any enthusiasm I will put that. "He's not very well turned out, it's been pointed out to him, he's made no effort to correct it, and his ability is far greater than what he has shown." ' (83: 4, 9)

Considerations of force recruitment, solidarity, personal experience and responsibility enter the assessment, but remain largely masked to all but immediate supervisors. An insight into the interactional and rhetorical devices by which TCs reconcile the role and assure supervisors their assessment is adequate is conveyed by a detective constable. It hinges on differentiating paper from real content.

'My assessment came over better by word of mouth than a piece of paper. I had a sergeant who was very good and we kept in close contact. So that paper was a very concise version. There's not enough room to swing a cat (on the form) . . . So the way we used to do it was we assessed each in his own way. If we went to a job and he made an almighty cock-up of it we didn't go harping back to the sergeant. I'd tell the probationer, and if the sergeant asked you don't say, "He's made an almighty cock-up," you say "He's progressing, see how he goes." ' (83: 5, 7)

There are problems in having one's work dogged by the probationer. 'It's all a bit of a bind and it is hard work. It takes twice as long to do everything to tell somebody to do it' (83: 3, 11). Gender problems also complicate rapport. 'My last one was a policewoman, eighteen and a half. Now who knows what's in their minds at that age, 'cos I don't. It's ever so difficult for a chap of 30 to relate to a young lass' (83: 4, 4–5). There being no allowance in respect of other duties is resented. 'I've got a workload already. Sometimes I have to say, 'I ain't got any time for you. But if I don't get this file in there will be repercussions so sit and read through some of my files'' ' (83: 4, 8). The need to present a variety of work could distort the tutor's normal style. 'Instead of you doing the village-type bobbying system, you cut yourself off from that. It's no good showing him the village, you've got to be looking for work for him' (83: 5, 4). It may even be that the probationer copies an 'aggressive' style the TC temporarily takes on to fulfil the requirements of 'variety'.

The role of TCs in promoting a contrast between training school and the 'real world' may well influence probationers' reconciliation of formal and informal modes of socialization. The TC's perspective on training is negative.

> 'If it's just going to be lectures and "remember parrot fashion the following definitions" that really is irrelevant to the job outside. As long as you can pinpoint that there has been an offence and deal with it, you can read up afterwards and copy it from a book what a particular offence is and what Act and Section.'   (83: 1, 3–4)

Another emphasized the pettiness of the TE regime. 'It's evil. You don't get any sympathy. If you fall behind you stay behind. And if you fall out with them on day one then on the last week you will have a hard time.' Personal experience was behind this harsh view.

> 'I picked up a chair at clearing up time in t'local boozer, and it just happened somebody had broken it. My course inspector said, "What are you going to do about mending that chair?" and I said, "Nothing at all, I didn't break it." That was my mistake. I ought to have said, "I shall pay for it myself, sir." Is that any basis for deciding how to work with that man for thirteen weeks and learning from it? So I struggled. Every time I lagged a bit, "RIGHT, YOU, what do you know about so-and-so? You don't! Right: come to my office tonight!" Huh! Silly.'   (83: 4, 4)

Probation and training distort initial service. 'First two years you're concentrating on getting your probation over. You don't really get sufficient time on the street to be good at your job. The next two years you're more on your own, you've got no courses to go to, you then learn a lot more' (83: 1, 10–11). The important point in these comments is the priority the TCs plainly give to practical experience.

Tutors were keenly aware of the lack of care over their own first beat attachment.

'When I joined, in three weeks, through staff shortage, I was put straight out in the unit beat car, and that was a rough area. I was dealing with fights, burglaries. I joined the shift at 9 a.m. and at 9.30 I was giving evidence in court through somebody who went AWOL, arrested him, straight into court the first day . . . I wouldn't want to do it like that again. I was in too deep. It left me . . . sort of shocked.'

(83: 5, 4)

The emphasis on 'experience' is not simply an endorsement of the 'sink or swim' approach to training; the TCs feel that care needs to be taken. Another problem was emotional immaturity. 'She had a few domestic problems, and what happens in life. We couldn't quite fathom her out, she cried with one, came to me, cried with me and went to the third one' (83: 5, 6). Every TC could tell a story about unsuitable recruits.

'There was a batch three years ago, a rather large influx from the forces. They reduced certain restrictions for these ex-services, and there was one chap, 43 when he joined. Even now there's a lot that he tries to deal with which you know is wrong but you can't tell him.'

(83: 1, 10)

Constables' ideas on the tutor role reflect their opinion of the organization. One compared selection as TC to the capriciousness underlying staff appraisals. 'I consider it to be an absolute joke. "I got on with X" and it reflected on the Staff Appraisal and "I didn't get on with Y" and again it was reflected' (16.5.83: 4).

Tutor constables bear attitudes that recur in the culture. They invest in and employ a rhetoric that binds them to other organization members, and plays a role in the replication of the culture. There is much that situates them alongside all other constables in the positions they strike on probationer training. Not the least reinforcement of their collegial identity is that the 'tutor' status is barely visible and has little tangible reward. Yet the rhetoric to which they can lay claim does have the added dimension, however limited, of their training role. At least in their need to 'explain' the organization as well as the work they have an incentive to sort out their own thoughts on the occupation. The interview data suggest that the training role has an impact on their own development and identity, and leads to a further refinement of vocabulary and access to one further way of expressing ends they seek.

Doubts, resignations and realism

As will be recalled the recruit's accounts of their experiences with TCs gave rise to broadly positive remarks, as though inviting them to reflect on when they first confronted the work called for a rehearsal of their passage from outsider to increasingly confident practitioner. This passage can be approached from another angle, by examining allusions to doubts about job choice and thoughts of resigning. These are instances of the negotiation of identity on taking up a career with marked consequences for existing relations. Even in the first week recruits seek the discriminating appraisal of the experienced.

> 'I asked them "as a policeman what do you think of it?" Because . . .
> I'm not fool enough to think what the recruiting people tell you.
> They've got a job to do, they've got to sell the police force, and some
> of it's flannel.'   (4: 4, 1)

Expressions of doubt were more frequent after a year's service, suggesting that, after trial by practice, they could be admitted to. This corresponded with data on resignation rates, showing a low rate in the first six months and over half the resignations between the seventh and eighteenth month:

Length of service	Number of resigners	%
0–6	3	10.7
7–12	10	35.7
13–18	5	17.8
19–24	6	21.4
25+	4	14.3
Total	28	

Resignation rates were high in two groups: the young and relatively highly educated, and the older ex-soldiers (Fielding and Fielding 1987).

This response, with its hint that the recruit is not certain he can see himself as a police officer, suggests that the initial experience of the work, and not the training, provides grounds for a decision, and that commitment remains provisional through training.

> '(Do you plan to stay until retirement?) That's a hard question to
> answer. It depends how it goes. It's an early retirement, isn't it, the
> police. (Yes.) It's hard to say. When I get on the streets I'll be able
> to tell you better. I don't see any reason why not if I like it. If I don't
> really like it of course I'll get out.'   (5: 3, 2)

In fact, he resigned.

The occasions which gave rise to thoughts of resignation after a year mainly arose from poor evaluation and performance assessment, as in this nicely 'socialized' adjustment of answer. 'A couple of times maybe, when you get told off by the sergeant . . . I say the sergeant telling you off but putting work in that was wrong, of course' (7: 2, 1). He contrasted his unease in training with his experience of the job; he found classroom instruction difficult, suffered a cautionary meeting with instructors, and experienced training centre as stressful.

> 'When I first started and went up to (DTC), I was a bit uneasy. But it's totally out of context with the rest of the job and it wasn't very good there. There was a great deal of pressure, but I never really felt like packing it in. I thought I could stick with it to the end . . . when I got on the street.'   (8: 3, 1)

Related to this source of doubt are worries about paperwork, the sole source of the 'many many' occasions this recruit thought of quitting.

> 'I've . . . literally got to the end of my tether. I've put something in my file and there's yet another form to be filled in. It's not that I haven't got any evidence together, because I had a lot of military police training prior to coming in. But there's so many forms necessary . . . it's the frustration. At one stage I got to walking towards the bus depot . . . thinking, "bus driver?" Then I thought . . . "No, I've got a reasonable job, I enjoy it and I don't know what else to do." . . . I must admit there were times I thought, "Sod this for a lark."'   (9: 1, 3)

Others console themselves that, in having doubts, even senior officers suffer.

> 'When things aren't going right, you've dropped a bollock and you're getting it in the neck from somebody and you think, "I shouldn't have done that . . ." But you all make mistakes. You get over it. It's happened to everybody, to chief constables and his career sort.'
>   (10: 2, 2)

He could not see training as likely to approach the responsibility and pressure of practice and therefore it did not present such occasions of doubt. 'All right, you're under pressure to get through exams but when you're out on t'street you're the one the county is paying to keep the peace' (10: 2, 2).

This tendency to identify bureaucratic requirements or the responsibility of enforcement as the principal cause of doubts and anxiety, illuminates the relevance of early patrol experience to the recruits' occupational imagery. They do not construct a perceptual apparatus and operating ideology merely out of belief in common sense as their principal resource, formal training as an irrelevance, and practice with an experienced mentor and in the company of veterans as the key value. There are variations of value and emphasis. Early practice is not just a universally valuable *rites de passage* but a source of anxiety and even danger.

> 'The first time you're outside on your own, you're frightened to death. You're wishing nothing is going to happen. You're thinking, "I won't know what to do." Sometimes you see victims of violence and you think, "That could easily have been me." Is it worth it all? As you get more experienced it becomes easier. It's the unknown.'
> (12: 3, 2)

The negotiation of identity, crucial to the officer's conception of role, is contingent; it is influenced but not wholly formed either by formal training or the model of the veteran. This respondent was asked if solitary patrol bothered him.

> 'It does, it does, because . . . the things you were taught earlier to do, you've never done before. Some people just can't report somebody for an offence. It's far easier to let them off. You say, "Oh, forget it, don't do it again". . . (rather) than report him and see him in court. You have to say, "I saw him doing that."'   (12: 3, 8)

Instructors recognized that for young recruits the job could be overwhelming and lead to resignation. 'For a lot of the very young recruits, ex-cadets particularly, it comes an awful shock that suddenly they've got to be policemen' (81: 5, 11). High unemployment, and high police pay, made officers suspicious of motives. A chief inspector said,

> 'Anybody who does join purely for finances does stick out. If they don't make the grade they will be got rid of now, whereas before they could be complacent because we were so short of recruits they had to be really bad before they'd ever be dismissed. While it's cruel to a few, it's very good for the job.'   (81: 3, 10)

This raises the pressure recruits feel.

The crucial period for acclimatization is related to the practice of patrol and not completion of formal instruction. Acquaintance with recurring events engenders confidence. When new events are continually occurring recruits cannot know whether they are worth becoming adept at. Confidence is related to perceiving a 'pattern'. I've been in 14 months. It's only these last four months when the majority of work is starting to come into a set pattern' (7: 1, 4). Repetition and not simply the TC's model was effective here. '(TC) showed me what to do, but when I was on my own for the first five minutes it just didn't click. I had to ask how to put this up, but now it's just starting to come into place' (7: 1, 4). The broad legal and administrative framework of action can be taught, but the contingency of real-life situations is too great to tackle other than in practice.

> 'They tell you if you see a person doing something you can arrest them, but it's completely different when you're out there, depending on what sort of person they are and what they're doing. There's no real point in telling us *how* to arrest somebody, they have to tell us when you *can* arrest somebody, under what circumstances.'
>
> (7: 2, 2)

One should not conclude that after a few months of patrol recruits regard their competence as fully developed. Again this is to do with the nature of events which do not recur frequently. This recruit assessed his understanding after a year: 'Very basic. I should think I've got a hell of a lot more to learn' (8: 2, 4). The respondent's emphasis on perfecting routine practices indicates that they wish to maintain a 'learning' perspective on the work. This exists in tension with the desire to resolve the transitional status blocking full membership of the organization, to be cast off as soon as practice skills permit. Some indicate limits to their knowledge which are worrying in light of the reliance of forces on probationer constables for routine policing. Particularly disturbing are those who feel their legal knowledge is inadequate. In the following, the recruit seeks to demonstrate his competence in interpersonal skills, a competence only necessary here because he has to cover his limited legal knowledge.

> 'I think I've got a good understanding of the public and the problems, but an extremely poor understanding on law . . . I will bluff . . . I'm the foot bobby in the town centre, I couldn't give you a pig licence. I wouldn't know what to do with one. So I go up to this farmer. He's a funny old bugger. He said, ''I suppose you know as much as the rest of them?'' ''I know nothing about pigs whatsoever but I'm required to come and look and you show me seven stalls and assure me they're in good order.'' There's 200 of them up there, so I said, ''You come and show me.'' We get talking about all sorts of things. When I get there, they're all fit and they're all there . . . and he's got them separate and they must be the ones. He's kept his book and he's signed it. You say, ''Make sure you keep your book up to date . . .'' and you go. If you go there and say, ''I want to see your pig,'' he'll tell you to fucking go and get on with it . . . That's what the job's all about.'
>
> (9: 1, 7)

The job is 'all about' making up the deficiencies of formal training and the disjunction of legal and social reality by personal skills of negotiation, bluffing and liberal use of the 'Ways and Means Act'.

After a year even those with high prior police contact feel they could not have anticipated the nature of the work.

> 'I was in the cadets and I had a bit of insight. . . . (I have) a lot more than I did, but you learn something new every day . . . about paperwork or the job or an aspect of the law or people on your beat. I've got a growing knowledge of what the job's about, more than somebody that's just joined our shift. But I'll ask him, if he knows.'
> (12: 1, 15)

Apart from emphasizing willingness to learn from any source, including those of lower status, this common emphasis on the continuance of practical learning informs their negotiation of organizational identity. 'CID, I'm not sure what they do, or traffic. But as a beat bobby I know it pretty well, what we do and our side of the story' (12: 2, 7). One can glimpse the recruit's forming posture towards the occupational culture – 'our side of the story'. What beat officers do comes to be distinguished from what beat officers feel about what they do. The beat officers' version of their activity becomes important in addition to their action. It represents a crossroads in the negotiation of a police identity. The recruit speaks conjointly of the expectations he has and those that others have of him. 'Obviously you've got an idea now being on the streets for nine months, what you expect, what's expected of you. But obviously you can't account for every eventuality you're going to meet' (12: 3, 11). The street still holds promise of challenges to his assumptions and any interpretive apparatus based on them must reserve room for upset. In a sense, his value system relies on the challenge of the unexpected. 'One of the ironies of police work is that the recruits were attracted . . . through the unrealistic expectation that (it) . . . would be exciting and dramatic. Yet the experienced officer knows such activities are few and far between. Once the man has mastered the various technical and social skills of policing (he) must sit back . . . and let his experiences accumulate' (van Maanen 1974: 97). The recurrence of routine events and the long wait for the unusual will characterize later socialization experience. Inevitably their focus shifts to the realities of police work and away from training. As it does so their recruit status fades.

4

Experiencing police work

The basis of occupational competence, according to police, is experiential. Policing is seen as a unique occupation, and expertise in no other area, nor any formal education, can prepare one for it. This stance may well be a reflection of the educational philosophy which presently informs police training, for it emphasizes experience as the great teacher. The police's assertion should be treated seriously, because they construct the practice of policing we experience. The emphasis of old hands and recruits alike is that it is only through the work that one can learn the craft. Experience of the work and stock reactions to i˙ suffuse the occupational culture which serves as the resource from which differently motivated police fashion justifications for action.

Asked to rate jobs as most and least similar to police service, at induction the majority rated policing almost equidistant between two main groups, respectively teacher/social worker/civil servant and lawyer/military/public relations. The first cluster suggests a 'treatment' or service orientation. The second cluster suggests the contrast of treatment with control-oriented occupations. Different adaptations to organization and culture were reflected in stronger choice preferences after a year, respectively, for social worker, military, and public relations, indicating some polarization of responses, but a fourth group, the largest, saw policing as combining elements of these three occupations.

Structuring police work: the shift system

The shift system is a generic term for the deployment of personnel, including the practice of frequent transfer and reconstitution of 'shifts' or groups of workers, as well as the division of patrol cover by time. The organizational unit for the patrol is the relief, comprising 13–15 officers; each has two sergeants and perhaps two probationers. Reliefs are organized into shifts, working different times each week for three weeks, having a long weekend and starting again. The late turn (2 p.m. – 10 p.m.) is consistently busier than other shifts, with early turn (6 a.m. – 2 p.m.) next and night duty (10 p.m. – 6 a.m.) lightest. In towns, however, the night duty (up to about 2 a.m.) can generate as many calls as early turn.

Shift work enforces the social isolation of police but also confirms their bond to others who must suffer it. 'Working shifts you've really only got friends on your own shift so it is difficult to get friends outside the force' (8: 1, 1–2). Such feelings are particularly strong after the first encounter with the system. 'I hate it. I was a cadet and it's just such a shock. I think we ought to be introduced to it slowly. I'm having to do seven nights all in a row and I've never done it before' (10: 1, 1). Shifts cut across work friendships as well as outside ones. 'You're going off early when he's coming on for "afters" and he might be on nights when you're off' (10: 2, 5). Consequently he did not 'socialize' with colleagues and led an increasingly family-based existence. But working values compensate for unsocial hours. A recruit explained 'normally people don't like nights, but it's part of the job and nights, theoretically anyway, is the time when you're supposed to collar more offenders' (12: 1, 3).

Tracking police work: paperwork

While the 'occupational culture' validates both resistance and acceptance stances towards the shift system its posture towards paperwork is less ambiguous. This is so for sergeants as well as constables. 'When asked which duties posed the greatest problems and difficulties, the majority of each type of sergeant mentioned paperwork' (Jankowicz and Walsh 1984: 6). In a group discussion, paperwork was immediately raised when comment was invited on problems faced by constables. An officer remarked that police culture was rife with paper, that a lot of it was 'back-covering' and due to laziness by senior officers and court staff (field notes, 16.5.83).

Paperwork was the subject of the most forcefully-expressed criticism of any aspect of the occupation, so much so that it invites one to speculate just what is so repellent to police about filling in forms. Even at induction 82 per cent agreed there was too much paperwork. This increased to 93 per cent by year one and 95 per cent by year two. That the activity contradicts the image police hold of their occupation has been noted previously. Moreover case files represent threats to autonomy, and this is so not just for novices whose files are being evaluated closely. Formal rationality hinges around the file. Files can be used to check the quality of work (Manning 1980: 228–9).

Attempting to account for the vehemence of hostility to it leads one to speculate that paperwork serves as a cipher for police administration, or even as a metaphor for the bureaucratic model of organization which jars with the officers' experience of the messiness of the real world, a disorder that permits their action. The freedom of action accruing from the legitimation of discretion, which underwrites their tolerance of the job's worst features, is denied or even contradicted by paperwork. Their relatively unfettered action on the job, for reasons hard to state, on hunches difficult to pin down, has to be filtered through the sieve of a formal account of their action. To add insult to injury the exercise requires skills that their generally mediocre educational performance shows they have never seen as essential. Paperwork becomes a symbol not just of rational police organization (with the ultimate *irrationality* of its assumption of objective and measurable behaviour) but of civil servants who are just those people the men of action have never wanted to be.

> The police define their 'real work' as face-to-face interaction with people in need of help or control . . . concretely defined in terms of persons and events, only converted by administrative fiat into paper after the social significance has been drained off by officer decisions.
>
> (Manning 1980: 220)

The disjunction of paper and social reality is amplified by the constables' knowledge that by this means their actions are assessed and even reformulated in the office.

> The arresting officer may or may not have a part in this negotiation . . . The issue is precisely how the rules and procedures of the organisation can be recast, describe or rationalise decisions taken in complex, chaotic, sometimes rapidly-occurring events.
>
> (Manning 1980: 222)

At induction the recruits' performance was chiefly oriented to paperwork exercises such as tests, and it may be this to which their early intolerance of it may be attributed. Paperwork occupies a star place in the demonology of the 'occupational culture' and it is hard to separate the influence of 'experience' from that of 'occupational culture'. Interview responses indicate that the culture acts as a repository of coping devices to enable attribution of positive or negative qualities to objects of experience, and that the cultural repository has mainly negative attributions for paperwork. It contradicts both the preferred occupational imagery and the ideology of the officer as employee with certain rights. Paperwork refers recruits back to school and to discipline imposed by senior officers. Both challenge their competence.

The demands of paperwork are seen as unduly particular. Confronted by forms which require 'a man's name and address on a file seven times at least, and his place and date of birth' the officers' preference to keep their cases in the form of 'scrawled notes on napkins, bits of paper torn from notebooks, telephone message forms and other handy bits of paper' is understandably challenged (Manning 1980: 230). A young WPC cited it as having caused thoughts of resignation; note her counterposing of this with outdoor activity.

'There's times when the paperwork gets so much on top of you, you're stuck inside doing it all, especially one time I had to get all my paperwork done because I was going to have a month off and I felt like screaming.'   (10: 1, 1)

Paperwork not only stands for 'book-learning' but interferes with constables' freedom of action. Since paperwork is a criterion of an officer's performance the activity of 'back-covering' by generating appropriate paperwork can actually impinge on the enforcement activity it supposedly describes. It is also a means by which another person's crisis is converted to a unit of work.

'You've got a crime report to fill in as soon as a crime's happened and if you're not very careful, you start thinking of the paperwork before you think of what you're doing. There could be an offender there and you're getting your paperwork out before you've assessed the job. In the long term the paperwork is more important because I'm in my probation and you can get in trouble over your paperwork a lot easier than if you arrest somebody unlawfully. You can get a refused charge and you're OK but paperwork going in seems to make a big effect.'
(12: 1, 4)

These complications are aggravated by contradictory procedural demands, creating the impression the 'supervision' itself does not know what to do. The way this develops into occasions calling for subsection loyalty is also indicated here.

'You have to fill in a form for your previous convictions which takes three days and on the other hand the supervision like an offence within twenty-four hours and I don't know what the admin. are doing. I thought that was their side of it. My particular section doesn't like you staying in too long and doing the paperwork. They almost don't recognize that you've got to do it.'   (12: 1, 5)

This culminates in deviance from administrative rules.

'I was wondering whether to say it actually because you're not supposed to take stuff home but I have done. Sometimes it gets a bit worrying with certain things that have to be in so many days after the offence, certain pieces of paper.'   (12: 1, 5)

In the interests of their own survival recruits learn the crucial importance of satisfying the organizational demand for paper. Yet recruits are not made party to the rationale which supports these activities, so their value remains the defensive one of protecting their position rather than one they might grudgingly endorse. The following responses contrast the feelings of a recruit with no real information to justify this work with those of one whose previous occupation furnished him with an appreciation of the need for administration. Asked why the same form had to be completed several times one speculated that it might be thought necessary to have it in the officer's own writing. 'Wrote down in your writing I should think. I don't really know. Get it in and that's it. We're not told where it goes' (12: 2, 3). Another officer used his experience with paperwork to locate its value in providing management's basis for officer effectiveness evaluations.

> 'There's a lot of paperwork to do but . . . my previous job stood me in good stead. If you've worked in the civil service there's not half as much paperwork as there is there. I haven't found that as difficult as lads, say, out of industry. No disrespect but sometimes the paperwork lets them down. The emphasis might be too much on whether you can commit pen to paper. (But) that's how they judge. There's got to be a standard.'
> (12: 3, 4)

One had resolved the contradictions of his role by opting for an unambitious survivalist stance – you just 'get it in and that's it'. The second had taken the role of the other enough to see how administration's need for the information could be made to serve his own interest. The production of good paper had become a vehicle for organizational advancement, not an irksome chore.

> 'The file's got to go in and the paper's got to be there. You can do a hell of a good job outside. You can catch a burglar. But at the end of the day, you need the evidence in court and if you can't put pen to paper, that's how you're judged. The first thing your chief inspector and prosecutions department knows of you is the written file. He doesn't say, "Oh this chap can't write very well but he's good outside." He doesn't know. So if you're on top of your paperwork that's the first thing that gets you noticed.'
> (12: 3, 4–5)

There could be no better instance of the canny career-oriented recruit, whose valuation of paperwork is not on his terms or the 'occupational cultures' stock imagery, but on the coincidence of his own and the organization's shared interest.

Experienced constables suggest the problem is eventually overcome by familiarity; only those concerned that paper will expose deficiencies of practice continue to worry and complain.

> 'I had two very bad years when I first joined the job but now . . . I'd class my work as fairly proficient. . . . I needed a lot of assistance and supervision. . . . But it's just . . . the same basic standard approach and type of report once you've mastered the wording.' (83: 5, 1)

The ability to cope well with such work becomes a source of pride, and a resource for distinguishing oneself in the eyes of supervisors. Officers in such a position can presume on a 'play ball' relationship with supervisors that reinforces their autonomy.

> 'I'm in a fortunate position, whereby the persons above me appreciate that if you're doing work then you must be doing files and paperwork as well. So therefore without a time limit on how long it takes you to do it.'   (83: 4, 2)

Experienced officers also admit the utility of paperwork in 'back-covering'. 'If they got rid of everything and just had the bare form you'd bear the rap' (83: 2, 1). The organizational pressure they experience evokes coping strategies which ultimately can be used to increase their control over the working situation. Chatterton (1983) shows how 'defensive writing' is developed into a fine skill in response to officers' perceptions that they had to anticipate criticism and take necessary precautions. None of one's jobs should rebound, making work for the bosses or obliging them to render an account to their superiors or, worse, outsiders. Paperwork is not only a bugbear but affords considerable advantage to the experienced in supporting their conduct of the work according to their preferences. Chatterton slyly notes, '*the low visibility* which has been recognised as a feature of police work is as much an achievement of the lower ranks as it is an intrinsic feature of the environment in which they work' (ibid.: 113).

Doing police work: beat work and specialist duties

While examining aspects of organizational practice which spell 'trouble' for the ranks renders some impression of the subjective meaning of identity transformation, the subject of their attitudes to patrol and specialist duties gets to the nub of the matter. 'All officers share a sense of the importance of police work on the streets. It is the baseline function and the central locus for comparisons in police departments' (Manning 1980: 49). Gaining experience enables recruits to differentiate the organization. After both one and two years of training 55 per cent agreed that specialists reaped the benefit of routine police work. It has been remarked that the police organization is marked by a paradox – those at the bottom of the organization have the greatest degree of discretion. As Black (1980: 9) notes, patrol is 'invisible, non-reviewed (and reviewable) and highly discretionary'. Yet the *irony* which marks this *paradox* is that within the organization the patrol division is least 'powerful' (Manning 1982: 7).

Within this organizational context the contrast between the needs of recruits and of experienced peers points to a discriminating calculus by which the utility of a certain period of beat service is determined.

> 'Beat work is the most important part of police work . . . (How about the others on your shift?) Some of them agree, it's just that some have put in five years on the beat and they're getting a bit tired of it, weather and shift work for a start. I think you need to spend four years before you specialize.'   (8: 1, 4)

Recruits generally sensed that more experienced offices valued beat work but this does not imply they are unaware that other valuable work may come to be regarded as more desirable.

The recruits' perspective is not necessarily enduring; they see the returns of beat work in the building up of a stock of situated expertise.

> 'I think basically it is valued. Most bobbies I've found tend to be rather proud of the fact that they do beat work and collect local knowledge and it is a very valuable thing. . . . It's surprising the number I've found that are quite happy to stay on the beat. They enjoy themselves, they know everyone on the beat and it's like social work in the end.'
>   (8: 3, 4)

His 'surprise' suggests that, as well as the scarcity of experienced PCs on patrol, those that were available were often disillusioned and cynical.

> There were those . . . who were dedicated to beat patrolling but viewed with deep suspicion and cynicism the way they were treated by the organisation . . . those who aspired 'to get off the beat' in order to develop their careers . . . and those who had been sent back to the beat after some transgression.
>   (Jones and Winkler 1982: 107)

Return to uniform service can be demotion.

> 'Sometimes you hear about people thrown out of CID back into uniform, walking the beat as if it's a punishment. I don't see why it should be but it's probably to teach him a lesson to get back to what he should be doing.'   (7: 2, 3)

The officer gone astray can re-discover the essence of police duty in the reservoir of the beat.

Consequently there is a recurring interplay of themes of ambition, experience, promotion and status. The specialist, promotion-conscious are seen as embracing a different conception of the work.

> 'They're all oriented towards status and rank and I think that's probably a fault in the police force because if it wasn't one would

accept, as the public do, that if C. is a good bloke it doesn't matter if he's a police constable or a police sergeant. Then the beat bobby would be a great bloke to know. At present the status isn't in that work, so everybody wants to opt out of it.'　　　　　　　(9: 1, 6)

That suspicion more simply expressed – 'I think most of them would rather be out in Panda cars' (10: 1, 4) – leads to an early awareness by the probationer that one has to reach a decision about one's own service orientation, and that it will involve either bargaining personal valuation against status reward or career prospects against personal values. A shift can 'hold' a view on promotion and specialist duty until someone breaks ranks.

'From what I've seen on our shift . . . most of them do appreciate the work they're doing. It's like every other job, it's not a bed of roses and they've got their gripes. Usually everybody's got the same gripe. Unfortunately the shift is young in service and in consequence they're not eligible really, but one or two may know what they'd like to do.'
　　　　　　　(10: 2, 6)

The 'age' of a shift closely affects attitudes to promotion, and the recruit's basis for interpretation of culture. This is reinforced by views which identify the beat with 'action'.

'You find most of the blokes like to be out walking the streets. We've got a very young shift. . . . They all want to be out on the street . . . they don't want to be stuck in, writing paperwork. They're at it, even one or two of the older blokes who've got one or two up-stages, they're beat work, they don't want to be stuck in a Panda.'
　　　　　　　(11: 1, 5)

The way the collective value system castigates deviants is shown in this reaction to the ambitious on a shift.

'Not all (of the older officers want specialist duties). Some of them like to think of being the big glory boys, and want a big salary. We've got one or two who just want to be good bobbies. Which is just being out in the street.'　　　　　　　(11: 1, 5)

The gulf is apparent to recruits.

'You've got different schools of thought. There are people obviously who prefer specialist work, and narrow their field down, there are people who enjoy being part of the community, being that figure in the community. So you've got a vast amount of difference there.'(11:2, 4)

A large concentration of recruits may be posted to a tough area where they will 'grow up' fast.

'I'm down . . . centre of Derby and my own particular section, we're all pretty young and keen like. A lot of them are probationers and they need to do the work and they get it done. So they all do a lot of work and don't moan.' (12: 2, 5)

On sections where older men predominate a very different impression prevails.

'You find that as they get older they dislike walking as much as they used to do. Once they've had a car beat, they're very reluctant to go back to walking. I'm sorry to say but they dislike walking, some of them. Well, I've only known walking. I might differ me view if I had a Panda.' (12: 3, 8)

Solitary patrol begins surprisingly early in training. Recruits are also surprised, although they appear to appreciate the 'sink or swim' philosophy. Solitary patrol is not just for 'quiet' areas. 'In Derby I was all over the city. It surprises a lot of people that they send you out alone. Just have to have that confidence or you'll never go out at all' (12: 3, 5). Apart from the time with a tutor constable, patrol is generally solitary. Doubling up depends on the area; in a local mining town pairing occurred on Monday, Friday and Saturday – 'when it gets a bit hectic' (10: 2, 5). Attitude to beat work revolves around the important decision recruits face as to advancement, with transfer, or developing a stake in a local area, a decision for which abundant time is available as they go about the solitary patrol that comprises the bulk of their outside work.

Recruits are predisposed to see an affinity between ordinary patrol and specialist duties. Consciousness of 'overlap' is a component of the rank's belief that all other activities emanate from the basic constable role. This strong belief pervades the organization. Its acceptance by senior ranks indicates that it is an important part of the police operating ideology, an article of faith. There is a powerful feeling against divisions and in favour of the group in the police service; its resonances are perceptible in pay negotiations, Federation conferences, and public relations interviews, as well as recruits' thoughts on separate specialist forces. 'I don't think (there should be a traffic police). Because there again they're in a "them and us" situation. They will see the traffic police as being something apart from the normal police' (2: 1, 2–3). Reasons known to be effective organizational justifications are given against moves which could dilute the 'real work'.

'Otherwise you get devoid completely of this concept of a policeman, you become a traffic policeman and that's your sole object in life. The

British police force has got a great history and a British policeman should stick to what he is, he is everything.'   (3: 2, 3)

Specialist duty cannot be regarded in isolation from the beat. The qualities that justify a move into specialist duty are drawn from capabilities displayed in beat work.

'If you wanted to go into traffic, you'd have to report more motorists for different offences, and . . . if you wanted to go into crime you'd have to have a fairly good liaison with the people in CID, because if you do get a criminal then they invariably help you, or take over the case.'   (7: 2, 5)

But this necessarily carries with it a consciousness that if the beat is a 'common pool' it is the base from which one moves on.

Awareness that a decision to specialize has to be made represents a further stage in occupational socialization. It marks the beginning of the end of the recruit's self-identity as a neophyte, a not-yet-full-member of the organization. At this point management – 'the supervision' – changes its relevance. It is no longer evaluating a previous decision, the one to recruit this person, but becoming oriented to a prospective evaluation, the recruit's best place in the organization.

'Your main priority is getting through the probation successfully and then to get experience. If (you) make it known that you want to specialize, I think the supervision do take an interest. You'll invariably find that your inspectors, they've been on traffic or CID, and they can be useful for first-hand experience.'   (10: 2, 7)

Transfer from the beat is the first stage in advancement, a fact soon grasped by recruits. Jones and Winkler's (1982: 109) survey of 391 recruits in training found that 74 per cent had definite career plans but only 2.5 per cent expressed any interest in beat work after probation; the rest wanted to specialize, especially in CID (45 per cent). Supervisors actively encourage this perspective; 62 per cent of probationers with 18–20 months service had discussed career plans with supervisors, and in 71 per cent of cases they were encouraged to specialize. Some 62 per cent of promotions were from specialized posts yet these accounted for only 19 per cent of force strength.

Constables' references to the beat appear as a contrastive article of faith. The beat symbolises the 'common pool' which cements the police culture through shared experience. The parallel to subcultural theory is strong, with its emphasis on collective adaptation to shared problems and the priority of early experience. 'Once I've gained experience, perhaps in two or three year's time, I might start looking around. It's important for every policeman to have that grounding before he specializes' (10: 2, 8). After a year of training 64 per cent agreed that only another PC understands the job; this increased to 73 per cent after two years. Those with a year's experience know they need to learn more from the beat but are conscious that peers are beginning to consider specializing.

'You get conversation, "I'd like to go to CID," or, "I'd like to go on traffic," but at the moment I don't attach much importance to specializing. A few of my mates do but I'm not thinking much about it because I'm thinking of the disadvantages of each that I'm not experiencing now. On the other hand, you're thinking, "Should I show some aptitude in traffic or interest in crime to make it look good later on."'   (12: 1, 12–13)

Being on the beat is not simply a general learning experience but a grounding for later work. It not only has a strong effect on how recruits think of the police enterprise but influences tangible orientations to specialization. 'The more experience you have you feel right for crime . . . (or) traffic. You get to know yourself. You either like doing accidents or you don't. If you don't you should look towards CID' (12: 2, 5). The idea that one 'gets to know oneself' evokes the complex way in which the job and personal identity are entwined. Importantly the one-year stage did not correspond to any dissatisfaction with the mix of duties; the variety of work was still stimulating. Even after two years 58 per cent chose 'interest and variety' as the main factor in job satisfaction, only a 5 per cent drop from induction.

Crime control and social service

It has become a truism that police work combines an element of social service masked by an overt but symbolic orientation to the control of crime (Manning 1982; Packer 1968: 118). Their most successful relations with other agencies are often where police bear 'service' roles, such as between social workers and juvenile bureaux, and beat PCs and housing estate managers, but the predominant view of PCs is that more time should be spent on crime-related work. In one survey 82 per cent thought the most important source of public satisfaction was rapid response to 999 calls, 77 per cent the detection, prosecution, and arrest of offenders whereas only 54 per cent identified helping on non-crime matters (Police Foundation 1982). Reiner (1978) found only one in twenty officers saw their work chiefly in terms of social service rather than crime-fighting. Jones (1980) showed that the public chiefly evaluate police according to their performance as helpers or comforters, while the police evaluate themselves against technical proficiency in crime-fighting. The British

Crime Survey found 'consumer' contact (41 per cent) was over twice as frequent as adversarial contact (16 per cent) and research confirms that only a third of calls are crime-related (Comrie and Kings 1975; Ekblom and Heal 1982; Hough 1980; Punch and Naylor 1973).

The proportion of the recruits agreeing/disagreeing that police work includes too much social service work remained steady (40 per cent and 41 per cent at year one, 42 per cent and 40 per cent at year two). The greater reference to social service in the 'joining' essays than in later interviews was noted. While probationers increasingly complain that much 'social service' work is tedious, it is not marginal to their conception of the police role. They argue that such interventions bring them closer to the community and this is not only how they become attuned to local standards but how they get information useful in crime control. 'Social service' receives validation from its utility in 'crime control'. Bittner (1978: 37) argues that 'the police have always had to justify activities that did not involve law enforcement in the direct sense by linking them constructively to law enforcement or by defining them as nuisance demands for service'. The preservation of a crime-fighting occupational image must increasingly be viewed as an achievement at a symbolic rather than a literal level.

Order maintenance is seen as reinforcing the centrality of a police force to the very conception of the social.

> 'You're putting the icing on the cake for the way of life by having law and order, which comes from a police force. . . . All things come down to if we didn't have a police force then you would have crime, then you wouldn't have society. . . . This job's more than the crime-buster. If all else fails he (PC) is there. The bobby's motive is not doing good for the person, he's there to arrive at the best solution for society. That means telling Mrs Jones that she can't have her dog because it's bitten somebody, whereas the social worker may say, "We will keep your dog for you." We're not interested in the effect on Mrs Jones as an individual, we're objective.'   (3: 5, 5–6)

Social service embraces maintaining order, a fragile and continually negotiated forbearance from fighting out underlying conflicts. This is related to a further element of the police role in securing the 'consensus', their strict but non-military organization.

> 'The police were created for crime work (but) I can't help feeling they're a convenient body of men with a rank structure that will enable them to carry out certain duties that are nothing to do with crime. It's a good thing, it brings them into contact with the public that they would . . . not normally meet.'   (4: 3, 6)

Over the year another probationer moved from being unable to specify any non-crime duties to a 'social contract' version of policing.

'Sometimes you say, "Really I should be catching criminals," but I think you enjoy doing it. (The social service stuff?) Yes. If (colleagues) saw I was getting (social services) in (to help an old lady get her heating on) they would say, "It's good for the police to help people do these things 'cause then they get the support when they need it." They'd do it anyway, 'cause they enjoy doing it.' (7: 2, 8)

He makes play with the problem of definition of 'crime' and 'social service', perceiving they are related. Similarly,

'dealing with drug addicts is a social problem but it's also a criminal problem. A lot of crime is committed by people of this nature. . . . People (who) commit burglary and they've had a few too many to drink, if you can deal with them before they commit the burglary you're preventing it.' (8: 1, 8)

Probationers come to appreciate that brute force or the arrest are weapons of last resort, and that public encounters can go either way.

'I have purposely worked on crime, but the end result of the majority of juvenile files is social work. The Panda driver who I worked with, the majority of their work is social work – domestics, fighting, saying, "Now come on, it's just not on." The majority of our work on the beat is social work'. (9: 1, 11–12)

The proportion of such work was related to area characteristics. 'Seeing kiddies across the road, looking for someone's dog, there's a lot I didn't expect. It depends on how big your area is, what sort of property you've got on your area, whether or not you get crime' (10: 2, 13–14). Similarly, 'in the X Division, miles of countryside and tiny villages, he's a community figure, helps run the youth club, etc. That takes as much time as bringing criminals to justice' (5: 2, 6). A constable posted to inner-city Derby found the crime level 'a damn sight higher' than he expected; thus he thought policing was 'mainly to do with crime control' (11: 1, 9). The area posting exerts strong influence over the balance of crime and service-related work perceived by constables. It may lead to real differences of perspective and indicate points of tension within occupational culture.

Data were collected on groups the probationers could not easily deal with. Seeking to control those to whom one has until then deferred is a searing experience, as a PC with ten years' service recalled. 'For a good twelve months I struggled. As a young man of 19 . . . I didn't think I was capable of dealing with the public who were above that age' (83: 3, 5). The importance of maintaining the upper hand is evident in this probationer's determination to rise above provocation.

> 'It's sometimes people's attitudes towards you. Members of the public can get a bit of a bugbear, but you've got to grit your teeth, say, "That's the way it is," and contend with it. Providing, of course, you don't start losing your temper, then you're on a loser.'   (10: 2, 1)

Ethnic minorities were the most identifiable group with which police had difficulties. Some recognized 'your own personal bias which is built up over years that you have got to control.' But the widest emphasis was that 'they build theirselves into a community and therefore they are a community separate to us' (3: 5, 3). The sense of separate community was elaborated by a recruit who argued that failures to resolve a situation appropriately generally resulted from a lack of appreciation of the other's perspective.

> 'It would be advisable if you had coloured constables. They would know the lifestyle and customs of the people. They would know how to deal with them, like I know how to deal with problems of people my own age or interests.'   (5: 3, 4).

Thoughts on coloured recruitment reveal the power of experience to alter general attitudes. Probationers were somewhat ambivalent whether more coloured constables should be recruited (28 per cent agreed, 40 per cent disagreed), while attitudes to coloured immigration were more hostile (65 per cent agreed there should be a stop to coloured immigration into Britain, 11 per cent disagreed). However, ex-military recruits were particularly likely to favour coloured recruitment; whereas 20 per cent of non-military recruits favoured coloured recruitment, 39 per cent of ex-military recruits did. This was the opposite of coloured immigration, where 56 per cent of non-military recruits agreed it should cease compared to 76 per cent of ex-military recruits. Experience in the military prompted such recruits to see coloured recruitment as useful, but it was a segregationist sentiment. 'In coloured areas it would be much better with a load of coloured police because, of course, it's easier to handle your own.' The contradiction of belief in the need for more ethnic minority recruits in a society one wishes to preserve from further immigration reveals how experience invests response to general attitude questions with situated meaning. Thus 'we had problems . . . in the military police with the coloureds. Until we got our own coloured bobby. He succeeded where we failed.' This also suggests how recruits begin to draw on experience in reflecting on how best to achieve their ends.

Another concern is the element of power police can deploy in their dealings with citizens. Probationers become sensitive to the need to employ power in a finely tuned way.

'You try and be nice to the yobs and then they start. The next night they take it out of you. They've got over you, they've beaten your authority down . . . With most people, being polite, having a bit of respect for them, does work, they respect you back. But some just take advantage of you being pleasant. . . . You try to help them out almost, but if they rebuke you there's nothing further you can do and then you have to talk a bit more firmer than you usually would to get them back into line.'

(7: 2, 7)

As Holdaway (1983: 132) notes, their 'grammar of force' relates particular tactics to particular individuals.

Some recruits can draw on local knowledge in dealing with youths. 'That does a lot of good, talking to the young lads that are coming along. And they knew me before I joined the police force of course, and they know that I'm still Jane' (8: 2, 8). It must be recognised that adolescent youths can be puzzling for probationers barely older than they are, that youth provides no automatic insight into youth and that a rigid upbringing can blind the officer to comprehension of their attitude. Unlike blacks, whose hostility can easily be attributed to difference, problems with youth oblige young constables to recognize that similarity does not necessarily make for insight. It forces probationers to confront the social consequences of their going into uniform.

'Juveniles and young persons, they've no respect whatsoever. . . . You can't do anything about it. If they are like that what's the point in taking them home to their parents. . . . I wasn't like that you see, and my parents were never disrespectful. I can only reflect on how my life was. My father never brought me up with a rod of iron but he let it be known that if I ever brought trouble home I'd be for it.'

(10: 2, 12)

It is worth considering why constables sustain an imagery of policing which puts value on an element of the work, crime control, which they seldom perform. It reflects, somewhat trivially, the officer's self-concept and means of sustaining commitment. More importantly, it may indicate adherence to one of the ground assumptions about the location of law enforcement within the system of social control. It is an empirical question whether officers can accommodate social service while adhering to a crime-oriented conception of policing. 'You do a double act. Social services, I don't think a lot about that. All right, we are social workers in uniform, but let's face it, our emphasis must be on crime' (11: 2, 8). Good 'information' is what constables are taught to winnow out, and in numerous mundane ways facilitates their daily work. Muir (1977) argued that the essential tension in police work is that given rise to by the necessity of coercion; the practical face of the power in the office of constable is in the myriad decisions whether to escalate one's intervention in specific encounters. Whether power can remain implicit and compliance be secured by consent relies more on the information that social service contacts bring than on legal force.

Guns

As well as a negotiation of identity the interview data provide instances of a dialectic between organizational demands and individual preferences. Recruits' attitudes to guns provide evidence for tactics of 'resistance' as well as occasions of 'rehearsal'. Socialization is commonly associated with organizational competence. As such the notion suggests a certain rigidity and linearity. Organizational competence merely suggests awareness, appreciation of, and compliance with, the formal demands of the organization. The 'socialization' perspective allows discussion of 'transition' but assumes that arrival at an end-point of adequate socialization is inevitable. If not, the resistant are expelled. The interview data suggest this is overdrawn. The organizational picture must include the insurgent. It must also allow for equivocation. Indecision is different from disloyalty. Agents of training know that learning the ropes does not mean recruits will feel bound by them.

Probationers were like their more experienced colleagues in their negative attitude to guns. Experienced officers may well appreciate that having guns is not justifiable in terms of response time; the average armed robbery takes forty seconds and having armed officers ready makes little difference to the prospects for apprehension at the scene. To the probationer, though, personal security and images of British society counts for more. Most disagree with the police carrying guns; 77 per cent at induction and after one year, 89 per cent after two years. The 23 per cent agreeing at induction reduced to 8 per cent and then 5 per cent.

Prior experience affects perspectives. In his first week this recruit thought the police should be armed, and wanted to extend his marksman training from the army.

> 'There are terrorists in England. I've been out to Ireland seven times and I know what it's like to walk on the streets without being armed. I reckon the police should be armed at all times. It would put down crime a hell of a lot. Because they will probably be faced with a gun.'
> (1: 2, 5)

It was more usual to encounter the perspective recruits correctly identified as the official line; training should be taken in handling a gun, which would be issued as the occasion warranted. 'I'd prefer to be trained just in case the situation does arise but I wouldn't like to carry one. I wouldn't like to be in the situation where I'd have to use it' (1: 3, 2).

However some statements of personal disliking were followed by the charge that if they do issue weapons, the police should leave officers unfettered in their use of them. Organizational constraint seems to the recruit to contradict the presumption of competence the organization should make.

'I don't like to think of the idea of hurting somebody like that. I don't think I'd like to have that hanging over me. . . . The police, they arm themselves with guns but as soon as a shot goes off there's an inquiry. It's a funny situation. It's difficult to say, "OK, here's the guns but only use them if somebody's pointing the thing at you and saying, "one, two, three – fire."'   (1: 4, 5)

The view of those with military experience surely leads to a particularly dangerous assumption of comparability between military and civil order. Of those in favour of carrying guns, 3.5 times as many were former soldiers than former civilians (13.6 per cent former military and 3.6 per cent former civilians at year one, 7.9 per cent former military and 2.4 per cent former civilians after two years). 'Ten years ago I would have said no way but in the present world situation I think you've got to. I can see that time (when all bobbies will carry guns), I don't want to see it' (3: 2, 5). However, not all those with service experience with firearms regard them as useful in crime control. 'I don't want any more to do with guns. There's always that thought that someone's going to have a pot shot at you. I carried one in Northern Ireland for two years and I wasn't happy with it' (2: 2, 4). Similarly,

'If I carry them all the time they know they have got to carry them. Whereas now they know they can probably get away with a good hiding. Anyway, more military policemen got in trouble in Northern Ireland over negligent discharges than anything else. You have got a bunker where you empty your weapons. You unload it into the sand and if you don't do it right, if you've done eighteen hours on a stretch, one goes off, it's cost you £80.'   (3: 5, 4)

Also pertinent are occasions when the recruit has been on the wrong side of enforcement.

'In America and Canada . . . you see them throwing the guns around left, right and centre. In Canada you're not allowed to carry drink openly. One of me mates . . . came out of this pub and he decided to have a drink and from nowhere they all started to talk to him, and the next thing we were up against the wall with guns, these Canadian police, and I thought, ''In Plymouth . . . the police just come and say get him home.'' ' (4: 5, 3–4)

These perspectives compare interestingly with positions after a year. As noted, the survey showed a marked reduction even in the original minority in favour of carrying guns. The data show an affirmation of the 'occupational culture' position calling for weapons specialists, basic training but no general issue of guns. Those who earlier called for guns changed views.

'I know what I said to you last year. But now I've changed my mind because you're enticing people to come out on the street with weapons and for people to hide behind a corner and take it off you. So they shouldn't be armed at all.' (7: 1, 9)

A further response explicitly refers to peer group views.

'Only the specialist units. You don't meet people (carrying guns) that often. . . . If you start carrying them, they'll start carrying them more. There's a lot of policemen, most that I've spoken to, if they did start issuing firearms to carry all the time they'd leave. I probably would as well.' (7: 2, 6)

There was also the negotiation of the job's demands within one's social network. 'Frightened to death. I would seriously consider calling it a day. I've talked about it with my wife and we're frightened to think of if I had the power of life and death' (11: 1, 8).

These reservations, it must be emphasized, also pertain to some with military experience. Their experience of guns and a jaundiced, suspicious image of the public may have supported tough statements in early service that experience and discussions with experienced officers now counteracted. 'This is the first time in nine years I've never been armed and I wouldn't like to be armed in the present situation. It would be too easy to use it' (11: 2, 7). America remained the demon image.

'My father pulled a few contacts and we ended up in a black-and-white in San Francisco and the first few minutes we went to a triple stabbing by a transvestite . . . That's another thing against armed police, they don't seem to be deterring the amount of murders.'
(12: 1, 19–20)

Instructors similarly resist the extension of armaments. A chief inspector foresaw problems in the calibre of recruits. 'As to arming every policeman, we've got to look at the men that enter closely because I wouldn't like to arm some of these cowboys. I'm a bit worried when they get their truncheons out' (81: 3, 18).

The responses about guns show movement towards the perspective prevailing among serving officers. The movement is unsurprising, because both the formal organization and occupational culture are pulling in the same direction. There is no strong undercurrent of management philosophy in favour of guns, nor does the tough stance of the Police Federation and the ranks extend to guns. The first year of service makes recruits realistic about their organization's expectations of them as well as about the situation on the street.

Public relations and private meanings

At induction 65 per cent of recruits believed the public had a high regard for the police, but by year one, 84 per cent agreed and by year two, 94 per cent, a clear instance of the taking on of a view characteristic of police (Levi and Jones 1985). However, the somewhat resentful idea that citizens think they know police work better than the police gained 30 per cent agreement at induction rising to 40 per cent by year two. Complaints by the public represent a particular threat to recruits, who tended to assume they arose from people having 'a chip on their shoulder'. From the assumption that some groups bear special animosity to the police, the recruits inferred they would have to be scrupulously fair.

> 'You have to watch what you're doing more because they can take you to court and say you arrested them . . . because they are coloured . . . So you'd have to be more careful and more sure that it was them who committed the crime. Because if they were found not guilty then they could complain.' (1: 1, 3)

This is refined experientially, as the officer learns to justify action, primarily out of the necessity of satisfying organizational demands.

> 'There's complaints started flying around in the last few years more than ever. I don't think it's a bad thing but people are getting to know their rights and the law to the extent where, even if they know it's wrong they just do it . . . to make it a paperwork exercise for the police.' (12: 1, 14)

The recruit was working under a sergeant with a strict 'by the book' stance and a disillusioned approach to the public. Strong views were expressed in a discussion between officers and a group of 'senior constables'. A 'big percentage' of complaints were 'a load of bunk' and there were 'compulsive complainers' – 'they (the public) have got a complaints procedure, there ought to be some comeback for us' (field-notes, 16.5.83). An inspector said there were some genuine complaints, but some that were 'to do with getting the person off'. Animated discussion resulted from a consideration of recording interrogations, with officers suggesting that if interrogations were on video they could rebut the complaint that 'a guy had been belted'. Complaints served to concentrate thought on more artful means of getting a result. An officer remembered a detective inspector who would come in and 'bollock' the interrogating officer if no confession was forthcoming, the idea being to build a rapport between interrogator and suspect which the interrogator could use as a lever (field notes, 17.5.83).

At induction, 37 per cent of recruits picked public relations officer as the occupation most like policing, with figures of 36 per cent after one year and 37 per cent after two years. Although 'public relations' may suggest itself as an apt description of the job to recruits the term takes on new meanings through experience, acknowledging that policing is more constrained by the public than it used to be (1: 4, 1). The police cannot be effective without public co-operation, and the community cannot be regarded as passive.

> 'They're looking for somebody that doesn't take the law to its limits. There's your grey areas and you've got to take a lot of things into account. You've got to be able to get on with people. Rather than shout at someone, "You will do this," say, "Let's discuss how we are going to do it."' (4: 4, 3)

Officers depict their style as dictated by the area they work. Asked what lead to his interest in CID one said, 'The area I got assigned to . . . (had)more of those problems . . . There's a beat and it all depends what property you've got on it, what sort of people live there' (8: 3, 7). The response seeks to locate the officer's work in relation to readily-apparent, uncontentious features of the area. Crime becomes a physical feature, associated with certain ecological characteristics. The 'fact of crime' may be applied to other areas possessing these physical traits.

The attribution of some stereotyped trait to an area can lead to differential enforcement when police are faced with crime without 'clues' and with an unlimited suspect population. Ecological stereotyping can be seen as myth translated into fact by the officer's belief that it is fact. When I first contacted the training establishment I was given a 'thumbnail' description of Derbyshire's social and physical terrain. A year later I heard the description again, in an interview. 'It's like you can split the county up the middle. You've got the countryside on one side, the west side, and on the east side you've got all the industry and mining' (10: 2, 6). The similarity of the stories is not the point. Physically this broad description is valid. However, this innocent description illustrates the way a story of obvious utility becomes lodged in an organization. It is circulated through the organization because it conveys important information in a readily orally transmitted form. Acquaintance with the story becomes a mark of organizational socialization. In the process local knowledge, the experiential signal of validity in police organizations, becomes divorced from its experiential base and is launched into the repository of organizationally underpinned 'facts'. Its veracity becomes an article of belief. To this point can be added a further touch. In the version I first heard the social description went beyond this. The trunk road which divided the county also divided it politically; on one side were the Labour voters, the working class, on the other, the Conservatives, farmers and landowners. Such stories have analytic utility but endow each of their elements with veracity by virtue of the apparent truth of the core, physical description.

Such practices have their basis in the presumption that local knowledge is highly pertinent to successful policing. 'Derbyshire born and bred. Without a doubt it works well (for me) in the police as well. I know a lot of the local villains' (11: 1, 2). Because it is a relative rarity to possess local knowledge prior to joining, the story may be taken up and used on the basis of its 'self-evident' rectitude. No more stringent test is ever applied, and once the story is in use it achieves its own validation through a practice of policing based on it. Mulling over this minor tale reinforces the importance of bringing into account the experiential basis of the recruit's nascent operating ideology. There are cases where recruits referred to the inaccuracy of certain stories officers used as sieving devices to build a coherent, because selective, version of social reality. One recruit found the standard of public behaviour 'generally better' than he had been led to expect.

'I expected, from the few stories I'd heard from the police officers, that the people they meet are low-down, nasty people. The stories that are told and the things you remember, are the nasty situations. But there's countless times that I've met people and their attitude to me is marvellous. Which . . . I didn't expect at all.'   (8: 3, 9)

One cannot read the recruit as a cipher for the occupational culture. The occupational culture has to make its pitch for support, just as the agencies of the formal organization exert their influence through control of resources. The stock stories of the occupational culture must be effective as a means of ordering perception which maximizes desirable outcomes. If they contradict the recruit's gathering experience they are likely to be dismissed. Increasing experience lays open increasing grounds of contradiction. Like the formal organization, the occupational culture has to make its pitch early if it is to supply enough of the recruit's perceptual apparatus to make its filters work and its version of reality sufficiently consistent to secure affiliation.

5

The police employee

The probationary period, particularly the first year, is a time of variety and new experience. Recruits gain rapid acquaintance with the work and are exposed to alternative but not wholly contradictory analytic frameworks for perceiving the work, leading to particular priorities and methods of work, justified according to particular abstract beliefs about policing's aims. Internal performance measures intended both to produce loyalty and 'results' have increasingly encouraged policing's definition as visible, recorded activity: 'that which could be measured by calls, by despatched runs for service, and by arrests, clearances and traffic tickets issued' (Manning 1982: 64). To tap the norms endorsed by the ideology of professionalism, what could be measured was in large part what could be glossed as crime. Such considerations define the rhetoric whose terms the recruit must learn to use. Experience helps recruits to choose elements of the package on offer according to their own combination of biography, academy and patrol experience. As they gain an appreciation of the work they also take up the role of the police employee.

Entering the ranks

In the past the entry of all recruits as constables may have been an organizational practice whose 'democratic' appeal only matched its pragmatism; when recruits were hard to come by the police had to take who they could get, within the minima. With economic recession the qualifications of the applicants improved and cases where entry at constable rank chafes may well have increased. Accelerated promotion of graduates may relieve the most vociferous pressure, for former soldiers perceive the system as fair, compared to the military.

> 'A direct entrant into Sandhurst . . . although he comes out as a fully commissioned officer still does not know about basic man-management. . . . Being a senior NCO I've come across this many, many times. I have been cried down for doing something I know is right and it's been proved at a later date.' (3: 2, 2)

The experience gained as a PC is qualitatively different to that as an officer. Experience within the organization *per se* is not enough to instil an appreciation of the basic work.

Former civilians speak in precisely equivalent terms. 'If you go straight into inspector, you don't really know what it's like to be a policeman on the beat. Therefore you can't advise or teach policemen if you've never done it yourself' (1: 1, 2). Comments such as these address the experience of training the recruits are going through; they may be founded in the 'all in the same boat' feeling which compensates for some of the trials of training. If they are to suffer drill, hard exercise and swotting the law then the rest should suffer too. There is another dimension to this. It is not just that effective officers need experience of the basic work; the officers' credibility and claim to rank rests on the constables' consent as well as their practical capability.

> 'It would be a "them" and "us" situation if people join as chief inspectors. . . . (If) he doesn't know anything about the police service, never worked in (it) before, they've no time, no respect for him, and they will probably ignore his orders.'   (2: 1, 2)

Recruits put a clear emphasis on the need for superiors to secure the ranks' consent by gaining their respect. They also re-emphasize learning by practical experience. It is better to 'start working and making mistakes when you're at the bottom as when you're at the top of the ladder' (3: 1, 2). There was little change in agreement that police administration is out of touch with the ranks, with figures starting high at 76 per cent and settling at 72 per cent after two years following a dip to 68 per cent at year one.

One should not underestimate the importance of such considerations because of a reluctance to perceive officer/ranks relations as an instance of industrial relations. The 'direct entry' point elicited some of the most vehement expressions of view in the interviews.

> 'You get a jumped up son of a – one particular person cost me a lot of promotion. He was absolutely incapable of taking advice. He was young . . . his father had estates. He was a spoiled brat and he had some of the finest NCOs and senior NCOs and just would not listen. He eventually got flung out for incompetency. He could have just sat back and let people run it . . . The better officers come through the ranks and have a little bit of experience about how other people feel.'
>   (3: 4, 2)

The example revolves around the privilege of commissioned officers and their insulation from criteria of efficiency, offending the recruit's notion of equity. The officer went even further to demonstrate his (officially confirmed) incompetence by not allowing the men who did understand the job to 'carry' him. Another deeply felt case hinges on the need for a good managerial style, one which respects the ranks.

'The majority of officers that have got any respect from the men are what we call "rankers", the blokes who have made it. The others . . . cannot relate to the man on the ground. An officer from the Hong Kong police joined the military police and he thought that we were all related to his house-boys in Hong Kong. . . . When a file was wrong, instead of saying, "All right, why is this like this?" . . . he'd say, "Hey, you, sort that bloody thing out." This is the man who has got the problem.' (3: 5, 2)

The criteria recruits use is the need for the officer to be assured of the compliance of the ranks. Loyalty was crucial if constables were to trust officers enough to respond without hesitation or misgiving when ordered to act.

'A police constable has got probably the most important job in the police force. (E)very officer, even at the most senior level, should gain this experience because there will come a time when he's got to make a decision which is going to affect all his men. They're going to say, "How can I take notice of him, he's never done it." . . . Officers who have worked themselves up from the ranks command far more respect when they say, "Look, lads, it's going to be done this way," the blokes all know he's been through it all. It can present some (other) problems . . . We used to have an officer dealing with men 30-odd, married with families, and he was about 22.' (4: 4, 2)

The contradiction of seniority by inexperience makes for an environment in which more experienced recruits may be uncomfortable. One recruit's quarterly progress reports noted against the 'personal relationships' category, 'he has found it difficult to settle into the Police Invironment (sic), being in many cases older than his fellow officers by some years'. Older recruits have problems in managing their orientation to promotion while remaining within the ranks culture, as this comment on the 'Leadership' category suggests: 'he has qualities, but tries to subdue them, probably because he is young in service'. A reminder that the issue is about manager/employee relations, not simply loyalty, is from one of the explicit references to class.

'It's good that everybody starts at the same level. To become an officer you've got to merit it. The army system, being commissioned, I'm not in agreement. I'm from a working-class family myself and just because we've got no money doesn't mean we can't have the same opportunities.' (5: 2, 3)

After the first year's service it was increasingly seen as important that police management appreciate the problems of the ranks, not simply to secure compliance but so the ranks could exert pressure through the flow of communication upward in the organization. 'It's necessary for them to know it otherwise they go straight into admin. jobs, don't know why a policeman does such-and-such a thing out on the street, and it probably baffles him' (7: 2, 4). Constables are anxious that their managers should appreciate this mystery of police work. 'You need the experience of being on the beat to understand it . . . How can you understand a PC's problems, the problems of walking on the beat, if you've never done it?' (8: 2, 4). An instructor referred to it as being 'brainwashed into being a regular bobby' (field notes, 27.10.81). A chief inspector felt that without common experience of the beat, the police would copy the military's mistake by imbuing officers' rank with status while denying them *personal* respect:

> 'An officer class would alienate the recruits more from the officers. When you see some of the academics we're encouraging into the force, they are not the best by any means. A lot of drop-outs are using it. . . . Our standards are too low and frankly I would hate to see them (promoted) because it would get a snob class. It would alienate the public from us even more.'   (81: 3, 17–18)

It is difficult to underestimate the strength of opposition to direct entry; not just ex-soldiers oppose it but instructors, officers and ex-cadets. The issue provokes another prejudiced contrast with 'academic' training.

> 'I spent a long time carrying idiots, and a man that is academically sound and able to turn out knowledge at the flick of a switch is not always the best man to have with you when you've got problems. I speak from personal experience of five terms in Northern Ireland. I've carried many a young graduate through various incidents.'
>   (11: 2, 5)

The statement amplifies his strong feelings by the equation of 'academic' with the sort of 'idiot' who needs 'carrying'. During the year recruits start to divide those who have 'experience' from those who do not. Academic knowledge is taken in police culture as a reference to clinical knowledge of law, the most tangible intrusion of 'academic' knowledge into constables' work. The word 'academic' bears a pejorative implication in British culture; 'academic' knowledge is counterposed to practical, common-sense knowledge.

> 'A chap that's done eight years, he's got . . . not just the knowledge of the law which the chap in the college would have, but the application of it to the practical situation and even the small duty of talking

to people, communicating. It's not quite the same as in the classroom. You talk to all sorts of different characters and after the years you get to judge what somebody's like after you've had just two or three sentences with him. As well as listening to them, you think of what you're going to ask him next . . . It's this as well as the application of the law, thinking about the law and bringing it out like that, for which you need practical experience.' (12: 1, 15–16)

'Academic' knowledge is pertinent because it provides a framework for interpretation; the law is part of the officer's repertoire. But the skills salient in the public encounter are not learnt in class.

Assessing performance

Knowing their vital concern with public standards, one would expect the police to apply a model system of assessment to themselves. Yet assessment by immediate supervisors is inextricably bound up with shared norms, implicit assumptions and strong assertions of autonomy. A report is submitted monthly on probationers by the sergeant (annually on others), and bad reports can entail dismissal. Formally constables are assessed on appearance, determination, initiative, oral expression, presence, professional knowledge, reliability, and written expression. Yet sergeants' criteria vary. 'The same activity that is appreciated and perhaps demanded by one sergeant is treated indifferently by another sergeant . . . To patrolmen, such idiosyncratic policies, while sometimes difficult to understand, provide a margin of safety in . . . a very uncertain work environment' (van Maanen 1974: 107). Autonomy is granted on the assumption that constables' situated knowledge gives them warrant to act as they think best. Sergeants, having operated the same way themselves, are reluctant to interfere, and the ranks sanction supervisors who do so without good cause. Autonomy can also be seen in norms against 'poaching' and information-sharing between officers. Yet outside formal assessment, constables assimilate each other's informal evaluations and criteria because it is self-protective in the short run, minimizing the intrusion of supervision and external criteria of success, and because in the long term it cements their autonomy.

Even so, one would assume the organization would set some store by those evaluations of performance pertaining to training and early service. However, van Maanen found no association between a rookie's 'street performance' and academy rankings, indicating that the criteria on which trainers evaluated recruits did not correspond to those used in the field. Field sergeants actually penalized rookies for the very qualities of motivation and commitment the academy endorsed (van Maanen 1975:

218–20). Further, policy is often neither clearly expressed nor understood. 'Officers cynically remark that calling a supervisor for assistance in a domestic fight usually produces two domestics, one among civilians, another among police' (Bayley 1986: 337).

Thus, complex informal undercurrents pertain to what may appear a straightforward exercise. Quarterly progress reports typically take the form of a checklist of qualities and a rating system; sergeants assess constables, inspectors assess sergeants. Ordinal ratings are made on appearance; vitality; professional ability (practical); professional ability (written work); oral expression (ability to communicate verbally); detective ability (crime investigation, interrogation); temperament (self-control, stability, reactions); personal relationships (work with others, social adjustment); leadership (control and guidance of others); judgement (assessment of people and situations, perception); reliability; and self-confidence. Instructions on one such form demand that, 'Judgement is to be based on the standard of performance of officers in the rank generally and not merely by reference to the local standard.' Thus evaluators are told that it is possible to make assessments of general applicability on some universal standard. They are led away from precisely the local criteria which may mark an appropriate accommodation to community standards and expectations.

Limited space is also given for comment. Such comments subvert the blandness of the ratings by affording a modicum of insight into the person whose character is being appraised; it is in these that allusions to local standards creep in, e.g. against 'vitality' one report reads, 'Keen to involve himself in local problems on his beat.' On probationers these appraisals endlessly repeat the need for experience; 'he is short on service and can be considered average, he will improve with Experience' for professional ability, or 'Again it is experience that he needs, but his work shows a steady improvement.' How one might confirm such assessments as the supervisor of the supervisor, is unclear, for the form permits no room for evidence nor for evaluators to make plain the way they interpret particular categories. In many of these reports, too, the sole reference to the actual conduct of the work refers to crime work, e.g. 'Although not tested, he shows some flair for Minor Crime Investigation,' and one can infer the assessor's orientation to crime control/social service from negative assessments such as this on judgement – 'generally no problem, he wants to see the nice side of everybody. Not always a good thing' – which was classed 'has shortcomings'. The progress report completed by the immediate supervisor can also bear summary information from that person's supervisor and recommendations for training/employment, but there is only room for three lines of typescript and this information is often derivative.

The final report on probationers is at twenty-three months. There is no class rank, and overall performance in TE and DTC is not compounded. The 'quick think' daily quizzes of ten questions keep staff aware of probationers' performance in case they need special tuition. The three week TE course at the thirteenth week culminates in the last TE examination, when all four TE marks are summed. If probationers do not get 70 per cent at TE they receive extra tuition, but there are no re-sits, due to lack of time. At DTC there are intermediate and final exams, on a mixture of procedural and legal topics. The DTC course pass mark is also 70 per cent and performance below this entails remedial tuition and a re-sit (field notes, 27.10.81). Force establishment affects assessment. After their big recruiting drive the force went over establishment by eighty posts and the Home Office obliged them to 'lose' fifty officers (Constabulary Annual Report 1980). There was more 'weeding out', testified by the raising of required exam scores whereas 'in the old days you would be assisted to get through' (field notes, 8.3.82).

Informed references to the system of evaluation were rare in the initial stages. After a year attention centred on the DTC assessment, seen as a demanding series of objective tests and field performance evaluations which went on one's organization file.

> 'You've got a test every Monday morning and you have to know fifty questions . . . on all different parts of the law . . . You learn a week's work, have two days off and come back and take an exam . . . I failed my very first one. I went in front of the inspector and got a right telling off for it. Said, "Pull your socks up or you're away," and every one after that I passed . . . There was a lot of people that failed the first three. It's something that people just can't take, they seem to go to pieces.'   (7: 1, 3)

Some tests are seen as unfairly literal.

> 'That's the trouble, some of these questions are a play on your understanding of the English language . . . The term "admissible evidence", you had four choices, "never allowed in court", "seldom" . . . "sometimes", and "always". You can start reading things into it. The answer was "always" but in a practical sense, you could think of your tone of voice (in saying) "Well, that's admissible". It could be "often" rather than "always".'   (12: 1, 8–9)

Nevertheless DTC re-sit policy was generous. 'We just had retakes till we passed it. If you didn't pass it (after two retakes) it went down as a fail. It was three failures and it was up to your force whether to dispense of your services' (12: 2, 3). In 1983 the Police Training Council discouraged automatic dismissal for failure on 'slip tests'.

Reports are also made at the DTC.

'You've got a report at the end of the course from your class instructor. . . . With the pressures up there one or two people haven't got
a good exam technique but they can be very good in class and this
allows for those people.' (8: 3, 3)

The PTI's report includes 'your bearing in class, your involvement with
the class, how you conduct yourself generally . . . a lot's to do with it
socially' (10: 2, 4). Intense scrutiny is assumed.

'They're watching you all the time. You can tell that, the way they're
always looking at you, your dress, the manner in which you conduct
yourself, the manner in which you wear the uniform, even when
you're standing having your cup of coffee, whether you stand leaning
against the wall with your hands stuffed up your pockets. They take
it all in. All the staff here have a role in that. Mainly instructors
though, because they know who you are.' (11: 1, 3)

Judgements about which type of work recruits might be suited for
were not made in the TE or DTC.

'No, they assess you on practicals when you're out in the field. Some
of my friends have been to domestics and they've been sent away
because they don't look old enough and it's embarrassing for them, but
other people have gone and sorted the situation out. So the people in
the field would take note of that, put on your file, "did well in this
setting".' (7: 1, 3)

Recruits confirm they specifically address matters of competence on the
part of colleagues. Everyone in the station spent time 'rating' others.

'There's probationers starting at the police station at the moment. I
look at them and see what they say when they've done a job, see if
you rate them or not . . . The operational side, your inspector, your
sergeant, they're the most concerned.' (7: 2, 4)

Despite its universal interest, formal assessment is for designated
individuals.

'It starts at your sergeant, your immediate supervising officer, and you
put all your work in through him, he reads every file you submit and
knows the general standard of improvement, the work-rate. He also
notices how you get on with your colleagues, knowledge of the law,
and he will put this in a report. It's basically down to the sergeant and
inspector.' (8: 3, 4–5)

Recruits are very conscious of bases for assessment other than formal criteria. '(H)ow you behave generally, your appearance, your attitude, your willingness to learn, listen, ask questions, how you get on with the shift' (10: 2, 6). Adjustment to role and, particularly, commitment and loyalty emerge as salient concerns. 'Far more thorough than they do at the training centre, they go into your mental attitude to the job, your adaptation to your fellow colleagues, and domestic scene as well as their going into your job' (11: 2, 4). Peer contact and sociality are included. 'They really judge you on what self-initiated work you've done and what sort of personality they think you are from what conversation they've had and ask a couple of your mates informally what you are like' (12: 1, 13). Some experience inspection of patrol activity.

> 'Occasionally they walk around with you, see how you're getting on with your work and what sort of bobby you are and assess you on that. The inspector will come out and watch you on the beat . . . Our inspector's pretty good, comes out on shift with us . . . He looks after us all. We're all in the same boat. Whoever he meets first (he) walks with them for 10–15 minutes.'   (12: 2, 6)

This kind of direct check on performance is more likely to be by the shift sergeant.

> 'Obviously the man who's most qualified to write a report on you is your immediate supervisor, which is your sergeant. He knows, 'cause all your work goes through him. He comes out with you on the occasion. He signs your pocket book more than anybody. He knows what you're doing, he gives you work. He works the same hours as you . . . knows what you're not doing, how smart you are on duty.' (12: 3, 10)

This is a substantial catalogue of factors thought by recruits to pertain to field performance evaluations. Importantly, it is information only indirectly available to senior officers.

Promotion and advancement

The avid attention given to promotion is evident in the front page column regularly appearing in the constabulary newspaper, listing promotions and transfers, and in the feature article on outstanding police work. Such features signal the work which gets one noticed. They cover those high-profile, crime-related, action-dominated episodes so central to the imagery of policing, as in the three-column account 'Bravery award follows chase across county' featuring an armed man suspected of killing five victims, a high-speed pursuit through narrow country lanes, the overpowering of the suspect after a town centre crash, the pride of colleagues at the award ceremony and the presentation of a bravery award by the county's lord lieutenant (*Ramparts* 1980: 1). One may also note awards for those in training. The baton of honour is annually awarded to the cadet who has performed well in all aspects of training; in 1980 it went to a 17-year-old who was described as having special all-round qualities 'not only in the academic and physical side of training but also in self-discipline, attitude and pride' (*Ramparts* 1980: 3). Such awards signal the ideal. On the award day parents see the award-winners on parade and performing PE displays (rather than reciting powers of arrest or counselling distraught spouses!).

It may be conventionally assumed that what is in the thinking of those 'up the chain' is highly pertinent to the ambitious recruit. Van Maanen's research on American police training undermines such assumptions. Immediate supervisors are not only the most important people in the constables' immediate working environment but the most important to their prospects for advancement. Ironically, van Maanen found the recruits who were least motivated to work hard were rated as better officers; early socialization taught recruits not to be overly zealous and to develop strong loyalty to peers rather than looking to ways of advancement over peers.

> 'The best solution to the labyrinth of hierarchy, the red tape and paper-work, the myriad of rules and regulations and the dirty work which characterizes the occupation is to adopt the group norm stressing "stay out of trouble". And the best way to stay out of trouble is to minimize activities.'
> (van Maanen 1975: 222)

This suggests a basic tension between the desire for personal advancement and the need to maintain strong co-operative relations with peers. It is unsurprising that many constables resolve conflict in terms of the latter, for the rationale to secure personal safety and loyalty is a theme which pervades the organization, receiving reinforcement from senior officers and occupational culture. In examining thoughts on advancement one must be aware of this basic tension, but may also perceive such material as bearing on recruit perceptions of their (changing) place in the organization, on the organization's fairness, and, importantly, as a further 'angle' on their gathering grasp of the 'essential' nature of the police role. The uncertainty and danger which provide potent (and manipulated) images of policing are concretely rewarded by the organization. Although dangerous encounters take up less than 5 per cent of patrol time, violent and dramatic incidents dominate those singled out for commendation and award. Since they are entered on officers' files they will be used at their promotional hearings.

A first pattern in response to enquiries about the promotion system concerns the need to present an image of oneself as coping ably with any contingency, maintaining proper control over situations and oneself. 'If you can keep supervision over other people. The other thing they're looking for is whether you're not frightened to make a decision. You don't want to change your mind – if you say something make it stick' (1: 2, 3). The response asserts the primacy of control as an occupational image and therefore as a mark of organizational competence. Other recruits may have some difficulty in gaining promotion. 'It's just getting your head down and showing results. And asking plenty of questions, trying to show that you're competent' (6: 1, 3). Such a tactic as 'asking a lot of questions' may be interpreted as showing the opposite of competence. One who was keen for promotion listed 'leadership qualities and understanding of the job and not being too sloppy in your job' (2: 1, 2). A more hardened view was held by a former soldier who was 'not bothered' if he got promotion; 'if you scrape and grovel' one would be promoted (2: 2, 2).

While these comments bear several resonances they share a focus on individual qualities. A different category emphasizes co-operative, collegial qualities. Here promotion is perceived as, by definition, 'breaking ranks'. These may be accommodative individuals oriented to maximum autonomy and reward within the present rank, or the indifferent, who seek neither upward mobility nor lateral movement to obtain greater informal rewards (Manning 1981: 2417). Such 'laterally bonded' officers emphasize solidarity whereas the ambitious 'seek lateral moves within their rank . . . because these promise greater visibility or opportunities for vertical promotion' (p. 2417). While still invoking the centrality of control, recruits relate this to an individual's ability to enlist the co-operation of others. Thus 'the most important (quality) is man-management. If you can't get the men to do what you want there's no point in having the rank on your arm. The ability to relate to your equals on rank' (3: 5, 2). The emphasis is on relations among peers and reveals reflection on how to advance while retaining the all-important loyalty of colleagues. Ability to handle both practical and 'theoretical' aspects of the work is related, as in comments on direct entry, to ability to enlist the support of colleagues. Thus competence is itself defined in terms of co-operation and empathy.

'You've got to be able to do the job from both sides, both practically and theoretically. It's all right sitting in the office knowing what to do, but getting out there and doing it is another matter. If you're going to send a man into a dangerous situation you've got to be prepared to do it yourself.' (5: 2, 3)

Specific and purposive accounts of promotion emerged after a year. At the one-year stage recruits have gained operational experience which encourages them to adopt a reflexive attitude to their own practice. In the throes of developing a set of categories with a close fit to the world experienced in patrol, they emphasize a capacity for assessing events and circumstances.

> 'For promotion, the assessment of situations is very valuable, which you tend to pick up with experience. You've really got to know how to quickly assess, and general man-management. It's not just being able to do the job, it's being able to tell others how to do the job well, and without causing any friction.'   (8: 3, 6)

The recruit has moved beyond simple practice skill to the need to be reflexive about practice skill so as to share knowledge.

While the co-operative imagery is a seductive one, value being put on ability to be self-regarding so that one's experience can work for others, the police is a competitive organization, where promotion can lead to rancour and jockeying for position.

> 'Unfortunately the police force is an egotistical society. We are all motivated by rank, position, years of service and specialism. I got some very good advice: if I want to know anything, find a bobby that's been in the beat sixteen years. If you can get it out of him it's good advice, but unfortunately we're all motivated, and I'm just as bad, I want to be a CID officer. They're all either motivated to drive around in big white cars with a big red stripe looking the part or they're motivated to wearing civvies and being CID officers, fitting them up with a TV image. It's terrible. I saw a chief inspector six weeks ago, there was a vacancy for a superintendent, and my God, the bloke was forever brushing his uniform and doing things that were completely different to his pattern of life, all because of this. I watched the inspector laugh 'cause he was the one that told the bloke there was a superintendent vacancy '   (9: 1, 5–6)

Promotion-mindedness actually affected public relations.

> 'The announcements that are made on shifts, "PC so-and-so's been accepted into the force," "Police Sergeant so-and-so has passed his inspector's exams." "There were thirty-two officers from Derbyshire to pass the sergeant's exam, the others were a total and abysmal failure" . . . these were the announcements made, so they're all orientated towards status and rank. That's probably a fault in the police force, because if it wasn't one would accept, as the public do, that a PC is a good bloke. . . . The public see no difference between a police constable and a police sergeant.'   (9: 1, 6)

Attitudes to promotion are formed around perceptions of what ambition does to others; several recruits contrasted their easy-going stance to the anxiety to please of others. 'I am ambitious . . . with a small "a"; if it comes, it comes. Obviously I'm going to do everything in my power to move it on a bit but I'm not going out of my way as some people do here' (11: 2, 5). Both promotion-mindedness and loyalty to colleagues register in the 'industrial relations' rhetoric of recruits. Here the loyalty theme is related to the demands of power.

> 'For (promotion) to sergeant, if a bloke knows his job inside out, (and) . . . when the cards are down he's on the bosses' side, which is what all managements got to be, and if something happens he can sort it out or certainly sort out the person that caused it.' (11: 2, 8)

It is necessary to consider whether, and in whose view, non-promotion is a stigma. Many constables insist they do not want promotion and are not only content as constables but actively deride the officers. 'You can evaluate who's . . . .. keen for promotion or who's quite contented with his situation in life and has no immediate plans to become the chief constable' (12: 3, 12). The ambitious who do not advance may take on an embittered perspective; 'secretly they do, to remain a PC all your life and look back, "I could have achieved a higher rank!" . . . The people who are quite content to just stay as a PC are probably the ones who realize they're not going to make the higher rank' (12: 3, 12). Numerous probationers said they felt no stigma in remaining in the rank they felt committed to.

> 'I've told everybody if in twenty years I'm still a constable that will be because I want to be a constable and there will be no apologies to anybody if I want to do that. By the same token if I want to get on I would like to feel that I can.' (4: 3, 3)

One could not duck the issue.

> 'There's different ways to look at it. There's the old-fashioned type, you want to be an area policeman, where everybody knows you and you know everybody else. Someone might say, "If you don't want to get promotion, you're lazy," there's that way of looking at it. You've got a choice. Not a very good choice. I think you do need to get promotion quite honestly. It's a pity you can't stay a constable on the beat. I mean the inspectors say, "Start swotting for your sergeant's exam now."' (7: 2, 4)

Promotion orientations indicate constable styles. Ideal-typical models of constable styles in the occupational culture provide an anchor for talk about competence. They bear nuances which mark routine tactical decisions, but it is vital to recognize that they are not prescriptive of action.

Rather they are resources officers may draw around their actual decisions, giving the appearance of resolve and solidarity to action which is mediated by self-serving or idealistic concerns they may wish to cloak from view.

Most new recruits rated themselves as more ambitious than WPCs and the village bobby at induction. Using recruit's views of rankings on the scale ambitious/unambitious the following scores were obtained, where the lower the score the more ambitious the role is perceived.

Police sergeant	2.15
Self	2.2
CID officer	2.5
WPC	3.15
Village bobby	4.3

Someone seen as a 'riser', i.e. the police sergeant, is ranked most ambitious, followed by self. Recruits may reason that CID officers have reached their ambition and are therefore less ambitious than self. The WPC is clearly seen as less ambitious. The short descriptive phrases the recruits were invited to use to help them think abut the roles revealed that the village bobby is often interpreted as a fictitious role and one that is by definition unambitious.

After a year the organization's rationale as well as its members' foibles become more evident. Early exposure to patrol work, the essential symbolic resource of 'occupational culture', along with a growing appreciation of the extent and limits of knowledge held by those classed as 'experienced', encourages recruits to see that, although their formal status is transitional, they are already provisional adepts. They may be probationers but they are not untried. What promotion means in the police culture becomes evident. In terms of breaking solidarity with peers there is but one promotion, that away from constable. But the same thoughts of status, solidarity, professionalism v. community standards, and duty v. fitting in may be invoked by specialist options within the constable rank. The recruit whose prospective orientation is towards traffic is withdrawing from the generic conception of the office of constables as much as the constable who passes the sergeants' examination. Such ambitions are enabled by an organizational index which supports the claimed expertise of the hopeful. As a measure of organizational work the police have a unit of exchange as apparently tangible, and actually elusive, as money. The article is arrest rate. There is a deep literature on police discretion which establishes that the arrest is anything but an unambiguous and concrete occurrence. Yet, the convenience of the measure largely precludes alternative criteria (Manning 1980: 241). The criterion of arrest rates is likely to become more, not less, central to police performance measures under present reforms of police powers of arrest. Although 'arrestable' offences are confined to those carrying at least a five-year prison sentence, many others created by statute also carry powers of arrest, e.g. 'going equipped to steal'. The extension of powers of arrest for minor offences not prosecuted on warrant reinforces the 'arrest' as a convenient index of activity.

Chatterton (1983) demonstrates that certain arrests are chiefly *competency* related and others mainly related to *style*. Style refers to an officer's working personality and fundamental orientations. Understanding how officers define and respond to incidents also calls on questions of competency. Both values and abilities vary. Officers recognize the different styles of policing which form the range of role adaptations in practice and, Chatterton notes, after a few weeks on the division a probationer would know which styles characterized the approach of others on the relief, including the 'snatchers', who grab arrests where possible, apply strict legalistic tests and minimize discretion; the 'dodgers' or 'cuffers', who put their own interests first, are not ambitious and work the system to secure an easy life, and the 'negotiators' who are concerned to ensure that those who deserved arrest 'had their collars felt' while those who did not were spared the indignities of arrest and trial. A knowledge of the situated and contingent nature of arrest (and 'process') pervades the organization, and many police strenuously deny that evaluation is based on arrest rate. Part of that denial rests on sensible appreciation that quality of arrest is more important than quantity. Indeed, van Maanen's research reveals that high arrest rates can be associated with over-zealousness leading to informal reprimand. Constables have to learn how to gauge the 'quality' of an arrest, and do so in relation to those who routinely monitor such quality; charge officers have a part as well as sergeants. Arresting someone, the PCs come to recognize, makes work for experienced colleagues whose goodwill they must cultivate and who interpret, categorize and judge the quality.

But sensitive recruits appreciate these qualifiers, discount the denial that arrest rates matter and recognize there is an element of luck in having a 'good pinch' attributed even partly to one's efforts. The great variation in 'business' available on a shift affects what is thought. All probationers are aware that 'arrests' are one of the concrete things which serve the organization's need to assess performance. All are likely to encounter denials that there is a 'quota' operating. However, only some will work on shifts where the volume of business is so high that they can afford to concentrate on quality.

> 'Nobody said, "You're not doing enough, go and knock somebody off." It comes to you on the street, you don't have to go looking for

it. It comes straight to you. And when it comes to you, you just knock
them off for the offence. You don't have to go and infiltrate people.'
(7: 1, 6)

This applies to urban centres. The lack of 'arrest pressure' is linked to
the idea of a 'busy station'. Thus,

'not in our station: use your powers, don't misuse them and you are
all right. They're pretty busy where we are. They don't need to
motivate people so hard, nothing's said to me. You get a lot of work,
there's a lot of trouble. In the day you've got shoplifting, theft. At
nights you get fighting and damage.'   (12: 2, 5–6)

No doubt this reflects a kind of experience, but the experience is
limited to urban centre policing (here a large mining town noted for
enthusiastic brawling) and also assumes the absence of a specific offence
type favoured by the supervisor. Perhaps the type case of the supervisor
with a favourite offence is given by Rubinstein (1973) in his account of
Philadelphia sergeants, whose keen interest in vice supported an
elaborate complex of unstated, rule-governed practices by patrol
officers. To locale and offence-type sensitivity may be added the performance of one's peers. The usual unit of analysis is the shift; if one's
performance suffers by comparison then increasingly explicit prods are
elicited. Full establishment contributes to the effectiveness of the prod.

'Now we're up to strength and they can get rid of you just like that
in the first two years, there is pressure to get arrests. There's a light-
ning campaign on at the moment for vehicles, and that's come from
headquarters to every station. So there's pressure on you to bring a
certain amount of work in. You have to caution people for the first two
weeks, and the second two weeks you're solely reporting them for it.
That is a pressure, and there's people sacked for not bringing enough
work in. If there's a bobby working in a town centre on one shift
getting plenty of arrests and you're getting none of course you're out.'
(7: 2, 3–4)

Pressure of this sort can be provoked by a force-wide policy, as in the
example, but a decision to dispense with a particular probationer is not
force-wide. It emanates from local assessments and the record of formal
training. Therefore comparisons of the sort at the end of the quotation
are most important. It is there that assessments are made in light of the
supervisors' knowledge of local standards.

The drive to get arrests is not a universal pressure. One survey found
marked gaps between PCs and supervisors on arrests; only 18 per cent
of PCs thought that always looking for and making large numbers of

arrests was undesirable but 90 per cent of supervisors thought so (Police Foundation 1982). Pressure falls especially on probationers.

> Probationary officers, who are most concerned about productivity, pursue the few things that are possible to proactively generate, namely traffic, liquor and narcotics violations. During one shift an officer constantly referred to his monthly activity sheet and the upcoming assessment of his status. He felt he could produce more 'brownie points' by proactive rather than reactive work and said he longed for the day when his probation ended so that he could 'relax' somewhat.
>
> (Ericson 1982: 59)

Asked if he noticed any arrest pressure a probationer replied,

> 'Not on my section, although I have noticed on other sections in the same station a certain amount of pressure from the supervising officers to get arrests, breathalyzers, there's a sort of unofficial quota in some cases. I don't think its quite that bad in all sections although there are one or two instances. And of course there are the campaigns that are put out by headquarters, breathalyzer campaign at Christmas, which is not really to do with the stations – it's a force campaign. I've never found any pressure on me certainly, to get arrests for traffic offences or anything. As long as I do get some, there's no pressure on me to go out and get everything I can possibly find.' (8: 3, 4)

An interesting point is the recruit's regret at the use of arrest pressure, which is not 'that bad in all sections'. Coyness over what is clearly a necessary pressure arises from fear on the organization's part that the public will assume that where quotas exist differential enforcement ensues but the point also signals the inception of an employee's perspective, where arbitrary quotas can be imposed without regard to local difficulties in finding sufficient offences without upsetting community standards.

Such a sensibility is a major element of socialization towards competent practice. Doing arrest is a learning activity for recruits. This leads to a different sense of arrest pressure.

> 'Nobody ever said to me, "Go out and get some bugger tonight," but when I got an arrest I was either told that that was a good arrest or, "Did you really need to arrest that man?" So there was a certain element of pressure because my motivation was evaluated all the time.' (9: 1, 6)

The recruit speaks of the pressure arising from having his performance assessed, and, as he notes, in the recruit stage one is not only learning standards but also making mistakes, which affect citizens. 'I was aware of that evaluation, therefore I did feel pressure. I don't feel yet that I have arrested somebody unfairly. I've arrested people and then found out afterwards that I had the power to either arrest or report. But most times (I've done about thirty-five) the majority of them I've thought to myself, "Anyway, I wouldn't have reported it, he was such an unreasonable person and the situation at that time warranted me getting him away." But, yes, there is a certain amount of pressure on arrest' (9: 1, 6). The officer suggests that pressure to get arrests can lead to mistakes.

Both organizational and individual performance assessment is by crime detection rates and arrest/report-for-summons figures. Of 1,000 commendations in one force, 73 per cent were for crime detection on the evidence of crimes cleared or arrests made, 16 per cent for 'good police work' supported by enforcement figures, 9 per cent for bravery and 0.5 per cent for 'responsible leadership'. There were none for beat work or peacekeeping unless supported by enforcement figures. Officers who failed to produce a desirable number of arrests/summons reports were openly criticised and probationers were unlikely to be taken on without a list of arrests and reports at appraisal time. Those wishing to specialize also had to show a good arrest or traffic summons record (Jones and Winkler 1982: 111).

Several probationers vented strong feelings about the fairness of arrest rate pressure. One who thought there 'definitely' was such pressure observed that

> 'the bobbies all say, "I haven't had an arrest for ages, I'll have to go out and get an arrest tonight." I just don't agree with that at all. Chief inspector in charge of us is one of these that likes you to knock off everybody you see. I just don't agree with it. If I see somebody doing something wrong, or know they are, then OK, I'll go and arrest them. But if it's just somebody shouting in a street who's had something to drink, I'll not go and arrest him for that. I'll not go and knock kids off for riding bikes on pavements and petty things like that. Some people do. I suppose you are supposed to, but I just don't agree with it.' (10: 1, 5)

There is a dialectic between community standards and full enforcement; it is mediated by police discretion. 'I'd rather solve a crime than report a motorist. That's my feeling and I think that's better policing . . . But . . . the CID notice you if you nab a burglar . . . There's a certain amount of luck in it' (12: 3, 12–13). The point is that notions of equity are hardly the only influences on the exercise of discretion; there are organizational pressures. What is worrying is the chance that, as these recruits discovered, organizational pressures can structure practice for organizational motives which run counter to public conceptions of the organization's mandate.

'I've got to be quite honest – you are expected to put a quota in. But I'll have to be careful how I say that. They don't just want you to go out for the sake of getting arrests. If they're there by all means bring it in. Not just arrests, that covers a wide spectrum of things, process, traffic. I don't think that's designed to just bump the figures up, I think that's for the bobbies' benefit, to gain experience, but there is a certain pressure on you.' (10: 2, 6)

The instigator of the pressure is most often the sergeant, who lays off 'old stagers' and only kicks the probationers whose 'self-motivation' is waning. A recruit who reported pressure 'to get work' but not necessarily arrests said,

'there were a hell of a lot of pressure. You've got to be out there all the time searching for it. Your sergeant puts on the pressure. He'll book you up if he thinks you're not doing enough. But really it's self-motivation, because at first you want to get as many as you can to get the experience. But if you start tapping your feet the sergeant comes and kicks you up the pants for it . . . They don't tend to bother too much with the old stagers . . . But the probationers, you've got something to prove. . . . The pressure's on you all the time . . . to prove your worth. But once you've proved that then the pressure moves off.' (11: 1, 5)

The recruit begins with a distinction between pressure to get arrests and other work, but then equates getting experience with getting 'as many as you can'. The seductive 'measurability' of arrests makes for the equation of arrests and work; if recruits are deemed lacking in experience of a particular aspect of patrol work they are encouraged to find an offence in that area and learn from doing summons, report and arrest on it. A self-defined 'ambitious' recruit noted,

'You're expected, as a probationer, to prove your worth, which is only natural. Which is not to say that people stand over you with a big stick and say, "You will go out and get an arrest today." They would say you hadn't had enough experience at this work and, "go out and see if you can get such-and-such." (That was coming) from the shift sergeants, (but) it emanated from an inspector.' (11: 2, 4)

The final variation in recruit's experience is the priorities of different supervisors.

'It differs from one sergeant to another. . . One sergeant, if you're not working, he'll let you know . . . Some sergeants will pressure you into doing offences where others, they're not as keen. They don't give you an ultimatum. I haven't been given an ultimatum anyway – "You must report somebody before you come in today." I've never had to do that.' (12: 3, 9)

Whether or not one's sergeant will give one a kindly warning or a sharp prod, one must assume the worst. The recruit negotiating a transitional status, in conditions of hopeless regional unemployment, and full police establishment, is conducting a campaign. Their tactics must proceed from worst-case assumptions.

The depth of the division between the 'practical' perspective in the occupational culture and the approach taken by the promotion-minded was forcibly conveyed by this experienced WPC. She was anything but a naive proponent of crime-bashing, rough and ready values. One learns about the occupational culture as well as promotional issues from the advice she would give probationers on how to get on.

'I would like to say, "you stick at doing your work, do it well, keep being enthusiastic, pass your exams and you'll get on," but it doesn't really work like that. The good practical policemen stay good practical policemen and one relies on them. You've got to show that extra – Oh it's difficult to put into words and I hate it because its so wrong. You've got a degree behind you so people are looking out for you all the way, or perhaps you can be the type that will conform to certain things because you know you're going to get on. You'll devise some wonderful scheme that's got your name on the bottom, people notice it. It gets back to the frustrating part of it, the more that you're a good practical bobby the longer you'll stay one.' (83: 3, 8)

The values of competent practice as a constable actually militate against advancement and promotion-mindedness.

That constables assess evaluation criteria in terms of their own notions of fairness implies another lexicon in the available vocabulary. Perceiving something as a criterion transforms its organizational significance. For example, a recruit who had been reprimanded for having 'lost interest' (his inspector found him rather dozy after 'a bit of . . . night-life') said,

'I told him that I haven't lost interest in the job at all. If there was a certain number of offences he wanted every week, why didn't he tell me, but I didn't want to say that, it sounds sarcastic. They like you to get, say, three a week, or, at the moment, I've started to think about one a day to try and get this report back up again.' (12: 1, 9)

The comment illustrates how an *assumed* management orientation becomes confirmed in practice whether or not it is intended, precisely because it is seen as an assessment criterion. It also shows how, acting on this assumption, the practice of the officer changes on the street – people on his beat will be under closer scrutiny. His further remarks bring out how the beat constable is in competition with specialist squads; he begins with the idea that some arrests are 'worth more' than others.

'If you get a good arrest perhaps. But on the beat, walking, you think about traffic more than anything because crime is very difficult to come by. CID are straight there at a call. Or if there's something happening, a burglary, a car's straight there. Car'll pass you, you're looking at the tax discs, checking vehicles, checking property. Which, if you look at a definition is preventing crime. Anyway, that's the only way they can judge you. So you have to start thinking of what they can see rather than what you know you're doing.' (12: 1, 10)

The officer lays bare the probationer's necessarily instrumental criteria for orienting their performance. It shows the potential damage in terms of skewing practice, and the kinds of experience and expertise gained, in order to conform to criteria of practice which can actually be assessed. It suggests that, far from taking on the 'lay low' version of appropriate practice embedded in occupational culture, some recruits try to play the system. For them the occupational culture is less an aggressive, bloody-minded support for notions of policing divergent from formal policy than a defensive redoubt for those whose ambitious tactics fail.

Partners and gender

Of course 'the' occupational culture is actually many subcultures; nuances and colourations arise from regional differences, differences of ambition, divergent perceptions of the police mission, varying experiences of the organization, and so on. Although there is no inherent warrant for assuming that the chief divisions within occupational culture correspond to gender and class consciousness, the manifestation of these central sociological concerns in the police is especially telling.

While women have long been employed in the police, and still comprise a great proportion of 'civilian' employees, it is relatively recently that women have been able to pursue a career as constable with equal duties to men. Smith found only a moderate gender difference among Londoners considering joining police: 22 per cent of men compared with 15 per cent women aged 15–44 had considered it (Smith 1983). Yet the male-oriented ethos of the organization is continually apparent not least in the scatalogical humour indulged in regardless of gender (field notes, 16.5.83). At induction 82 per cent of the recruits chose the village bobby and WPC as more similar out of the triad of village bobby, WPC and CID officer. Reasons ranged from 'same job' to 'involved with general public'. Those that picked village bobby and CID officer as most similar mainly saw 'experience' as the distinguishing trait, although several responded with remarks like 'vs. women's lib'. After a year 72 per cent saw WPC and village bobby as similar, while 23 per cent now chose CID and village bobby. Reasons again centred on WPCs' inability to deal with serious crime and claims they were usually relegated to routine work – 'mainly useful in dealing only with women and children'. They were also perceived as less ambitious.

One of the several reasons for endorsing women as colleagues and patrol partners was that mixed teams are better able to supply a range of services. A female recruit felt 'there are various points of the job which will be easier for a woman to tackle, more delicate matters, and there are points which we can't tackle' (4: 1, 2). One of the ironies of the role for women is that in order to make their way in it some women emphasize women's 'traditional' qualities, such as sensitivity and talking rather than punching one's way out of difficult situations. Asked to imagine herself as a coloured constable dealing with white citizens she continued, 'it would be easier for a female coloured officer to be accepted than a male. Because women are more likely to be more sensitive over such things' (4: 1, 3). The point about projected images of the female constable is that both the 'female as having useful gender-specific qualities' and the 'female as tougher than the tough guy' versions are encountered. The irony is that the WPC who hopes to make the police a more 'humane' organization, to achieve progress in organizational practice, has to emphasize 'traditional female virtues'. These qualities may not be those deemed appropriate by other females entering the occupation.

It is difficult to disentangle the sources of occupational and gender-relevant organizational imagery; there is no neat fit between respondents' sex and attitude towards female police. Several males were adamant that sex made no difference to the constable's ability, although they were prepared to acknowledge differences which seemed to 'favour' the case for WPCs. One who attributed his favourable approach to mixed schooling challenged the conventional line that WPCs' relative lack of physical strength limited their utility in disorderly situations.

'No, often they do it much better. In a violent situation it's very difficult to punch a lady. It doesn't go down as well with whatever cause you're violent for . . . Also, the lady constable . . . knows she's liable to get a smack in the end anyway, so as long as it didn't worry her it wouldn't worry me.'   (5: 2, 4)

Although none of the female recruits resembled the stolid behemoths sometimes alluded to in the lore of the ranks, it was not unusual to be assured that most WPCs were not so delicate as to be a defenceless liability (5: 4, 2).

A year's experience did not alter these respondents' views. A recruit with patrol experience with a WPC thought 'they play a valuable part in policing', and reported no problems in violent situations – 'they seem able to pull their weight so you treat them as though they were anybody else' (8: 1, 6). Pertinent here is the 'chivalry' idea, that the male constable working with a female constable may place himself in dangerous situations more often because of his anxiety over the vulnerability of his partner. The notion resonates with the emphasis on the loyalty of partners, and for constables to be able to rely on the loyalty and defence capability of their partner in planning their own action. From this perspective, where 'woman PC' equals 'weak partner', a fundamental working code is challenged by having female constables in all spheres of police work. Again it is hard to distinguish the paternalistic view from the apparently pragmatic one that each sex has its merits and demerits. Asked if he felt obliged to come to the aid of WPCs or was more concerned than if he were partnering a man because WPCs are vulnerable, this respondent said, 'Yes I (do) feel that way, but it is balanced by the work that they do in, say, indecency problems' (8: 3, 7–8). Some further nuances of the 'violent situation' problem, which acts as the nexus for dispute over the utility of women police, were suggested by a respondent who spoke of women's physical strength as the 'obvious reason' for 'their disadvantage'. Nevertheless

'they've got an advantage inasmuch as it's very embarrassing for a man when he's out with his mates at night to get arrested by a woman and that's one aspect . . . where it can be to their advantage, and the other one, in dealing with women. Although there are one or two policewomen I could think of who would just go into a punch-up and pull their weight . . . for Friday and Saturday nights I'd sooner have a fella stood next to me.' (10: 2, 9–10)

This equivocacy marked the 'pro'-women replies by men; the year's experience did not assuage early qualms based in policing's tough image nor the 'traditional' feminine qualities. Grudging acceptance is a more adequate description than 'pro-women PC', even when allied to a consciousness that things could be otherwise. A recruit who had done 'a lot of criminal matters with WPCs'(!) felt

'obviously they're not as physically capable, although some of the women PCs are. But I suppose you do find yourself a little bit protective towards them. Whether that's a man/woman role you've been brought up to . . . I'd be very . . . upset if I was with a policewoman and she was assaulted.' (12: 3, 14–15)

The more thoughtful struggled to express this concept of cultural change around the crystallizing instance of violence.

'She knows as much law and she's as good at the paperwork as you. In certain situations her presence is accepted even more but under certain circumstances she's not taken seriously. And there's one thing, that if I'm with a woman PC, especially if it's on nights, you get an uneasy feeling because if anything did happen, then afterwards (colleagues say), ''He's the PC that let that woman get assaulted.'' You get a moral sense of duty to not only look after yourself but to look after the woman as well, who's supposed to be equal.'   (12: 1, 17)

The segment 'he's the PC' hints at the salience of (male) traditional beliefs in the recruit's reasoning. He may be echoing what he has learnt as 'the line' on WPCs, but conviction was evident in his tone of voice. It is as if he is speaking of a reaction by colleagues he would will to be otherwise. He continued, 'yet if you put that to the woman (she'd say), ''I can look after myself.'' That is their pride, if they said the same to you you'd resist too. But there is still something there, I'm not quite sure of . . . It's all part of the new way really' (12: 1, 17). While some men recognize the cultural-groundedness of their protective feeling, they seem unable and unwilling to abandon it; after all 'chivalry' and 'good manners' are a 'good thing', and are generally taught to boys by women. If even those men with insight into the problem are unwilling to abandon their own traditional stance, one they find heavily supported by the occupational culture on apparently plausible practical grounds (loyalty, 'strength'), the obstacles to wider change are more rigidly set by the prejudiced. The recruit who had done much crime work with WPCs highlighted the obstacles as he expressed his reluctance to wholly relinquish a traditional stance. 'You are obviously a bit protective towards them. It's just a thing you've been brought up with, but I'm not openly against them . . . Some policemen just openly dislike women police officers' (12: 3, 15).

Even respondents who condemn female equality in the force often discern some role for women; the police culture abounds with references to the fine work traditionally done by women as clerks.

'They're a funny lot, the policewomen. I've known cases where a policewoman has been at the station after briefing and they have said, ''I'm just waiting for a policeman to go around (with me) to give somebody a summons,'' that sort of thing. I don't think they should have been allowed equality in the force. I'm not a chauvinist pig but for their own protection. I am thinking of the way they have gone about it and gone the whole hog. Before they were doing a nursemaid job and something was needing to be done and it should have been done in stages until they got to the stage they could cope with, stop there. I don't think I'd fancy being in a scrap and expect some policewoman to sort it out.' (1: 4, 4)

Most 'anti' respondents rather bleakly accept that women are in the police to stay, but emphasize physical limitations.

'They have their uses, we have to accept it now, women's lib, etc. When I was in (the police) last time, after eleven o'clock they were only in the station house to look after female prisoners, and that's the place they should be. The idea of having one beside me in a spot of bother, you tend to think more about looking after the policewoman than you would after yourself . . . They're not physically built for that type of job.' (3: 4, 3)

For Cain's (1973: 116–17) police, women fell into two sharply divided categories, the rough and the respectable. Respectable women were innocent, ignorant and needed protection. Policewomen could be resented because they caused confusion of the categories.

The view that a woman constable's place is in the station house and not the street points to the image of policing carried by the respondent. It is another arena for the preference of crime control over social service as an occupational image. The 'physical' approach to policing underlies comments which otherwise appear only to voice prejudice. Thus,

'I've worked with women before. I try not to be biased. I've met one or two good ones. If you get a good woman she is brilliant and she will leave you standing. But the majority are, quite honestly, something to hang a uniform on.' (3: 5, 3)

It is interesting to compare this with the elaborated answer given a year later by the same respondent. The early views are confirmed but invested with the extra 'credibility' of 'experience', which here seems to pertain more to inhabiting the occupational culture than working with a WPC.

'I've walked the beat with one once but I avoid it like the plague. There's three reasons. One, if that woman gets injured I would feel a lot worse than if a bloke gets injured. The second thing I don't like about women is they seem so indecisive and giggly. They frustrate me at work. I don't mind them giggling in bed but I don't like them giggling next to me at work. And, three, a lot of them only join the job to find a husband, and I just haven't got time to tolerate them. A lot of blokes, when they're out working with policewomen, their motivation's not to do the job well, but to impress this female. And I am a male chauvinist pig, no two ways about it.' (9: 1, 9)

The point in examining these comments is not to document prejudice, but to examine the way prejudice can be excused in the account by reference to aspects of the police role which are unproblematically defined as desirable. Despite his self-attribution of the label 'chauvinist', the respondent's evaluation is expressed in terms of role requirements. In his conception of the police role, dedication to duty is a signal value.

> 'If my job runs over . . . I'll just give the missus a ring, and say, "Hey up, lass, I'm going to be home late." "What, again?" "Look, it's putting food in your belly, don't complain," and put the phone down. But there's girls saying, "Oh, I've got a hair appointment," or they're engaged. I say, "Sod off and leave the file to me to sort out," but it happens so often that it makes you cross. They're not conscientious about the job.'   (9: 1, 10)

In a final version, the alleged unsuitability of women is presented by two rhetorical devices. The idea of WPCs arises from the 'admin.' who lack a grounding in real policing, and even the WPCs themselves do not wish to work on patrol.

> 'The previous system, the WPCs section, was far better than where they've got this what they call "equality". When I refer to "they" I mean the people who work in admin. I've worked with WPCs who are rubbish, and with WPCs who are better than some men. But as a whole I don't think they feel they should be out on the streets. It's a matter of physical difference and attitude.'   (11: 2, 6)

The 'disadvantaged' group is seen as reluctant to accept its own 'advancement'.

The overlap between this perspective and a paternalistic approach is apparent. What the paternalist gains by a denial of prejudice he does not, as it were, lose in the depth of his assumption that women prefer to be treated as delicate and unworldly. Some responses move beyond paternalistic protectiveness to consider the advantage to the benefactor of taking responsibility for a female partner.

> 'They are more or less the weaker sex, aren't they? You can't expect them against most blokes to stand up for themself (sic). So really it's quite good for them to walk with a bobby. They're a bit more secure. Even the bobby's probably a little bit scared, like. If there's a woman at side of him he's got to put that fear out of his mind.'   (1: 2, 4)

The paternalist's answer to the 'violence' problem is to keep the WPC away from such situations.

> 'I find them a bit of a bind sometimes . . . But I'll work with them providing if you get the odd punch-up you can generally leave them

in the car or something . . . But the girls I've worked with have done the self-same job as me.' (2: 2, 3)

Even experience of working with women in combat failed to overcome the belief that women cannot cope with violence. The army's policy reinforced the stock male view, and the comment quickly translates to a traditional view of women's 'nature'. The recruit had worked many times with women soldiers and had

'no problems except when it comes to violence. I appreciate a lot of the girls can handle themselves but when it comes to firearms and things like that you've got to push them out of the way. Like in Northern Ireland where the girls go on the street, you're armed but they're not, that policy. But you've got to have policewomen, you've got to if you're dealing with women, especially hysterical women.' (3: 2, 3)

The lingering pertinence of the assumption that the job is in large part a 'physical' one is so general that the 'physical' aspects must be subdivided; this quality concerns much besides actual fighting. Stamina and psycho-motor co-ordination are as pertinent to success in the physical work of policing as fighting, if not more so. All constables spend some hours walking about in vile weather, need to be able to run, to focus quickly on distant objects and so on. Not one respondent, male or female, mentioned any physical quality other than those relevant to fighting. Nor were the allusions at all specific; the art of handling fighting drunks probably depends more on holds and hand grips than it does on the pounds force per square inch potential of a particular muscular configuration. But it is precisely the brute force image of the constable which these accounts draw on.

'I've worked with them, sometimes a bit temperamental about the work. The only worry I'd have is in a situation where there was going to be some physical violence offered to me. I've no doubt they can muster a WPC that's six foot tall as well as broad, but there's not many of them knocking around.' (4: 4, 3–4)

The response works towards a dualism whose mutual exclusivity – a thing is either one or the other – obscures the interconnection of things. The WPC belongs to the feminine world of emotion, sensitivity and academic niceties like paperwork, the PC is the man of action and strength.

Locked into this frame of reference even officers with experience contrary to the stereotype manage to ignore it. Responses like the following suggest the mythic character of the chivalrous/paternalist response in fights. 'You tend to look after them a lot more. If it was two bobbies walking around it's all right but if you've got a woman and there's a bit of aggro . . . you tend to look after her and you end up getting thumped in the process.' Asked if this had happened the recruit, who had worked 'a lot' with WPCs over fourteen months, replied, 'It's not happened, no. The ones we've got . . . will get stuck in as much as a bobby would if there's fighting . . . They are good policewomen at our place. (But you'd still have some reservations?) You would, yeah' (7: 1, 8). Respondents still oriented to the myth rather than what experience 'taught' them, so that they interpreted experience as 'confirming' initial belief.

> 'I know I said last time, you do feel slightly protective towards them. They're still a woman when it comes down to it. Even though some of them are very good, better than a man in certain situations, to calm a situation down.'
>
> (7: 2, 5)

It matters little if a thing is a myth when it is believed to be factual and a basis for action. The purportedly superior qualities the WPC does have can hardly be tested if, whenever a fight occurs, the 'talkers' are pushed to the rear. The disadvantage of belief in the myth is clear when one considers the sole example offered by a 'paternalist' in support of the 'violence' claim.

> 'On the whole they are a good thing but . . . I've been on football duty with a WPC and we went into a crowd situation and all the time you're looking around, "Where is she, is she all right?" Not thinking about the guy who's about to clobber you. Whereas with a bloke you would never think of this.'
>
> (11: 1, 7)

Performance is based on the questionable assumption of a higher prevailing duty – protect the 'defenceless' female – rather than the task at hand.

Reservations about WPCs arise from the 'problem' of physical strength. There were some expressions of concern over female frivolity, lack of commitment and about female predators hunting for husbands but these 'problems' would arise from any female presence in the organization. The conception of policing based on physical strength may itself represent an inappropriate occupational image, but the myth is embedded in occupational culture and more than the gender-specific resonances of the operating ideology would have to change to bring about a change in practice. What clinches the view that the myth has a staying power resistant to even direct experience is the attitude to female officers as opposed to female PCs. Female officers are presented as no problem at all; male and female PCs respect them and even become 'gender-blind'. 'I don't mind (a female superior officer). A superintendent came to some of our informal meetings. I didn't really think anything about it. It was just another police person' (1: 4, 4). A positive cast is put on *la différence*.

> 'You normally find they are more prepared to listen than a man in a senior position. If you've got a point they're more prepared to accept what you've got to say and then throw it out if they don't agree with it. Whereas more often than not a male person in charge will not take notice.'   (3: 2, 3–4)

The female superior is as intangible as any in the world of officers. A female recruit commented,

> 'I wouldn't find any difference if it was a woman or a man. You wouldn't be able to talk so easily. You wouldn't be able to say what you want to say with a boss, even if it was a woman. You would be a little uneasy in case you did anything wrong.'   (1: 1, 3)

The responses imply a clash of stereotypes in the recruits. They have little experience of the organization or its officers, bar their immediate supervisors. They do have enormous experience of the resources of cultural meaning which preserve two highly relevant mythic images. One is of the police force as a crime-and-disorder-controlling, mission-oriented, dispassionate and tough body of men. The other is of women as emotional, weak, sympathetic and service-oriented. The nexus of the conflict between these images of women police is the situation of violence; in so far as female officers, like all officers, do not directly experience that situation, the gender of the officer is irrelevant.

The early impact of occupational culture is such that it can provide a perspective on experience before the recruit gains direct experience. This respondent specifies how his initial, favourable, attitude has changed in discussion.

> 'That (working with WPCs) doesn't bother me, but I suppose I've been talking to people, PCs and that. They're most worried about it if they ever get into a fight, and I suppose it will be the same for me. . . . If it's a fella (PC) who goes in they're not going to bother about him, they will just carry on. Probably take a swing at the other person. But they're not likely to take a swing at the woman, they're more likely to take one at the bloke (PC).'   (5: 1,3)

It was 'a liability' patrolling with a woman. Although it is true that, as one female recruit asserted, the experienced officers 'all have to start from the beginning', her feeling that this constrained the experienced from 'hassling' her as a woman is more dubious. Her comment invoked the occupational culture idea that, as all police start as constables, there is a basis for solidarity. The evidence of male respondents is that the occupational culture, in so far as it preserves a consensual set of values, is a resource more particularly available to some groups within the ranks than others.

The two broad strategies open to a disprivileged group entering a formerly closed occupation are to seek to transform the organization to better fit their qualities or to transform themselves to better fit the organization. Attitudes brought to policing by women could be drawn on to change the everyday practice of policing, if not its fundamental mission, although such skills as negotiation ('talk') should be separated from their supposed basis in female qualities and be recognized as qualities accessible to anyone subject to particular patterns of socialization. However, unlike North America (Martin 1980), the few studies of British policewomen suggest the rarity of female entrants wishing to promote change and reform (Southgate 1980).

A female senior officer who thought, 'You've got to be a lot better than a man to be classed as an equal' (81: 3, 1) nevertheless suggested that 'as society gets more violent we've got a less important role. There is no way I see a woman on the front of a PSU' (81: 3, 1–2). This is a hard core 'police perspective', and a mark of the conquest of biography by the occupation. Certainly the female recruits expressed conventional views. They were young and wanted a career in police work prior to marriage with a view to returning after raising children. An early entry age was an attraction. They expressed a complementary view to males on mixed patrol. For personal safety they would prefer male patrol partners, although female company would be more satisfying.

> 'In a way it's (patrol with a male partner) rather an advantage. I'd rather be walking around in the dark with a man in the middle of the night than with a woman. Most girls would. But in a way it might be a disadvantage. You might find it easier to talk to a woman.' (1: 1, 3)

They also thought 'mixed' patrol could improve effectiveness by combining 'specialist' qualities (4: 1, 2). Females preserve their domestic options and are realistic about what this implies. While the male recruits accurately sense their female colleagues' domestic orientations they extend this to a view of women as lacking commitment and, in extreme form, only being interested in the police as a source of marriage partners. As the men are, for the most part, career-oriented, they discount the commitment of those who cannot realistically give themselves wholly to a police career. The steady increase from 50 per cent at induction and 69 per cent at year one to 77 per cent by year two in agreement that a wife's first duty was to her family may well reflect the impact of police work on constables' own domestic situation. There was also a slight decline in disagreement that abortion should only be available in cases of grave medical danger, from 53 per cent at induction to 46 per cent at year two.

The entry of women into the office of constable is one of the most potentially divisive and controversial recent developments in policing. It is not difficult to collect scathing, ribald, and openly hostile comments about WPCs in conversation with male (and female) constables and officers. The curious thing is that the female recruits put forward an attitude that is not so much complacent as matter-of-fact, not so much reformist as thankful for a chance at work. These 'sensible' female workers express little resentment of the labour market, household politics, or the police organization. They are set to conform to what is required of them, and regard the police mission as unproblematically defined by those who have come before. Few even express the anxious enthusiasm that marks some of their male peers at the recruit stage. Their views are remarkably similar to the men's. The similarity of views extends to the most controversial issues, such as the role of WPCs in violent situations, as if to suggest that the clamour is generated by men. While the opening up of the office of constable to a disprivileged group inspires some outrage amongst old hands the stirrings seem merely ritualistic. On this evidence, novices operate with a high degree of consensus about the meaning of their status as employees of the police organization. The real controversies of employment in the police are largely shared by male and female employees.

The Federation and trade unions

During the late seventies the police enjoyed pay increases and other benefits which the government denied other public sector employees. While some saw this as a mark of the government's trepidation about the maintenance of order in conditions of economic depression, the police tended to see it as acknowledging the special 'industrial relations' position of the job. Like a small number of other occupations thought crucial to the maintenance of the social order, the police do not have the right to strike nor to organize a conventional trade union. The Police Federation is the representative of the ranks in pay and benefits bargaining, and is not affiliated to the Trades Union Congress. Studies of attitude shift suggest a growth in 'instrumental' attitudes and a decline in idealistic attitudes as one gains experience of police employment. Agreement that the Police Federation should be more closely consulted rose sharply after two years of training, from 56 per cent and 57 per cent at induction and year one to 72 per cent at year two. Similarly, support for legislation against unofficial strikes fell from 67 per cent at year one to 56 per cent at year two (at induction only 29 per cent of a later intake agreed). Yet a characteristically high level of agreement (78 per cent) was maintained through year one and two that trade unions have too much power.

It would be fair to summarize the recruit's knowledge of the Police Federation as minimal and few expressed any interest in redressing their ignorance. Nor did recruits grasp the Federation's peculiar position as regards the trade union movement; it was usual to regard the Federation as a union itself. Knowing about the Federation was not seen as being informed about one's professional representative in bargaining and disciplinary matters but as a political matter. There was a gradual rise in opposition from induction through to year two (71 per cent to 76 per cent to 85 per cent) to the police playing a bigger part in politics. Recruits had spent very little time thinking about unions. 'Gor, struth, I don't really know much about the Federation. I haven't got much time for unions anyway' (2: 2, 2).

Many foresaw conflicts of loyalty in police work involving industrial disputes; they accepted the reason for non-affiliation to the TUC. 'It could cause complications. . . . You couldn't really be an amalgamated union and then have to go out and break up a meeting. If something gets unlawful it wouldn't be a good thing' (1: 4, 3). The respondent had worked for two years as a dustman and had been a trade union member. A former carpenter suspected 'they wouldn't get a very good reception from other trade unionists' (3: 1, 3). The former DHSS claims investigator, who stressed his working-class identity, argued that split loyalty effectively precludes affiliation; on occasion doing the police job meant enforcing anti-union legislation.

> 'As a policeman you've got to attend TUC-orientated strike meetings and demonstrations. So to be sympathetic towards the cause of, for example, the steel workers, you'd rather not prosecute a steel worker and you've got to keep order at these strikes. If you're a member of the TUC you might feel, "We can come out in sympathy towards that." But then you would not be doing your job . . . if you don't want to do the job you might as well get out.'   (5: 2, 3)

Anti-union sentiment was also evident. A long-serving soldier who later worked in a warehouse referred to non-unionization as a reason he joined the police. 'I could take the orders from my (warehouse) bosses, but I couldn't take being told what to do by the unions' (3: 2, 1). Another, more sophisticated tack was taken by a recruit who argued that the possibility that the police could be seen as taking sides by one section of the population was more important than the esteem the officer might have for unions.

> 'The policeman should in every respect be seen to stand on his own, not to have ties to anyone. The TUC might be an admirable body in a lot of ways, but people can make subjective judgements about that.

Therefore to one group of the population it might seem a good idea for the police to show solidarity with the rest of the working classes and to other people it might appear a very bad thing.'   (4: 3, 3)

Attitudes towards the industrial status of the police employee affirm support for the *status quo*. It is noteworthy that no mention was made of the Federation's role in supporting constables involved in disciplinary matters. Industrial relations matters were also approached by discussing recruit attitudes toward the right to strike. It may be thought that 'affiliation' is more innocuous than the right to strike. However, several respondents who were disinterested in the Federation and opposed to affiliation were prepared to entertain a police strike and to consider their own involvement in it. One who endorsed the right to strike went on to qualify this.

'But they should all go out on strike at once. It would be trouble for them as well as everybody else. Because when they're out on strike everybody else would be causing trouble and when they came back they would only have more work to do clearing it up again.'
(1: 1, 3)

Nevertheless, she would support a strike 'if there was a good reason for it'. Another recruit, while rejecting the right to strike, thought 'it wouldn't be bad to have the choice to threaten to strike' (3: 3, 2). Limited industrial action was contemplated by another.

'I'm rather split about this (right to strike). Possibly yes. But I think there should be a limit about how long they're allowed to go on strike. I think there should be boundaries. (You wouldn't rule it out if conditions were bad?) No.'   (4: 1, 2)

The former DHSS inspector was less equivocal. 'Yes, but it's got to be a last resort. If the cause was justified then I would use it, 'cause it wouldn't take long before they realize how badly they are missing you and that's the ultimate weapon' (5: 2, 3–4).

Former soldiers think such activity is simply incompatible with military or police service and, since this is self-evident, anyone who thinks otherwise must have erred in joining the occupation.

'Because they serve Her Majesty, and it's just like the army. It's unfortunate but you're serving the Queen so you sign on the dotted line. If they wanted to go on strike they could have joined a different job. They knew before they joined that they couldn't strike.'
(1: 2, 3)

The 'sign on the line' idea suggests the recruit sees the job as 'a package' and the strike ban as an inherent, essential part of it. Another ex-soldier even identified opposition to strikes as a feature of people drawn to such services.

> 'You find that with most servicemen. They like to get on with the job and they don't like strikes. That's one of the reasons for going into the police force or civilian jobs where there's no such thing as strikes.'
>
> (3: 4, 3)

Another cited experience.

> 'I worked with the Dutch marines and they've got a union and it was farcical. We were on an exercise, everybody was camped for the night and they say we've got to move . . . When the attack went in the Dutch marines weren't there . . . The union had said no. Can you imagine it in a war if, "Let's go on strike 'cause there's a chance of us getting killed."'
>
> (4: 5, 3)

Another approach was to invoke the danger of anarchy – 'if people see the police striking they will think anyone can strike and it will break down law and order completely' (2: 1, 2). Several felt a ban on the right to strike ought to be extended to other vital occupations.

> 'Certain jobs have to be done irrespective of any other factors, and the police force, the military service, medical services, social services, definitely have to be. There's no way they should strike. There's various jobs where they shouldn't be allowed to strike either.'
>
> (4: 3, 3)

Others who thought 'it could bring about anarchy' wanted to consider some other protest than the strike, such as working to rule (2: 2, 2–3). A young recruit who had not worked thought 'they shouldn't be able to strike, but we ought to have a means by which to get a fair deal' (5: 3, 3).

Rejection of the right to strike does not imply lack of consciousness of the industrial problems of the police. A former military policeman makes plain his sense of grievance over the treatment of public employees and yet adamantly (and contradictorily) refuses to consider any form of industrial action.

> 'I am against unions, always have been. Trade unions are OK if you've got a genuine grievance. I'd like to see something more positive for the police because this country's getting its priorities wrong. The wrong people are getting pay rises. Certain governments think, "These people have got a sense of loyalty." And loyalty doesn't pay your gas bill, your rates, your mortgage. It's the same in the forces and the nurses and the firemen. Without these essential services this

country would just go rock bottom. (Does that imply that you would be against the police going on strike?) I think so, yes. I disagree with strikes. Perhaps if we had a strong opinion about something it would be taken note of. You see, we've got nothing to back it up with. You may have some very senior officers or a member of parliament speaking up for you, but that's not good enough. The unions strike and they hit this country where it hits them hard.'   (4: 4, 3)

There are several inconsistencies in this statement. Although the recruit speaks in terms of industrial 'muscle' he ignores the potency of strike threats by such public sector groups as he mentions. His catalogue of barriers to a fair deal for the police establishes a 'genuine grievance' yet he is 'against the trade unions'. He suggests that 'if we had a strong opinion' it would be acknowledged, but asserts that even the support of chief constables and MPs is ignored. The rhetoric of frustrated loyalty bespeaks the poor position service-and duty-oriented people are in when the employer uses the paternalist relations it maintains with them to get their services on the cheap. But the most interesting inconsistency is that at the time of the interview the police had received the first of a series of generous pay increases. Thus his comments express a surrogate resentment on behalf of the other public sector workers. The sense of solidarity that fuels much successful union action is there, but the recruit opposes unions.

These induction stage responses delineate the ground over which the individual recruit's approach to police industrial relations will be fought out. The basic conflict between idealistic, service-oriented approaches and instrumental, policing-as-work approaches is transected by contrasting notions of loyalty, comparability, grievance, and the danger of anarchy. The industrial relations position of the police in no small measure invokes the essential nature of the police mandate and relation of the police to polity. Comparison of induction and one-year responses indicated the principal change was in the elaboration of earlier positions and closure around opposition to unionism. For example, the former soldier who felt police should not strike as they were 'serving Her Majesty' now offered the 'anarchy' answer (7: 1, 7). The ex-soldier who resented taking 'orders' from the union as a warehouseman echoed the idealist notion of policing where constables provide a moral model.

'The pride of the job is to uphold the peace and the laws of the land, and if we went on strike there just would not be any . . . It is a bad example for the police force, who are supposed to be the pillars of society, to go out on strike.'   (8: 3, 7)

Those who had been equivocal at induction moved into line with opposition to affiliation and strikes or maintained ignorance. The WPC who saw the utility of invoking a threat to strike was now strongly opposed – 'It would begin to look like America wouldn't it, with lots of strikes' (8: 2, 5). After a year another recruit complained 'sometimes a memo comes round, you think, "What does that mean? That's not going to make my job easier." And they ask you to vote, "This is your representative," even though I've never heard of him' (12: 1, 16).

Attitudes of instructors were consistent with the probationers in shunning the further 'unionization' of the Federation. A sergeant who had been a Federation representative thought there was 'no need – we've got better results as regards our pay negotiations than any other union in the country' (81: 1, 8). However, while he would not strike he was not averse to use what he called 'the power of lies and deceit'.

> 'For example, there was a referendum in the police service a few years ago, "Did we want the right to strike?" and 80 per cent of policemen said we did. That's a lie. We all lied, I lied, because we knew that saying that to the government would worry them. And it did of course.'   (81: 1, 8)

Whether this is a 'reading off' of his views onto others, or a reconstruction of a past mood of opinion from the contemporary position of good pay, it is evident that the 'industrial relations' views of police are a good deal more complicated than stereotypes and surveys suggest. For many the issue was a perceived conflict between the 'political' and 'bargaining' elements of their role. Affiliation to the TUC was rejected by a sergeant with twenty years' experience 'not because I'm anti-trade unions necessarily (but) I can't say that trade unions are necessarily effective in the way they ought to be . . . They've become far too political' (81: 2, 11). Even strikes 'might not be so bad if it was in defence of a genuine industrial grievance but there are so many political grievances'.

Reiner's (1978) respondents were much affected by their current relations with the employer. The present respondents were enjoying a benign period of industrial relations. However, some recruits had been involved in duties relating to industrial disputes. A strong opponent of affiliation and the right to strike at induction had come to support an extension of the Federation role.

> 'I don't think the Police Federation should be in the TUC . . . and I feel more so than last year because I've done picket work. I won't discuss the politics of the issue when I'm on the actual line. They're ordinary blokes like you and me . . . They've got a job but they can't go, not because they don't want to work but because some berk has said,

"Don't go to work." That's a sickening situation. I was on the steel strike and that shook me rigid. These were reasonable blokes, saying to the bobby, "Come over here, its warmer." But . . . when the pickets get around the lorry, ringleaders go and the others collect round afterwards. As though there's an obligation they're seen to do it. So we don't want anything to do with the TUC. The Police Federation ought to play a bigger part in the police force, it ought to be in a position to sway decisions, be consulted far more. Because, unlike many trade union representatives, *they* do know what the job's about.'

(9: 1, 9)

The recruit entered with an anti-union orientation, joined an occupational culture bearing an anti-union approach, worked under favourable pay conditions during the twelve months, and directly experienced the control of industrial picketing where confrontation seemed ritualized and organized by outsiders.

Experience of policing industrial picketing appears to convince officers of the humanity of strikers even as it fuels their rejection of conventional strike tactics. Like his colleague, this constable emerged a strong supporter of the Federation. 'Our Federation is ours and not some looney that's going to go round shouting, "Let's go on strike"' (11: 1, 7). He calls on experience as a striker and of policing an industrial dispute to explain his feeling that some less extreme bargaining power is necessary for public sector employees.

'I don't think they should have the right to strike but they want some more bargaining power. I was in the fire service and I didn't agree with their strike 'cause I don't think you can leave the public without some means. (Have you done any work on industrial picketing?) Yes . . . It was the hospital thing. I agree with some of their views but not the way they're carrying them out. All this shouting and banner-waving and the cranks who come in just to picket.'   (11: 1, 7)

Some feel the conflict between duty and a fair deal more than others by virtue of their experience. As a probationer the DHSS investigator maintained his ambivalence and explicitly related duty in industrial disputes to the industrial position of police employees.

'You must appreciate that we're a disciplined body. You don't get a lot of chance to express your feelings about trade unions. Sometimes we're up against a trade union, picket lines. It would be impossible for us to go on strike'.   (12: 3, 13)

Despite this contrapositioning of the 'disciplined body' and the strike, he adhered to his position at induction – police should have the right to

strike but not use it. 'I feel they should have the *right* to strike because
. . . it's never come to it' (12: 3, 14). Opposition to the right to strike
does not indicate total complacency about employment status, and these
comments illustrate that this issue is alive even in times of police
prosperity.

Being the power

Consideration of recruit approaches to their status as (prospective)
members enables one to approach the various meanings of the 'essential'
nature of police service by several routes. They orient to a culture which
invests particular belief in a crime control version of policing, and
projects a moral stand in which the police serve the community, not only
at a practical level, but at a symbolic level as exemplars of citizenship.
At induction 53 per cent agreed that a police constable's behaviour must
be exemplary. This rose to 67 per cent at year one and 84 per cent at
year two. Recruits strongly felt obliged, both at induction and year two
(95 per cent and 92 per cent), to perform police duty even if it involved
extra hours. However, agreement that a PC should never stop being a
PC fell from 58 per cent at induction to 44 per cent at year two, and to
the statement 'work shouldn't interfere with their private life' there was
increasing agreement from 53 per cent at induction to 68 per cent at year
one.

   Thus, the idealized notion is not an accurate representation of the
'organizational reality' or even the old hand's inner, realistic conception
of policing, but serves the police well as a status-conferring and utility-
confirming device in a world where objective criteria of success are
unknown and impossible to achieve. Because the system is closed and
self-confirmatory, it lends itself to the generation of symbolizations that
serve as ritualistic affirmation (Manning 1980). Thus the meaning of
apparently objective measures is symbolic. The recruits' evaluations of
the occupation are also primarily in symbolic terms; they do not speak
of cautioning for litter but of 'making society'. Constables derive great
satisfaction from what may be termed 'being the power' on the street and
in their other dealings with the public. Inspiration, enthusiasm, and the
other affective pre-conditions for perseverance in an occupation as
dreary and routine as any other, and more dangerous than most, must be
derived from such intrinsic features of the role. Their first experiences
of patrol, first arrest, and first time out alone can be intimidating, but
they soon gain self-confidence, if only from the realization that most of
us know even less about what is 'right' than they do.

   'Being the power' refers to the feeling that, at this time and in this
place, one is the representative of rectitude and the moral order, with its

accompanying complex of externally confirmed values. Comments which bear on this sense of affirmation through reference to an external, dominant value-set intersect with certain sources of job satisfaction; comments as simple as 'I wanted a job where I'd earn public respect and a feeling of well-being' (3: 5, 1) address this idea, and are not mere expressions of an undifferentiated idealistic sense of duty. The recruit suggests that respect must be 'earned', and 'being the power' is not simply about reinforcing one's ego by feeling that work is duty or about getting a kick from strutting about in uniform. These ideas are very much tied up with status, but a status derived from the organization the constable represents, and behind it the whole edifice of British justice, rather than from what is in fact occupancy of the lowest rung on the ladder of one of the largest employers in the country. One may recall the recruit whose frustration with paperwork led him to consider another job.

> 'I got to . . . walking towards the bus depot thinking, "bus driver". Then I thought to myself, it's strange, and I know it sounds conceited but I've got the British Empire Medal and bus drivers don't drive around with the British Empire Medal on their jacket. And I thought, "No, I've got a level in society, that is my level and my status. I'm not giving that up, and I'll go back and have another go at it."'
>
> (9: 1, 3)

Cynics may deride the pride that fuels this man's loyalty. But what cannot be ignored is the symbolic reality of the role as well as the routine and distasteful aspects of the job.

The symbolic reality comes through as plainly as the wet streets and mundane routine and cannot be taken away because it is inherent in the role.

> 'I then went out on the streets and I walked out of doors and I was on my own. But it's surprising how quickly you adapt. And it's a fantastic feeling. You are the bobby. You are the person responsible and these are your streets when you're on shift, nobody else's. You're the chief constable of those four or five streets, and it's a lovely feeling.'
>
> (9: 1, 5)

Of course, while they may become mindful of their autonomy, they need not perceive this simply as power but as neglect by senior officers. Those with a high degree of discretion feel both autonomy and isolation (Manning 1980: 93–4).

Status and duty are uniquely related in the police, as the recruit senses. Symbolically it does not matter whether one is a PC or an inspector, the law is the law, and, in a sense, one is responsible for everything in one's domain. In one's eagerness to debunk the crime control myth one should not ignore the basis of the constable's sense of worth in that heady feeling – 'you're the chief constable of those four or five streets, and it's a lovely feeling.' To understand how a basic grade employee of a large organization can feel, halfway through a two-year probationary period, that 'money . . . it's not a great thing', one must acknowledge the satisfaction the employee derives from the basic activity of the occupation. The feeling these comments describe is more than a sense of duty, a feeling of autonomy, or variety. 'Being out amongst the people, able to talk to them, just do whatever you like, whenever you like, and all the different walks of life that you meet, that have different opinions. That is very good' (11: 1, 1). When one learns to regard policing as work, certain concerns are dictated, practical matters such as promotion, discipline, industrial relations. Consideration of these matters alone suggests that the police are relatively disprivileged and backward as employees. That this does not square with the vigour and enthusiasm of the recruits points to the importance of the symbolic reality of the constable's world.

Supervision and authority

Asked if 'the admin.' understood the problems of the ranks a recruit said,

> 'They don't know you, they just see paperwork coming in. They don't think of the job you're doing. If it's all right then it's accepted, but if it's wrong . . . some hassle will be handed out. So it goes, all the way down the line.'   (12: 1, 21–2)

One cannot expect sympathy or interest from officers; the only way one's name will be noticed is if one causes a problem. It is necessary to consider whether this negative image of management as essentially an agency of punishment extends to officers in general. This has much to do with constables' assessments of the co-operativeness of their officers. Relations with officers are affected by station and shift assignments. 'It just depends what station you're at. Ours is a subdivision, so obviously we're more familiar with superintendents, chief inspectors and inspectors. At a small station there's only you, the constables and the sergeant' (8: 1, 5). Because operational decisions are effectively made by sergeants, the nexus of authority is in the shift sergeants' relationship with their constables (Tifft 1974). Sergeants stand midway, adjusting and mediating demands of constables and the expectations of senior officers – they 'crucify or justify' (Manning 1980: 102).

The 'experiential' basis of organizational rhetoric suggests that the greater the distance from the core practical work, the less credibility one is accorded. Indeed, constables are watchful for signs of unrealism in their immediate superiors and sensitive to hints of an ambitious lusting after rank on the part of their peers. Understanding is extended, and a presumption of understanding is accorded to, those who have shared the rank of constable. High levels of agreement that only PCs could understand the basic work of policing were found, with 82 per cent at induction, resolving to 73 per cent at year two. Yet constables do not suffer an innate inability to understand the sergeant role.

> 'I get on with them very well, but then I'm old enough to know that just because be calls you a stupid bastard . . . doesn't mean he hates you. It really means that he has so much in his in-tray, and the inspector wants to know where the hell this was and I put in front of him the biggest load of rubbish he's ever seen. They take a lot more pressure than I ever do, and good sergeants take the pressure off probationers . . . If a file comes in late and it's totally unreasonable then the sergeant is done with neglect of duty, vicarious liability. But I'm always guarded with supervision 'cause I could lose my job.'
>
> (9: 1, 6–7)

There is a further parallel to the military.

> 'I know now there's two officer classes in the police force. You can see sergeants mentally telling themselves they're hoping to pass over to fit into the inspector class. Then there are senior officers. Now some senior officers are damn good sorts, and some are out of touch and try damn hard to see they don't get too involved.'   (9: 1, 8)

Similarly, 'the higher levels (get out of touch). Not the shift inspector, he'll be out on the street and not the chief inspector, 'cause you tend to get them coming out on the street. But above that you tend to become office-bound' (11: 1, 6). Experience, recruits feel, inevitably becomes dated. 'When they were PCs there weren't a deal to do. It was straightforward, one piece of paper and that was it' (12: 2, 12). Thus, the value of experience erodes.

> 'He can't say, "When I was on the beat this happened," because we've progressed a long way . . . Twenty years ago when they went to a football match it was a family outing. But now he's stood directing what you do at a football match. He's not stood back of goal with 300 screaming skinheads and he doesn't know.'   (12: 3, 20)

There are also martinets whose style chafes.

> 'My particular situation, he's got a bit of a reputation, you've got to try and make sure you don't know him before you even meet him. After the initial shock, I think, "If I can work my probation under him

I can work under anybody.'' That's the attitude you've got to take. Before you speak over the radio you think of what he's going to say first.' (12: 1, 14)

As recruits, novices first encounter a problem which applies throughout their service, dependency on officers for good reports while they are also highly dependent on other constables to 'show him how to make his work interesting, introduce him to easing facilities and provide the necessary 'backing' (Cain 1973: 197). These competing forms of dependency are partially resolved in the sergeant role.

'Sergeants are in many senses members of the colleague group and will judge the probationer by the standards of the group . . . Thus conforming to the norms of the colleague group may indirectly stand a probationer in good stead with senior officers as well.'
(Cain 1973: 197)

Sergeants mediate the play of the organization's formal requirements on constables' practice.

'They're pretty good, sergeants. They will always help you with paperwork, put you right when you're wrong. The ones that we've got on our beat aren't too strict. If you make a balls-up they get a bit heavy on you. But they put you right.' (12: 2, 6–7)

Sergeants are in their own organizational predicament; an Irish study found that 25 per cent were dissatisfied with the interest, instruction, and resources given to them by senior officers and almost half were dissatisfied with the opportunity they had to influence decision-making (Jankowicz and Walsh 1984: 9). An experienced sergeant felt that integration could be improved – 'there could be more discussion between the higher ranks and the lower ranks, better management techniques' (81: 1, 9). It seems unfortunate that the officer saw no forum for such points to be discussed other than his own promotion board. A second sergeant described senior officers as 'far too removed' from lower echelons. 'Certain officers, when they become promoted from sergeant to inspector . . . are told that now you're somewhere above the rest' (81: 4, 12).

Remote supervisory relations are the other side of the coin to autonomy.

'I've very much worked on my own. I can't say I've had a hell of a lot of supervision. The sergeant used to work about eight hours during the twenty-four so if your shift didn't coincide with his you didn't see him . . . Inspector, you saw him once in a blue moon.' (81: 2, 10)

Constables generally take the attitude 'if I know what I'm doing I don't want supervision, but if I'm stuck then I want supervision'. The index of competent supervision from the PC's perspective is availability and preparedness to 'muck in', and that underwrites the view that the crux of relations between the ranks and senior officers was how close the latter's function was to operational police work.

> 'A lot depends on the job that they're doing. If you get an inspector, a chief inspector, even a superintendent, who's operational . . . he can't fail to get some feedback from his men. On the other hand, a surprising number of senior police officers come up through this admin. side and they do lose touch.' (81: 2, 10–11)

The gulf between operational and office-bound police employees was complicated by the presence of 'civilians' in the latter group. The issue was not ability but shared perspectives arising from experience on the ground.

> 'The girls (in operations room) are very efficient, don't get me wrong . . . (but) the policemen don't like being told what to do by a civvy (operator) because they . . . don't understand the pressure and the problems that shifts place on somebody. At 3 a.m. you're not at your best when you fill that form in.' (81: 3, 19–20)

Like probationers, experienced constables set great store by the appearance of camaraderie and equitable relations with superiors and are particularly irritated by the disproportionate attention the latter seem to give to 'petty' matters. When the infraction is minor the gap between the constable and senior officer is accentuated.

> 'You get to the scene of a serious road traffic accident, people are injured, the last thing anybody wants to see you do is look round the back seat for your helmet first. But I've been dealing with a fatal and a chief superintendent . . . came past the scene and I didn't have my helmet on and I got told off for it.' (83: 1, 2)

Inter-rank relations exceeded paperwork as the worst aspect of police service for the experienced PCs. A WPC who spoke of there being 'quite a strain at times' saw this as interfering with the quality of service.

> 'A lot of obstacles are within the police service. Like I can see a need for something to be done but I can't achieve it. It's got to be done by somebody high-ranking, but to get that message through, it gets so distorted or forgotten. By the time you get up to a bit of rank, they seem to have lost the fact they were doing it once.' (83: 3, 1)

It bespeaks the struggle between individualist and collegial ties, the conversion of solidarity achieved on the street into the appearance of work visibly better than the next person's. Her comments pertain not only to inter-rank relations but the values of occupational culture and the nature of the reward and performance-measuring structure.

> 'When you get somebody of chief inspector level they're looking for the next moves up, not for the good of his men. If he does something for the good of his men it's to get his name mentioned. You don't really get anybody above inspector who's right behind the shift.'
>
> (83: 3, 10)

When officers were under pressure they would discover the consequence of the lack of personal loyalty.

> 'Come the riot, in inverted commas, that we had, they're the people that are leading you. They're saying, "Right lads, let's get this done," and you're thinking, "Well, should we?" Had it been the sergeant saying that you're right behind him because you've got that contact all the time. Its a world apart. They seem to be looking after number one. We ought to abolish the role of chief inspector and have something like a personnel officer . . . somebody that was looking after the bobbies.'
>
> (83: 3, 10)

Again, this is not couched in terms of values but of orientation to practical requirements.

> 'They would not be popular as bosses if they don't know the ground work. Some of the chief inspectors and above get respect without wearing a uniform because they are totally competent at doing the job that you're doing and you can take it from somebody like that. A lot of bobbies on the beat, after a certain time it draws their enthusiasm out of them when they see who's in charge. You only really get this picture over a few years . . . Get somebody with fifteen years . . . They don't want to be a sergeant or inspector because they don't want anything to do with them. They've seen some of the specimens that have gone through and they just blank themselves off.'
>
> (83: 3, 11)

The value system constables espouse is relatively uniform on these matters. Those who are more ambitious, align with officers and regard the police mission as including social service as well as crime control, tend to keep a low profile and not challenge the moral calculus of 'the street' and experience. Their silence does not indicate consent but an unwillingness overtly to challenge a value system with such a self-confident measure of worth. Thus the myth of a monolithic system of police values is reinforced. The somewhat unreflective and myopic vision of those investing in this stock view of organization and hierarchy reinforces the remoteness of officers from constables. Increasing experience of policing and its formal organization heightens the salience of experiential knowledge of 'the street' to the constable, and unsurprisingly it is on this measure, which they can apply to themselves, that constables evaluate the overall organization and higher personnel. They do not consider that the street as a metaphor may be limited to application to the work they can directly perceive from their own vantage point. Thus, while there is little enough comment on the work of higher officers, what commentary there is implicitly assumes comparability of the tasks of the ranks with those of all police officers. The conception of the 'real' work is stubbornly fixed at the level of these experiential values.

That this is a stance born of ignorance (and lack of contact with higher officers) is clear when one reflects upon the universal hostility towards direct entry to the officer class. Here the occupational culture preserves values which conveniently obscure the uneasiness constables may feel about more 'gifted' outsiders pushing their promotion prospects to one side. The strong rejection of direct entry does not, it must be noted, stop recruits feeling, after a year of service, that higher officers are remote from the job. The weight of constables' inclinations and of the experiential-oriented operating ideology, impels them towards the view that officers are out of touch. Only the fact that they have risen from the ranks affords the benefit of a doubt.

The divisions between officers and the ranks are met by the deployment of a unitary conception of the police mission and method. PCs are dependent on officers to protect them from public complaints. The enforcement of discipline is a perennial source of trouble. It is intrinsically divisive. Again, the matter is assessed in relation to the value the occupational culture puts on solidarity, in this case members breaking faith. One engaging point about the following extract is that the constable does not 'read' the carping attitude of the sergeants as a product of hierarchy and the conflict inherent in supervision, but rather as the disenchantment of jaded men. Further, the 'trouble' that is being complained of is essentially connected with the internal divisions within the ranks and not with a conflict of formal organization and occupational culture. Ambition is disruptive, posing not only an uneasiness about assessment relative to one's peers but inhibiting the forbearances upon which the smooth operation of the shift depends. This is presented as a struggle for alignment to common values which the PCs adhering to them have strong but silent means of re-asserting. The exchange began with the question of how the respondent got on with sergeants.

'There are one or two in the station whose attitude is, "I hate policemen," which I find is rather remarkable. They're nothing to do with me, I just steer clear of them. Basically they're getting on towards retirement. They are generally moaning about the declining standard of police officers. There are also others, and not necessarily old, probably up for promotion. They stay exactly to the book, which, as everyone knows, you just cannot do in any job. They don't allow any give or take and it does create friction. But the problem is generally on their side because the average PC will just refuse to co-operate with it. In a subtle way. But they eventually get the message.'

(8: 3, 5)

The constables' sensibilities are directed to other constables, chiefly those on their shift, and to their immediate supervisors. It is at the level of immediate supervisors that contradictory instructions, contrasting styles and uncertain direction become most evident.

'There's a difference of ideas within the force, how to do things. Not at this (training) establishment, where everybody in Division thinks, "They used to be policemen." The level on Division with sergeants and inspectors. If you have two sergeants, one says, "Do a report this way," and you submit it when that sergeant's away the other sergeant doesn't like it.'   (12: 1, 1)

A chief inspector leading a discussion asserted that the majority of the Scarman Report's criticisms were of higher officers. He presented himself as a loner. 'This blooming rank separation, power determined by rank, is farcical in my view.' He continued, 'I don't go to the mess nights and join the mess clubs and all these other clubs because it enforces separation.' There followed some dark references, clearly understood by the constables, to the rank-based informal groupings which are seen as determining policy among officers at a particular grade. The chief inspector had 'gone out on a limb to oppose the organizations they join' (field notes, 16.5.83). Such officers are important bearers of occupational culture.

The 'troubles' from which the ranks gain insight into the nature of 'their' organization under pressure are those in immediate proximity to their own work situation. Constables perceive the organization from a perspective firmly rooted in their own direct experience. The culture's rhetoric suggests they still want to feel led by people possessing personal authority who adhere to core values of policing rather than bureaucrats, and who understand the need for certain legal infringements rather than being rigidly rules-oriented. Frequent rotation also works against officers making their mark with small primary groups of PCs. Senior officers deprived of feedback from the ranks cannot plan nor identify problems effectively. Inability to communicate long-term goals to the ranks tends to produce a law-enforcement style of policing which is reinforced by the system of rewards in the organization.

6
Situating police competence

Attitude research on the police emerged in the face of widespread criticism of police practice in the sixties. The importance of 'attitudes' is still debated; the issue is their relevance to action. Psychologists seem less inclined to lay this ghost than sociologists, many of whom believe that the notion of *a* 'police personality' is analytically unhelpful and empirically dubious. They have moved to a concern with how police work is done and away from matters of motive, just as criminologists have increasingly concentrated on crime as a practical activity. Early concern over the 'police personality' stimulated research on socialization to identify the means by which this apparent uniformity was brought about (Harris 1973: Teahan 1975). Such work revealed the importance of informal socialization processes and, particularly, occupational culture.

Conventional socialization studies have neglected documentation of the *process* because they assume *an* end-state. 'Progress along the socialisation continuum in the police world can be seen as the gradual development of an "in the same boat" collective consciousness stressing a "don't make waves" occupational philosophy' (van Maanen 1975: 220). Van Maanen's caveat should be pursued. In a footnote he adds,

> 'a staged socialisation model . . . glosses over much of the detailed and principled ambivalence a police recruit feels while undergoing passage . . . (I)t suggests a sort of unilinear development of a career while overlooking the back and forth kinds of passages a recruit experiences – first viewing himself as a civilian, then as a professional.' (p. 220)

Socialization represents a mirror one passes through to look at oneself from the other side (Davis 1968), but van Maanen insists it is not a single passage but many.

Recruits are exposed to matters of debate which are already invested with values within the working culture. Like any pluralist culture, the 'occupational culture' overtly orients to bland and unexceptionable cultural 'universals', to which members are readily conformable. The vacuity of most of these 'universals', like the American cultural value on 'freedom', is precisely why adherence to them can be so generally effected. Values like 'never rat on a buddy' are available as vocabularies justifying action. Debate within a culture is almost never about such formal values, but evokes conflicting orientations when their application arises. This is illustrated by argument over the extent to which the value of solidarity eventuates in compliance with 'officer in trouble' calls. It is now accepted that there are circumstances in which compliance is not automatic. However, these qualifying circumstances are not treated as critical at the level of values; the 'core values' of the occupational culture are seen as intact. Critical analyses of police culture hinge on the rigidity of the 'occupational culture', and such analyses are not served by the suggestion that there could be another reading of the culture as a shifting and diffuse entity whose shape varies according to the call made at a particular time on the rhetoric available.

If 'occupational culture' is to serve as an empirically satisfactory concept as well as a theoretically necessary one, the sense of its internal variations and textures must be brought out in the same fashion as have conceptions of culture in relation to delinquency. In delinquency studies, conflict and internal differentiation are recognized and made part of the analytic framework. In contrast many analyses of the police suggest that division is less important than the cohesiveness police show when they face a challenge from the outside, either in the shape of crime or demands for accountability. However, what constables do varies, and once 'inside' the culture, no one is more aware of that than the officers themselves. It may be necessary to 'go along with' what one senses to be the dominant value, as Southgate (1982) suggests probationers do on race. But aspirants do this in full awareness that it is a tactic. Once confident of their place, and ability to use the necessary justifying rhetoric in relation to their own complex of values, officers begin to move in and through the culture to secure their own ends.

Police culture

The role of informal culture is reflected in the prominent place that anecdotes about practice have even in the talk of senior officers. Tales include how police enforce informal working norms, such as the revenge wreaked on a rate-buster who was sent dashing to his car only to find it jacked up on blocks, a story told by a very high-ranking officer (field-notes, 6.9.79). Many hinge on the idea that the police learn things others do not know. Their special insight into human nature makes them odd – 'we're a strange group of people, we learn who leaves their curtains drawn and undresses in front of them'. This common experience of secret knowledge makes for an ironic *esprit de corps*; collegiality is based on knowledge of the discreditable rather than the appearance of purity. Such tales enable officers thrown together by contingency to weld a temporary bond. Yet the disparity implied by typologies of policing 'styles' (Reiner 1978) challenges the idea that a solidary occupational culture puts forth a consistent 'line'. Such observations suggest that an 'occupational culture' is not a tangible 'thing' but an amalgam of experiences on the part of officers. Are 'loners' part of the occupational culture? Is membership simply contingent on working for the organization? Can one be more or less a part of the culture?

One way recruits are made to feel that links to the outside are being replaced by commitment to the occupation's culture is formal training; they are treated as peers who are essentially indistinguishable and who lack an identity other than as raw material. Marks of former status are stripped away and the pull of prior friendships lessened – the former soldiers lose rank, the former teenagers their more risqué acquaintances. The ex-dustman was clearly stopped short by a question about where he would find friends now he was a constable. After a pause, he said, 'I don't know. I'd not thought of that. I mean you usually do make friends by being with them, like. You're bound to, to make friends' (1: 4, 1). He was aware he was entering unknown territory, 'a different world, a different outlook on everything'. The force influences thoughts of appropriate friendships.

> 'I'll find my friends in the police, definitely, because from the first day we were made aware in no uncertain terms that you have to rely upon your colleagues. . . . And if you're able to depend on somebody then obviously you make friends with them . . . You depend on your schoolmates for certain things, that's basically how you make your friends, if you can ask them a favour. That's why a lot of policemen are friendly with other policemen.'   (5: 2, 1)

This reciprocity of favours implies pairings-off and other divisions within the in-group. 'Although we all joined at the same time we all have our little cliques of who we amalgamate with' (7: 1, 4–5).

Recruit groups *per se* do not form reference groups for long, as the training disperses recruits. The bulk of formal training is spent in DTCs, when recruits from the same forces may feel driven together, but this influence wanes as the shift assignment gains importance. The bond to *all* officers is functional and sociality is selective.

> 'We went out for a drink at night-time once we'd done revision, pressed the uniform, done your boots. We all live in different parts of the county. I don't see any of them at weekends or anything like that. . . . You're not at the same police station. You may be on the same unit at a football match, and you have to stick together as you're all on one side but whichever group you're put in you're a policeman and you have to work as a group. That's all it is.'   (7: 2, 3)

British training is marked by such regular change and reconstitution of groups as to preclude any real solidarity developing. Sociability rather than solidarity marks these relations. Peer reference groups formed during training feature friendly co-operation directed towards short-term goals such as surviving a particular course or activity.

> 'You go up to (DTC) and find there are only going to be three of you from the same force in the same class. . . . There's 300 up there from different forces. . . . So you stick with those. We do tend to get a class spirit and when you're relaxing you tend to stay in a class.'
>
> (8: 3, 3)

This is reinforced by the programme of the training centre, which encourages competition between classes. References to a group spirit during training referred not to the force TE but to the DTC, and are inherently short-term. One former army sergeant identified this as the best thing about the training centre programme.

> 'The *esprit de corps* between the thirty blokes was fantastic. My particular squad, I was in charge of turn-out and we won everything, we won the all-round trophy. It was that in-bred *esprit de corps*, although I was Derbyshire and he was Northumbria, we were the untouchables. The fact that that was bred into us was a good thing, especially with some who were not too sure of what their powers were, they had the confidence to do it.'   (9: 1, 4)

The competitive spirit and rigid regimen struck a responsive chord in ex-military recruits, unlike the tolerant 'after hours' scene.

> 'After a certain hour of the night . . . there was a lack of emphasis on discipline and they didn't sort enough people out in basic training. When we went over the pub there was females there dressed in the manner, there was an example of rowdiness and I wasn't prepared to tolerate it. They are the sort of girls you see out with the sort of people we are locking up, and there they were, policewomen. Not policewomen in this force fortunately. . . . Perhaps from different parts of the country they're different about what a good woman is and what a bad woman is. I hope I haven't got to walk the streets with them one day, but the younger blokes liked it.'   (9: 1, 4)

Asked about group feeling among the same 'induction group', he said,

> 'When you're back at the station and on different shifts you haven't got time for it. Evening shift, when you all flock home you hand it over and pass on your way. But once you come back here (TE) you see how the others are getting on and listen to them telling you about

this and that arrest. You weigh up in your own mind whether they're the same people. You get a bit of a group thing, not the extent at (DTC), but then, you're not thrown together.' (9: 1, 5)

The group spirit promoted in training was functional and short-lived. 'In any training session you always develop a group spirit. That falls off the longer you stick together because obviously you become more individual. But we have, certainly, a group spirit in this shower. It's definitely an advantage' (11: 2, 2–3). Peer reference groups figure most importantly when people are 'thrown together', where there are intense demands that require co-operation. More significant bonds are formed around station assignments.

'I love the area I work. I get on with me workmates very well. It's just a small station and there's only a few of us there. There's one area that's very rough and we get a lot of trouble from there and the other housing estates. Very nice really.' (10: 1, 1)

One emphatic difference between induction and later interviews is the increase in the probationers' reflexive orientation to change in their self-image. These matters are hardly remarked at induction, but there is clear interest in what one's (probationer) peers, fellow constables and supervisors make of one's performance thereafter. This entails some wizening of one's perspective on fellow employees, and a more jaded, cautious stance.

'I've never lost interest but little things have put me off a bit. . . . If anything you do wrong, it's round the place before you know it. I noticed it when I first came because my father was a superintendent and they all knew me before they even met me.' (12: 1, 2)

He recognized that he too now evaluated newcomers joining his shift. Individual bonds may exist but must be subsumed by the need to feel one can depend on all other officers. There were three from his induction group at his station.

'We do tend to stick together, yet as soon as we are accepted into the shift, it's a job where you've got to rely on somebody. I noticed that when I was there ten months and somebody else new came, and they're a bit quiet. You start getting an opinion of them straight away. You've got to speak to them and get them out, and in a period of two or three months they are into it as well. We're all now back into the one family. I don't think you can . . . let one be out.' (12: 1, 10)

He was asked if the ex-soldiers 'stuck together'.

'When we have these courses they do. They're the ones that are laughing at something different to what we're laughing at. We still talk to them, but it's older family really. But when we're out on division there aren't that many of the same on each shift so we're back together again. We know our place.'   (12: 1, 11)

Early bonds were of declining importance as training receded.

The experience of formal training encourages a feeling of collective endeavour. These bonds are short-lived, and are replaced by a formal ideology stressing the need to rely on all fellow police and by an informal practice of association with members of one's shift. The formal ideology remains an abstract, generalized commitment because it is evoked by extreme and relatively rare events, such as officer in distress calls. The important point is that it is working together on something all define as important which effects the social bond. The commitment is generated by work, and not by a 'police personality'.

'You do form a loyalty because I spent ten weeks with a lot of these lads, ten weeks out of your life all pulling together. There is a loyalty to your colleague whether you've seen him for a year or not. More than you'd feel to somebody from another course or a policeman from another county.'   (12: 3, 7)

From autonomy to solidarity

Growth in the probationer's reflexivity implies an orientation to evaluation of the performances of others. A few had experience as a citizen to support an early, critical perspective.

'I go and watch football every week. Some of them deserve the fines they get, others are unfortunate, they happen to be there at the time. They can very often get arrested for doing nothing, which I've seen done. Though I'm glad it's (the tape) anonymous. The police have a hell of a job at a football match but I do feel sometimes that they're a bit heavy-handed, in that they can cause a lot of the trouble themselves.'   (5: 3, 5)

Another had never seen prisoners 'being knocked around' but was aware 'they do have a few left who do that . . . you get good and bad in any group' (field-notes, 5.11.80). More accessible were evaluations of immediate colleagues. 'The occasional one says, "I'd rather be at home than round here." . . . Some don't like walking around in the uniform, don't like going round in Pandas; the ones that aren't interested in the job usually find an office job' (7: 2, 3). A year's work gives probationers enough confidence to criticize those they feel no longer bring sufficient

energy to their work. 'There's one I don't particularly get on with . . .
He comes in and says, "I've got better things to do today." . . . He says,
"Oh, persecuting a motorist," if you report someone for a genuine
offence.' (7: 2, 4).

More disturbing are comments concerning the racial attitude of
constables. Southgate argued that probationers might go along with
expressions of racial prejudice in order to 'fit in' with occupational
culture. Something very like this is described by this probationer.

> 'Policemen *say*, "Oh blacks, hanging about and causing trouble," but
> in fact they get talking to them and have a chat. They're not
> prejudiced, you see, they're like sheep. They don't like to be different,
> otherwise it looks as though they're a puritan. I don't think they're
> really prejudiced.'   (7: 2, 6)

But he did admit of worrying exceptions.

> 'I'd say there was the occasional one. . . . I don't like telling you, I
> know it's on tape, but he says he's teaching his daughter to say things
> like "wog". It's his daughter that will get in trouble one day, and not
> him. If she does call somebody a "wog" and they're about six feet
> tall, she's only a little girl.'   (7: 2, 6)

The point is that there is movement during the probationary period
towards a more evaluative regard for the police culture. Socialization
does not indicate movement away from individuality and towards
unthinking compliance with the dictates of occupational culture. At the
same time, one does not need to see the probationers as drawn together
and into the culture for purely instrumental reasons.

This observation raises the change in interview responses from
emphasis on the constables standing on their own to an emphasis on their
receiving support from colleagues. It was a preoccupation of probationers but not among recruits. 'The policeman should be in every
respect seen . . . to stand on his own, not to have ties to anyone' (4: 3,
3). Lacking the experience on which they could distinguish the institution
from those who practise it, recruits stress a role they feel the police as
a force represent, independence from partisan influence, as if it were a
personal quality. However, independence is not the quality the police
organization and occupational socialization emphasise. Cadets and ex-
soldiers have already been exposed to emphasis on team-work and co-
operation. Those without such an entrée, such as this ex-factory worker,
were favourably surprised by the collegial aspect. 'The main thing is
comradeship, which I didn't expect so much of' (8: 3, 1). This sense of
comradeship was specifically with fellow constables, not higher officers;
he reported 'a lot of resentment' towards officers who 'appear to be

totally out of touch with the working officer'. While this bespeaks the underpinning of occupational culture in a friendship pattern based on mutuality and which does not readily cut across the rank structure, the commitment to others which friendship brings can also be perceived as a drawback. 'I don't go out of my way to get on with people. . . . I know it's avoiding relationships. . . . Once I've got the job cracked, or I decide that I'm giving up in the promotional stakes . . . I might start looking for friendships' (9: 1, 3). The needs this recruit had in probation he satisfied by turning to supervisors; he did not rely on peer help.

Respondents applied a tactical sense to issues of friendship, reputation and interdependence. The person who is most popular is

> 'somebody who is very funny, as everywhere. People talk to them more because they expect something funny. Also what you've got to do is not copy anybody. Be your own personality so that they'll come back and ask you something, rather than if they think you're following somebody. I like it when somebody comes and asks me advice. One of these older blokes on my shift asks me things and I can ask him things. It's not that one of us thinks we know more. . ... You respect each other's knowledge.' (12: 1, 11)

With rewards such as confirming one's probationary appointment or establishing a case for a specialist post depending on the quality of one's organizational knowledge, it is apparent that co-operation is useful but that one should not be seen as being without any knowledge of one's own. He saw a need to manage his requests for information from his supervisor, which led him to regard the inter-compensating nature of expertise on the shift as 'symbiotic'.

> 'I've got a growing knowledge of what the job's about. More than somebody that's just joined our shift. But I'll ask him if he knows . . . the shift is a party of different, various knowledge. It's like a symbiotic relationship. You just rely on each other, ask each other questions. The sergeant doesn't like you asking somebody else, he likes you to go to him and yet you're thinking, "If I go to him, will he say you should already know it."' (12: 1, 15)

The facts of supervision inhibit the probationer's relationship with supervisors.

The importance of these reflections on the cultural infrastructure lies in their suggestion of changes in the way recruits regard the organization as they gain a working acquaintance with it. The particular sense they make of it is less important. It is of no great consequence that a probationary constable regards the tactic most likely to result in popularity as being a ready wit. However, it is crucial to recognize that the police are not simply 'indoctrinated' into the 'police mind' but are continuously engaged in making an emergent sense of the organization. That sense is finely attuned to new information about the organization and about themselves; hence it is never settled, always responsive to new information and intentions. This self-regarding and analytic enterprise is pursued for instrumental reasons. Probationary constables construct their performance in close awareness of the projects they wish to achieve within and through the organization, whether these are strategic matters, such as confirmation or promotion, or tactical ends in the setting of the public encounter.

Police in community

Out of these emergent perspectives on the organization and occupation, constables lay claim to and fashion an identity as competent members. Their concern to effect unremarked usage of the rhetoric appropriate to particular organizational situations relies on the range of experience they gain. Appropriate response in the eyes of the organization and the public depends on their ability to develop a sense of the actions and justifications applicable to particular situations on the basis of experience. As operational service occupies an increasingly large part of their probationary period, the significance of legal knowledge will seem less important than a knowledge of correct procedure. More particularly, knowing how to proceed behaviourally in public encounters gains importance, for constables learn that gaps in their knowledge of law can be compensated by adroitness in handling citizens within the confines of the encounter itself.

The point is not that the police trample on the restraints of law. The wide responsibilities of the police make an ability to maintain the propriety of an intervention a signal skill, one relevant intra-organizationally and in dealing with the public. The starting assumption of the legal training is that recruits cannot expect to learn all the law there is to know in training, and that full enforcement of the law has never been a realistic prospect. Beginning from a presumption of selectivity encourages novices to see law as the final resource, to be used to warrant action which is challenged and secure compliance when efforts to resolve the situation within its own terms fail. Enforcement is interpretive work, and even the most incorrigible 'by the book' constable cannot escape the large measure of negotiation fundamental to it.

The movement towards 'human awareness training' (or 'policing skills') in the wake of the Scarman Report is linked to the vogue for 'social skills' training in other professions. It amounts to a formalization of things known implicitly by practitioners but seldom articulated. These are techniques of deportment, stance, and speech which facilitate encounters with citizens. Along with this, post-Scarman policing ideology has stressed the need for close contact with the community policed. While it is debatable whether this is a means for the public to have more control over 'their' police, the justification that makes such an emphasis palatable among operational officers is more apparent. It is a chance to get information useful in prevention and investigation of crime.

Learning competence

Comments which betray the probationers' growing orientation to regard their own and others performance in an evaluative and analytical manner are important. The ability to orient one's own performance to what are perceived as the dictates of the situation is the initial step in appreciating the influence of how one proceeds on the outcome of encounters with citizens. One has better information on oneself from a knowledge of one's own biography than of anyone else. By insight into one's own motives and how these are best achieved by the pursuit of particular interactional strategies in a situated context one can learn the skills of making plausible interpretations. Accurate short- or long-term prediction relies on the adequacy of one's analysis of the situation. Novice police can work to maximize relevant information and refine their conception of pertinent biographical material. This interpretive enterprise is continually being refined, both on and off the job. Part of the project is to learn what kinds of situations cause them trouble, not just to regulate but to glean information from. Unlike other professional/client relations the police cannot seek control over their work by means of their working environment. They must maximize knowledge of the environment and develop a normative standard of the proper use of space. Their territorial awareness is governed by 'normal appearances' and the use of what Sacks (1972: 193) called 'incongruity procedures'. The 'normal' varies between areas. Becoming alert to and refining deportment, conversational style, and interpretive insight is dictated by practical requirements of the everyday working situation, as well as the goal of securing confirmation. This process having been begun it is much more straightforward to also become interested in how other parties to interaction proceed.

As both the quantitive and qualitative data imply, recruits are keen on 'public relations' as a job description which draws together the essential aspects of police work. Its central skill of negotiation embraces component activities, including bargaining, manipulation, conveying a sense of one's own character and approach, negotiating low status membership of the organization, being alert for information, and using firmness, anger, and the staged use of force to cause minimum aggravation of the situation. The need to get involved in the community is also seen; 'getting amongst the people, find out problems before the problems pop out, the people who have got the trouble' (3: 1, 1). Even when car patrol officers see their function primarily as deterrence they conduct short-term interventions and employ what Mawby (1979: 77) calls a 'method of suspicion'. Crime prevention, the officer's security, and the cultivation of amiable, informative local contacts are interrelated. 'We would stop and talk to people, gain their confidence and therefore we got respect off them. A lot of the work is public relations' (2: 2, 5). This special sense of public relations bears no great similarity to the work of public relations officers, but addresses working objectives and techniques that the recruits' cultural apparatus gives them little other way of expressing. Insight into its centrality may arise from considering one's own biography. There is a touching quality to this burly ex-marine's remarks about his childhood image of the police.

> 'What I want to do is a lot of public relations work. . . . I'd like to think that remembering when I used to be scared of policemen is carried with me. I'm 24 and I've just realised that the policemen are human beings. On my beat I will always stop and talk to kids so that they don't get scared.' (4: 5, 4)

At later stages 'public relations' undergoes a translation of emphasis. It becomes more subtly defined, and the probationer begins to distinguish accomplished skills from those yet to be refined. 'Public relations' is no longer a generalized catch-phrase but a term for clever performance of the interaction with which routine is filled. A constable remarked why he sensed the delicacy to pub regulars of police being able to afford drink when they could not.

> 'That comes from realizing that there's people's various attitudes and they've got to be thought of. You learn that, and that's quite a basic training, strangely enough. You learn that there's a way of talking to people, and fortunately I had some of it and picked some of it up very quickly'. (9: 1, 2)

Accurate role-taking is facilitated by socialization practices exposing novices to a broad range and variety of social relationships (Weinstein 1969: 763).

Addressing 'public relations' on the basis of experience prompts recognition that a 'bargain' exists in a real as well as a symbolic sense. The co-operation of the public cannot be assumed but depends on the officer's personal qualities and the character of enforcement in the locale.

'Sometimes (where) . . . you 'do' a traffic offence they think, "why do the police bother with this," sometimes it gets through to you. You think it's not very good public relations, not what you're there for. On the one hand you're trying to get through to the public and ask them to help you and then you put a ticket on somebody's car and you think, "Are they going to help me if I'm getting some hassle over the road?" Some people, if you put a ticket on their car they say, "Expensive Chinese (take-away)," and take it as a joke but others will stand there for half an hour arguing and it's hassle I don't really want.'

(12: 1, 19)

He regards his own image by casting it in the eyes of others. He does not simply reject their view of the situation but seriously examines its consequences for his own role. The gain from public support may exceed that from by-the-book enforcement. Images of the police are highly relevant.

'The particular section of the public where I've had contact, being reported . . . might picture you doing just that. Yet somebody who you've brought their dog back, think what a nice *person* rather than thinking of all the other jobs you're doing. If he had no contact he's going to go on what his mates say, "He's a swine, you get him you'll get battered round the house." . . . You've got to be fair in every case because you be unfair to one and there's going to be a few on that street who've got the message. You've had it if it gets back to your division.' (12: 1, 22)

These considerations raise the way probationers sense their performance is being evaluated by the public. Constables are obliged to tolerate a good deal of irrelevance if they are to nurture a positive local relationship.

'People like to chat to a policeman and you do get called to domestic situations where you can't do anything but just be a listener. You deal with it in the area of work simply because it's the way of life.'

(12: 3, 19)

It is a heavy burden if one assumes one's performance is crucial in determining overall images of the police.

'Your first impression of a policeman is the first one you meet. If he's not very civil or reports you for a trivial motoring offence people get a wrong impression. They speak from their own experiences. If they've had a bad experience they're quick to say, "Police force not doing a very good job."' (12: 3, 20)

These views chart a growing awareness that police work is not only reliant on good information but involves a reciprocal relationship. Probationers collect references to interaction involving mutual attempts at manipulation and information-seeking ploys.

> 'The less barriers there are between the police and the normal chap the better feeling there is and not only that, the better you can do your job. (Officer W.) knew when to listen, when to not be a policeman, and he learnt an awful lot like that. There's no point going round aggravating people because you've got the authority to do it. I'd hate to be a minor official and nothing else.'   (4: 3, 1)

The negotiational stance is contrasted with physical intervention; 'when it comes to violence it depends how you can talk your way out of trouble, rather than getting back to the Stone Age' (6: 1, 3). As recruits discover that different emphases mark the organization their reservations about deviating from 'the book' are modified by the knowledge that policing is not widely regarded as a job for puritans. Response concerning policing's implications for private life and its comparison to other jobs shows that few recruits feel enjoined to be paragons, and the pattern of shift in view shows that this appraisal is reinforced by experience. Agreement that 'the PC shouldn't let work interfere with private life' showed a gradual increase (53 per cent to 63 per cent to 68 per cent). The negotiational stance is signified by the characterization of policing as more like public relations than social work or military duty. At induction 39 per cent of recruits picked 'military' as most like policing with public relations officer a close second at 36 per cent. Social worker was seen as most like policing for 17 per cent but teacher only claimed 2 per cent of responses. However, in training, public relations maintained a leading position, followed by military (down to 29 per cent), while social work fell to 8 per cent and teacher rose to 12 per cent. Using negotiation rather than force is more frequent in routine encounters than may be realized. Sykes and Brent (1980: 196) found that officers 'use mostly definitional rather than imperative or coercive means. Their most common successful technique is mere repetition.'

An amiable but goal-oriented relationship with the community need not imply passing offences by. Interactions defined as negotiational are marked by the core assumption of bargaining, that all parties will pursue their own interest. This necessarily involves anticipating the reaction of other interactants; actions should be judged for their consequences. As Mawby (1979: 177) notes, even 'residents of "disreputable" neighbourhoods are only too eager to involve the police in their lives on numerous occasions'. In the British Crime Survey only 1 in 100 incidents were initially discovered by police, and in only 4 per cent were police present when the offence happened (Southgate and Ekblom 1984: 13). Chatterton (1979) found that in almost half of 669 arrests for crime the public had provided the police with a prisoner. Officers must judge interventions against cost to long-term relationships.

'I enjoy talking to people on the street and if they're committing an offence then I'm afraid they get reported for it. But if you laugh and joke with them, they just accept it. If you're polite they're polite back, even though you've reported them. . . . After they've been to court, they're laughing and joking with you.' (7: 1, 3)

Because they too have invested in a long-term relationship citizens may see advantage in sustaining it.

The 'mechanics' of establishing a negotiational relationship are often first learnt in probationers' approaches to local shopkeepers. Rather than expecting citizens to 'have a go' in support of police the relationship envisaged was a routine, communicative one.

'I've had a few fights on the marketplace, but nobody's ever helped me out. . . . When I first went, I made myself known to all the shopkeepers. I made it my duty and point to go in and ask them who they were. I just got talking to them and have a cup of tea anytime. . . . If you're not prepared to find out who they are then you don't get nowhere. You've got to stop people, ask them who they are, where are they going, where have they been, who do they associate with.' (7: 1, 10)

One of the few studies which explored constables' rating of getting on well with the public established that this was acknowledged as important and that experienced constables were well aware of colleagues' short-comings. They told Southgate that younger PCs 'don't know how to talk to people' (Southgate 1982: 12). Probationers also acknowledged the centrality of talk but had reservations about getting caught up in discussion. 'The pressures on the young probationer turn his attentions elsewhere: to questions of doing things correctly and "by the book", keeping his paperwork in order, and producing an acceptable number of arrests' (Southgate 1982: 12). The present system of assessment does little to encourage officers to monitor their own performance.

Reciprocity does not just refer to the exchange of material advantage in a negotiational relationship. It also refers to an impression of shared experience.

'They've said to me it's nice to see a bobby walking, because they all used to ride round in Panda cars. Some of them wouldn't get out because it's warm in there and they didn't want to get wet. But if you're walking the street and getting wet with them it all comes back to, "Do you want to come in for a cup of tea?" You get chatting and get information off them, it's great.'   (7: 1, 11)

After their probationary service constables are able to specify how interaction with the public can bear desired results if it is skilfully managed. A constable retails his version of the ploy of pretending to a little information to get a big return.

'If you bring a chap in and you're on a wing and a prayer, you don't know if you've got a case, and blow me, he tells you everything that you didn't ever dream existed . . . that is a great satisfaction. Knowing that in spite of your lack of equipment and educational qualifications, you cleared this one up . . . That is the best part of the job.'
                                                                  (9: 1, 1)

The constable derives great satisfaction from skills of impression-management.

Yet the satisfactions from engaging in investigations that can be carried out if one has the 'in' afforded by good local knowledge are bought by sustaining reciprocal relationships. Police are taken as legal experts, sources of advice and inside knowledge about all the vagaries of officialdom.

'When I go into a pub if anybody says, "What are you drinking?" I tell them I'm a police officer and I leave it up to them to decide whether they want to drink with me. I get bombarded with questions on law and, "How do I solve this problem?" every time I go for a drink. But by the same token, three or four weeks later they'll come up to me and say, "Here, have your heard this?" And people are almost naughty; they're worse than policemen actually – "Mrs Jones's (car) tax has run out, did you know?" Now I tend to use this on occasions, I'll be honest. If it's necessary I take some course of action, but by people knowing who you are they can choose whether they drink with you or not. And you gain a lot that you wouldn't gain otherwise . . . But you gain pressure as well.'   (9: 1, 2)

This conveys what is meant when emphasis is put on the information value of this approach. It also establishes the criterion of voluntariness with which the constable satisfies himself that what is said can be used. He assumes that other interactants presume the information they bring can be used.

Earlier discussion suggested that 'information' is especially likely to come from those with a stake in it being used, such as shopkeepers. Officers build up their 'tea holes' where they know they can relax and chat. They should act as a site for information-gathering rather than an inducement to hear things from a particular point of view.

'If you're a bad bobby you can go from one tea-spot to the next without doing anything in between. I make a rule. I don't go to any more than once in a week and I won't go back unless I've had a look around; that way I get information as well.' (9: 1, 1)

All who discussed this most common 'perk' also noticed the motives of those offering hospitality.

'They look on it as crime prevention. The bobby goes in for a cup of tea, there's people inside the store see him, they stare: "We are doing nowt wrong here, what's he doing with bobbies?" You ask them how things are, if there's been trouble, and they do tell you a lot of it.'
(11: 1, 9)

It is information and not surrogate police which constables want. The bounds of the co-operative relationship is evident. 'You get help from people if you've seen an incident . . . they say, "I've seen him do this." Everything helps, but there are not many. (Pause.) They have to stand up in court if it goes that far' (12: 2, 10).

Not all the probationers find it easy to adopt the 'right' conversational style to allow the development of a relationship. Engaging in a negotiational, information-oriented conversation relies on each side revealing something which is private.

'It's possible to drift by, not expressing your views. . . . I used to do that in the cadets and I had a reputation, I still do . . . as being quiet. But then the supervision are never with me when I'm not quiet. In public, talking to people, I'm what I consider to be natural. Yet when I'm in an interview with a superintendent it inhibits me because you feel they are assessing you as you're speaking and it's like being in front of a TV camera.' (12: 1, 2)

An orientation to the construction and management of interaction begins with an ability to construe one's own efforts as a performance. It indicates that the probationer has initiated a process of reflexive participation in interaction which encourages the refinement of behavioural style and interactional skill.

Such an orientation only makes sense if constables believe there is more to policing than the enforcement of law by the imposition of legal force. The likelihood of their thinking so is related to their experience of public interaction, which varies according to the ethnic composition and prosperity of an area, and the degree of social integration (Banton 1964). The density of social interaction also affects police subcultures;

occupational culture is strong where the officers' integration in the community is weakest (Cain 1973). Recruits are aware that 'competence' is linked to 'experience', a quality not confined to repetition of similar situations and development of skills appropriate to them, but also to encountering a variety of demands. The experienced officer is able to cope with the unusual event. Self-reflexive officers are able to review their performance in demanding circumstances and learn how better to manage events if they recur. Having done so better suits them to dealing with the whole class of unusual circumstances.

At induction 65 per cent felt that citizens had a high regard for the police. By year two some 94 per cent thought so, citing cases of assistance by citizens. 'Often they're almost shy or scared in case you might tell them to get away. At accidents, if you're busy, they direct the traffic. . . . Lots of people would like to offer you a cup of tea' (7: 2, 7). The satisfactions in close contact with the public are remembered.

> 'You can be walking around town and the little old lady or middle-aged bloke pat you on the back and say it's great to see a bobby on the beat. . . . It makes me feel very proud. I grow up about 10 inches when they pat me on the back.'   (11: 1, 9–10)

Like the rest of us, police like to feel their work is appreciated. By the same token a cool reception is defused by assigning disrespectful people to disvalued social categories. At induction 65 per cent agreed that too many citizens think they know the PC's job better than the PC but by year one agreement fell to 60 per cent, and to 51 per cent by year two. They see a close association between the respect they receive and their being seen to derive from the same roots as the community they police. The police should not be an élite but 'our' police, respected because they maintain local ties.

> 'They have been disassociated with people these last few years, and that's just the economy. . . . They've got this rise now but I don't think they've done themselves any good by it . . . . There's the poor old teachers . . . the nurses and people like that. We have been lucky getting the rise because we've been a pet thing of Maggie's (Thatcher). I'd rather have seen everybody getting it or none. You've got the two pay rises. When it came out in September '78 it said you'd be getting half now and half then, that weren't too bad. But then when she came in and said ''automatic rise now'', cost of living thing in September, and there's the house . . . People are looking: ''Oh God, look at these police here, they're getting four rises when I'm getting one.''' (1: 4, 7)

Fractious incidents present officers with dilemmas in understanding hostile reactions.

'If there's a speed limit it's there for a reason, it has to prevent an accident, but I don't think they appreciate the reasons. If you get a group of lads and one of them's been in trouble . . . they try to impress the others with it. They try, almost, to get arrested so they can brag about it.'   (7: 2, 8)

Youths present a particular problem of respect, complicated by the fact that many probationary constables are themselves under 25 (52 per cent of our sample) 'The older people will stop and chat but people my age won't have anything to do with me. . . . An older one, even if they didn't like you, they'd say "hello". They've just got more respect' (8: 2, 6–7). Officers relate respect to youth mores but also to patrol policy.

'Where I work they seem to be anti-police. You talk to them and they don't respect you. . . . But from talking to other bobbies up (provincial towns) they're frightened and scared of you. (Ours are) just used to seeing us about all the time, every couple of hundred yards.'
                                                                                   (12: 2, 10)

Constables see their job as maintaining the established order by persuasion and manipulation. When the moral consensus (Banton 1964) in the community is weak police increasingly resort to formal enforcement, and come to define their task in such terms.

The probationer's relation to the public evokes thoughts which are self-regarding as well as outward-looking; this is one way they assimilate the special qualities of the role and how these affect their individual personalities. Their notions of the relation of police to community reveal their conceptions of what is right for them to be called on to do. At induction 53 per cent thought that society should not rely on the police to correct its mistakes, rising to 64 per cent at year one and 65 per cent at year two. Yet relations with the public often lead the constable a long way from social control in their perspective, as in this conception of the officer as 'adviser'.

'You see people's reactions when they see the policeman, may have done nothing wrong yet his heart will miss a beat. I'd do the same. It's because people don't really understand what police work is all about. . . . This relies on constables like myself to make contact with the general public. Let them know you're not an ogre in uniform, that you can have a sympathetic ear. And on the other hand, be stern. You see something wrong – and this comes into the grey areas – say, "Right, son, watch what you're doing." There is a barrier at present between the police and the general public. . . . I've seen a policeman assaulted and people just walk past it . . . .. It may be because they don't really understand what a policeman's job is about. They think

you're just there to get at people. . . . I think you're there as a friend
to them, an adviser.'   (4: 4, 6)

The difficulty of deciding the suitable role to pursue on a given occasion
is highlighted in 'the grey areas' of discretion. The 'right' relation of
constable to public is continually forced upon the constable, and is not
simply the concern of the sensitive.

These dilemmas not only touch those with a 'community' brief but all
officers in the routine exercise of discretion. This may account for the
frequency of emphasis on public contact, as if 'public relations' were the
ranks' equivalent of the manager's stress on 'communication'.

> 'You've got to get back to the . . . bobby on the beat, where somebody
> could associate themselves with them. You're more liable to be able
> to talk to somebody if you've known them for years. They're more
> likely to say, "I don't know about the police but PC So-and-so is not
> too bad and I'll see what he has to say."'   (1: 4, 7)

Off-duty performance is also relevant, as in the example of a constable's
sensitivity to what local men can afford to drink.

> 'I've . . . started drinking halves of beer now, there's no way I'll
> drink pints, not when the rest of the lads are sat around with a glass.
> I try and make it last all lunch hour because they're all out of work
> and you don't rub salt in the wound.'   (9: 1, 1–2)

This anticipation of the other's perspective enabled the constable to
maintain his claim to membership of the group of 'regulars'. It is an
instance of the centrality of skills of *negotiation* in the living as well as
the work of police. Skills of negotiation are intricately bound up with the
officer's use of the *power* his office affords; subtle negotiation can
absolve the need to employ the force that is implicit in the officer's
power, for power's utility is in its sparing, judicious use. Officers can
take great care to match their deployment of power to the dictates of the
context.

> 'If somebody turns round and calls you "Fat Pig", you've got to
> think, "He's right about the fat but I wonder where he got the pig bit
> from," and you laugh it off. Otherwise you can cause so many
> problems with all the other people around that feel they've got some
> justification for joining in, and the whole thing blows out of all propor-
> tion.'   (9: 1, 4–5)

This disposition is related to experience; 29 per cent at induction, 20 per
cent at year one but only 11 per cent at year two felt that force was the
only way to maintain order.

Police develop notions about 'human nature' not from an idle interest in mores but because the quality of their decisions relies on their skills of anticipating behaviour from the demeanour and disposition of citizens. Their investment in local information and situationally specific skills sensitizes them to rapid change. Rapid change is individually and socially threatening. Because 'modern society' is uneven in its emergence, the intervention of the police is needed to protect the vulnerable against too aggressive a pace of change.

> 'They are a stabilizing factor. It's hard for society to protect itself because there's an ethos (that) "anything goes". The police are the line that allows other people to have their democratic rights, and look after people who are on the sidelines against people who are pushing their democratic rights beyond reasonable bounds.' (4: 3, 1)

They were plainly aware of class divisions. The majority did not agree that Britain is a classless society (77 per cent at induction, 71 per cent at year one and 81 per cent at year two). Yet the split on whether there was one law for the rich and another for the poor showed a more complacent trend, from 53 per cent agreement at induction to 39 per cent at year one and 34 per cent at year two. While divisions were clearly perceived, their own part in law enforcement was related to increasing assertions that here equity was being achieved.

Cultures and ideologies

That the variety of idiosyncratic but patterned responses which small working groups evolve are not generally regarded as marks of subculture is clear in Reuss-Ianni's (1983) comment on the emergence of the two cultures of 'street' and 'management' cops. In the 'good old days not only the street cops but everyone in the department was socialised to this ethos . . . the values of loyalty, privilege and the importance of keeping department business inside the department. One monolithic culture permeated the department' (p. 2). Despite her analysis, Reuss-Ianni provides evidence of several bases for subgroups – 'age, sex, length of service, race, ethnicity, specialised expertise, connections and behaviour under fire' (p. 56). The existence of intra-cultural divisions is suggested by the numerous different sources constables may draw on to support an image of the work, an image of the self as it is realized and constructed in and through the work, or even a decision to follow a particular course of action. Yet others have argued that this contingency eventually subsides into what Becker (1961) called 'the final perspective' (van Maanen 1974).

The term 'final perspective' is misleading. The present data show that a number of competing value positions are in circulation. An 'occupational perspective' may indeed enable members to 'cope with the emotional reality of the job' (Schein 1961).

> 'In the police world these perspectives provide the perceptual filter through which a patrolman views his work life. . . . Such an ideology – rooted in common experience and knowledge – serves to support and maintain the codes, agreements and habits existing in the workplace.'
>   (van Maanen 1974: 101)

Yet one need not argue that all officers will eventually adhere to this operating ideology, only that it is in currency in the culture, forming a resource to be drawn on in assigning value to some action or providing a justification for some practice. Like delinquency, being a cop is not an 'either/or' but a 'more or less' thing.

7
Conclusion

This study began with the assertion that the place of training was central in the contemporary debate over policing. In recent times, as one notable commentator remarked, the 'tacit contract between police and public' has become so frayed that it is an 'open question . . . whether current efforts will suffice to repair it' (Reiner 1985: 62). The argument here is that no reform can hope to succeed that does not enlist the support of the ordinary constables who construct the reality of the policing we experience.

Understanding the changes people undergo in socialization to the police role affords critical insight into the criteria on which officers make decisions. In this study the early impact and subsequent dimunition in relevance of formal training was described, and the important but variable influence of informal socialization in the occupational culture was assessed. Socialization was examined as a process, and one in which the individual's place as both creator and creature of organization must be acknowledged. Those who give formal training or act as informal role models were studied as well as those who experience socialization. The focus was on individual experiences because socialization is a process of identity transformation, and variations in accommodations to the role tend to disappear in the aggregate.

At the outset, as we learned in Chapter 2, applicants have high ideals and great expectations. They see the work as marked by variety and foresee a relationship with the public in which respect is the best recompense for their duty and service. If they mention instrumental factors at all they emphasize promotion opportunities rather than job security or pay. Few applicants mention crime control compared to those who emphasize social service; many see themselves as exemplars who will sway the public by their personal rectitude. Communication and persuasion feature in their thoughts on how they will achieve their ends in public interventions. That the work involves abnormal hours and is outdoors only enhances its variety.

After they have been selected the recruits begin to acknowledge the implications a police career may have for their sense of identity. They recognize that they may lose friends and that their new role obliges them to reassess their values. Many say they could not police areas where people knew them before. Relatives emerge as more supportive of their career choice than friends. Even those from a background they regard as similar to policing see that things are different, and those with close contacts in the police are little better prepared. Yet the evidence was strong that, in opting for a police career, individuals avidly seek information about 'what it is really like'. Individuals confront what it is in their personality that has led them to the job, and speculate that it must be a quality they share with other recruits.

After a year they speak from experience on the impact of the job on friendship and family, and perceive the importance of work-based sociality. Also of rising importance are new concerns – job security, pay, the social status of police, and whether the satisfactions of the job outweigh disadvantages barely seen at induction. As instrumentalism grows, some of their early idealism is displaced. Also noted was the influence of experienced officers, especially instructors and tutor constables, on these feelings. Yet there were compensations arising from their sense of gaining experience and competence and an appreciation of the ways in which the qualities of police work can be used to derive excitement and validation. Considerations of duty and service still feature but are informed by a new conception of human nature and police authority.

Chapter 3 placed these experiences in the context of police training in Britain, with its division of labour between district centres run by the Home Office and the training establishments of local forces. Important lessons were learned as the novices discovered their personal limits and abilities in study skills and physical training. At district centres they also discovered some key themes: bureaucratic organization and quasi-military regimen v. informal coping mechanisms and easing devices, and the degree to which a common identity can be formed around organizational membership and neophyte status. At an early point recruits were found to draw a contrast between by-the-book and in-practice procedures, and this came alive most strongly after their first operational assignment under a tutor constable. The differing perspectives of training instructors and tutor constables conveyed the contrast of formal and informal sources of learning and socialization, while the unifying elements of the perspective of these two groups afforded insight into core beliefs of police culture. That socialization is no unilinear process was apparent from resignation rates and the doubts recruits expressed which prompted consideration of quitting; by the end of our research 22 per cent of the original sample had resigned. Whether they quit or were asked to leave, the effect of resignation patterns was to select those in the 'broad middle band' of backgrounds and attitudes. Poor performance assessments provoke thoughts of resignation more than loss of friendships or other factors but it is important to note the increasing cynicism probationers felt about staff appraisal. Equally significant was their conviction that anyone who has not experienced police work cannot appreciate its nature. This is one of the several signs of the probationers' increasing emphasis on the experiential basis of occupational competence. They were also increasingly inclined to link several elements of police work, such as crime control, social service, and order maintenance, under the banner of 'public relations'. Being inured to working conditions others would find intolerable, such as the shift system, becomes prideful to probationers.

Other stock features of police work proved less acceptable. Paperwork was endlessly criticized, yet it emerged that the canny probationer could see scope for autonomy here, and even inveterate grumblers acknowledged this as experience increased. Another significant division was over promotion (vertical advancement) and specialization (horizontal advancement). Perspectives on moves away from the beat revealed key elements of operating ideology and clarified one base for the differentiation of occupational cultures. Over half the respondents resented that 'specialists reaped the benefit of routine police work', with CID most impugned. But guns were no source of division; nearly all were opposed to arming the police. Likewise, thoughts on respectable and villainous citizens were cohesive, as were attitudes toward female PCs and the position of the police as employees. The most significant divisions were provoked by career orientation (those committed to the beat compared to those who looked to advancement), and conceptions of appropriate supervision. Data in Chapter 5 suggested that a bipolar categorization of police into a rank-and-file 'us' and a managerial 'them' was hardly sustainable. Loyalties to other officers were important but lacked the sharp divisions emphasized in other studies. Loyalties were several, including to those outside the force.

Research on police socialization has highlighted the influence of informal agencies and the very limited effect of formal agencies (Butler 1982; van Maanen 1975). The basis has been the measurement of change in a variety of 'attitudes', some of a highly general nature, such as Wilson-Patterson's Conservatism index, and some clearly focusing on police work, such as van Maanen's measures of commitment and motivation. The more subjective or qualitative data have normally been used as illustrative material. Yet the disappointing predictive ability of variable-centred models employing readily measured 'objective' indices of attitude implies that their explanatory power is less than the subjective aspects of occupational meaning. Present models of occupational socialization cannot correlate the bearing of a particular 'attitude' with actual practice; with a propensity, say, to reach particular decisions according to a cognitive pattern which could be measured (Bennett 1984). On the other hand, subjective data, emphasizing contextual and situational influences on practice and decision-making, seem less tangible than the limited information gained from 'objective' measures. Yet such qualities dominate the accounts officers give of competence. Whereas the image of the officer based on attitude tests is that of a cluster of attributes without a persona, the danger of ethnographic studies which emphasize occupational culture is their tendency to make a puppet *manqué* of the officer.

The object in examining individuals' accounts of experience and action was to compile a vocabulary of stock responses to the work which enhances understanding of the terms by which constables attribute competence to acts and to enable the anticipation of likely courses of action. These include thoughts about the meaning of work and types of commitment to it as well as the themes of dependence, uncertainty, autonomy and authority characteristic of occupational culture (Manning 1987). The term 'operating ideology' was adopted to describe the long-range career perspectives which help officers develop ideas of appropriate police practice and its consequences at a personal level. Such perspectives bespeak the officer's need to perceive consistency and scruple in practical decision-making; knowledge of them reveals the articulation between potential influences on action and decisions taken (and, in the current state of knowledge, ethnographic data may get us further than predictive modelling (see Sykes and Brent 1983)). There is much here on which training could build.

According to Reiner (1985: 64–5), concern over recruitment and training has played a part in policing's crisis of legitimacy since the 1962 Royal Commission. Standards of entry were not improved by the pay award recommended by the Commission, and poor educational standards remained a problem (Martin and Wilson 1969). Complaints that training was inadequate to the demands of modern society surfaced throughout the 1970s (Evans 1974: 187; Whitaker 1979: 215). The acceptance by the incoming Conservative government of the Edmund–Davies pay increases reversed the manpower crisis of 1977 but did nothing to alleviate the problems of inadequate training being applied to the flood of recruits (Reiner 1985: 74). The frustration of fervent demands for training to better recognize policing's substantial element of social service is an instance of the subversion of reform by operational officers; it is significant that these demands were most loudly expressed by very senior officers (Alderson 1979, 1984) and instructors at Bramshill (Brown and Howes 1975; Pope and Weiner 1981). Yet the importance of training was reiterated throughout 1981, a year Reiner described as 'a climacteric in the politicisation of policing' (1985: 167). Response to the report of the Royal Commission on Criminal Procedure raised the need to consider how any new powers could best be imparted but urban rioting and the Scarman Report (1981: paras 5.6–5.32) on the Brixton disorders most sharply posed the issue of trainings' role in strengthening control over rank and file action.

The 1982 Police Training Council Working Party (1983: 1) reviewed training 'with particular reference to the recent recommendations of Lord Scarman'. It accepted that many recruits joined with limited experience of 'life and society' (the average recruit age in 1981 was 22) and saw the probationary period as a two-year apprenticeship; recruits should not be regarded as trained until it was over. There was debate about distributing district centre training in shorter periods throughout probation, in case the initial ten-week course could be more easily assimilated in shorter doses, taking note of the low education and minimal life experience of most recruits. However, proposals to alter training's structure were rejected because delegates felt there was a 'survival kit' of knowledge recruits needed before they could start duty.

The Initial Course was extended. A one-week in-force Induction Course was now followed by a fourteen-week Initial Course; returning to the local force recruits receive two weeks Local Procedure, and a ten-week tutor constable spell, with brief specialist attachments (in year one a fortnight on a residential beat and a control room/enquiry desk fortnight). Between the TC attachment and the one-week Final Course there are three further fortnights at district centre for 'progress and monitoring', the last taking place after twenty-one months' service. Increased formal lectures on 'attitudes and social skills' were to meet reviews then under way on public order and community and race relations training. Assessment needs predominated in the new Final Course, rather than any more sophisticated input. Having opted for a longer initial course, the final course could only be a week longer.

It was further recommended that during patrol attachments no recruit should patrol alone, and that selection of appropriate tutors was vital and should not be confined to those seeking promotion since 'many officers who are content to remain constables have exactly the personal qualities of integrity and ''policemanship'' required' (Police Training Council Working Party 1983: 7). TCs should be trained to acquaint them with probationer training, explain their role in it and identify the deficiencies and skills they should focus on. In light of the limited input on community relations, it was later recommended that recruits should have a short course six months after joining, with more interactive teaching specifying the 'interpersonal and behavioural skills . . . needed to deal confidently and sensitively with members of the public, and providing racism awareness training', a tall order indeed. A significant problem in implementing all these recommendations is that the Central Planning Unit, responsible for police training practice, lacks the control its name suggests. It cannot control selection of training staff and hence the implementation of recommended content or procedure, this being a matter for individual forces.

Training must indeed attend to definable and measurable activities; it must start with what the police do or should do rather than non-behavioural concepts such as 'a deeper study of society' (Alderson 1979). Specifying objectives requires a behavioural description of necessary tasks, and while there is certainly a need to convey the social context of policing it must be clearly related to officers' tasks. As Reiner (1985: 199) remarks, over-concentration on crime-fighting 'has distracted attention from . . . how the effectiveness of the craft of "peace-keeping" can be defined, measured or cultivated by training and supervision'. Many problems stem from the separation of formal training from routine practice; 'programmes derived from theories about the role of the police in society will almost inevitably result in generalised proscriptive teaching which will fail to integrate theory with practice' (Taylor 1982: 3).

Interleaving formal training and 'on the job' apprenticeship requires an investment in supervision during the apprenticeship phase, and close monitoring of the probationer's negotiation of field experiences. This is patently not the present case. Tutor constables are unlikely to have received any training in techniques of instruction. Moreover, the probationer is often seen of necessity as a full member of the team. The unsystematic, non-specific, and uncontrolled character of the 'apprenticeship' renders it impossible to exert direction over the crucial first two years of service. It must also be more systematically assessed. A means is needed (a) to indicate that the probationer is still learning and developing skills and (b) to evaluate the achievement of these ends. To do so, core activities must be identified so that novices can 'proceed through . . . a range and variety of training experiences which might reasonably be regarded as encompassing the future constables' repertoire' (Taylor 1982: 8). Core activities could be specified by ecology (rural, inner city), function (beat, traffic), or behavioural skill (questioning, arbitration). Discussion of alternative procedures and planning ensuing practical phases would mark formal training's continuing role.

Identification of core activities, and associated 'theoretical' input would require the distinction of generic from specialized skills and the identification of specialized skills appropriate to particular activities. A growing corpus of ethnographic and attitudinal research which focuses on policing as work could facilitate this. The need for more explicit categorization and description of police behaviour is particularly marked with regard to verbal and non-verbal interaction techniques. Communication with minorities is still neglected. Race relations input is not tested despite the general emphasis on learning by objectives, and research proves this reduces the priority probationers give to it (Bull 1986). Skills-oriented material is absent from race relations sessions (Southgate 1982: 18). Enough must be conveyed about the lives and situation of minorities to demonstrate their essential 'normality' while provoking recognition of areas of conflict and misunderstanding. This represents what is needed generally in providing techniques and supporting justifications to enhance police/public relations. Special attention should be given to vehicle stops, checks on suspicious persons, and calls to disturbances and domestic disputes.

Training needs to address choice in specific situations, so probationers and instructors can discuss appropriate goals and tactics and the cues that should be used to shape decisions. This can be done by simulating 'street' encounters by role play, or recruits can be asked how they would respond to various written scenarios, with different approaches highlighted and the likely results analysed. Films and videotapes can be useful here. Experienced officers should not have classes handed over to them or be brought in to excite recruits with 'war stories' but should be used 'to help instructors explore the uncertainties of choice' on the street (Bayley 1986: 30). Field instructors are rarely trained to draw lessons from their own experience, may be blind to alternatives and so over-confident that they persuade recruits too much to their own version. As assessors they may intimidate rather than draw out complexities. Their involvement must be carefully managed.

In recent years training in social skills has made much headway in occupations where interpersonal communication is a core activity, e.g. social work, medicine. In these areas such skills are seen as prerequisite to the application of factual learning, but policing lags far behind. If training is to transcend exhortation, appropriate interpersonal skills must be identified and police-specific manuals devised (Hargie, Saunders, and Dickson 1981). The vagaries of recruitment according to law and order boom and bust exposes the weakness of learning by experience. The preference of police for experiential learning will not willingly be modified, but the present reliance on random personal experience cannot safely continue.

Appendix I: Method

The research reported here was a longitudinal study. A sample of 125 male and female recruits who entered the Derbyshire Police Training Establishment between autumn 1979 and spring 1980 were followed through their initial training, probationary period, and first year of service. Research methods included rating exercises, questionnaires, non-participant observation, and interviewing. Dr Jane Fielding was Research Fellow and the consultant was Professor Peter Manning.

The qualitative data accrued from two sources: essays written by recruits on application to the police and interviews with a sub-sample of recruits at various stages of training and service. The interviews were tape-recorded and transcribed verbatim. They were semi-structured by a thematic interview guide with probes and invitations to expand on issues raised; extracts have a code reference in text. Instructors, TCs, senior officers and experienced constables were interviewed in the same manner. Observations in the TE and documentary analysis augmented the interviews. A survey questionnaire comprising items on crime and criminal justice, law enforcement and social/political issues, and rating exercises on aspects of policing, was administered at induction, one-year and two-year stages. All of the respondents re-interviewed after training and a period of beat work recalled the initial interview and oriented to it by statements that their view on some matter had or had not changed (assertions which could, of course, be checked).

It is recognized that the meaning of the statements must be linked to the interpretive situation in which they occur. The consensual character of the stance struck on, say, police/public relations, can be either constructed or deconstructed not only by other participants but, notably, by the same participants as they address new issues under the interviewer's probing. Respondents often went to some lengths to devise qualifiers that did not undermine their initial, often sloganistic, response. This not only reinforces the need for alternative sources of data but for recognition that the measurement of 'consensus' on some topic is not always the most fruitful analytic exercise. Our interest should often reside not in attempts to mediate our subjects' consensus claims but 'the recurrent interpretive methods whereby variable symbolic products . . . are contextually generated' (Gilbert and Mulkay 1984). The intention is to identify recurrent collective cultural resources which are available to members and apparent in discourse. A knowledge of the police organization virtually obliges such an approach. Manning (1980: 250–1) notes that

in effect . . . since information control by agents at the lowest level covers their delicts, and supervisors have only *post facto* knowledge of most of what is done, the ways in which officers rationalise their actions take the form of accounts or verbal rationalisations for their actions.

The interview data was treated as topic as well as resource. These data can tell us much about the conventions and devices recruits use when asked to offer accounts of action or belief. One consequence of pursuing a multi-method and longitudinal research design was that it was possible to check single sources of data with others, and with the previous/subsequent responses of the same individuals. Subject to rigorous checking, the interviews offer data about the organization which would not emerge from other sources. For example, because any references to 'trouble' were matters for further investigation, it was possible to judge what pressure to increase arrest rates recruits experienced. Inconsistency between predictions of behaviour on the basis of expressed attitude and actual behaviour is related to the failure to appreciate situational variables. In the jargon, the typical measures of attitude-to-object do not measure attitude-to-situation. Numerous studies have shown that prejudice is a poor predictor of discrimination (Ehrlich 1973). The use of attitude data in this study is primarily as an index of personal change, to which the interest of given items *per se* is subordinate. As a rule more confidence is felt in the attitude items the more immediate their connection with police work and the respondent's experience.

Appendix II: Probationer training programme Derbyshire Constabulary

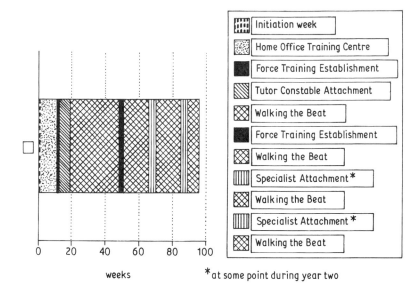

Initiation week	
Home Office Training Centre	
Force Training Establishment	
Tutor Constable Attachment	
Walking the Beat	
Force Training Establishment	
Walking the Beat	
Specialist Attachment*	
Walking the Beat	
Specialist Attachment*	
Walking the Beat	

weeks   *at some point during year two

Appendix III: _____
Instrumentalism items

1. The policeman shouldn't let his work interfere with his private life.

2. The policeman should never stop being a policeman.

3. The policeman is obliged to perform police duty even if it involves overtime or other interference with his private life.

4. When it comes down to it, police work is just like any other job.

5. The policeman should only be concerned to do what he must to earn a living.

Bibliography

Ahern, F (1972) *Police in Trouble*, New York: Hawthorn.

Alderson, J. (1979) *Policing Freedom*, Plymouth: MacDonald and Evans.

—— (1984) *Law and Disorder*, London: Hamish Hamilton.

Banton, M (1964) *The Policeman in the Community*, London: Tavistock.

Bayley, D. (1975) 'The police and political development in Europe', in A. Martin (ed.) *The Formation of National States in Western Europe*, Princeton: University Press.

—— (1986) 'Tactical choices of patrol officers', *Journal of Criminal Justice* 14(4): 329–48.

Becker, H. S. (1964) 'Personal change in adult life', *Sociometry* 27(1): 40–53.

Becker, H. and Strauss A. L. (1956) 'Careers, personality and adult socialization', *American Journal of Sociology* 62: 253–63.

Becker, H. S. *et al.* (1961) *Boys in White*, Chicago: University of Chicago Press.

Bennett, R. (1984) 'Becoming blue: a longitudinal study of police recruit occupational socialization', *Journal of Police Science and Administration*, 12(1): 47–58.

Bennett, R. and Greenstein, T. (1975) 'The police personality: a test of the predispositional model', *Journal of Police Science and Administration* 3: 439–45.

Bennett, R. and Haen, M. (1979) 'Criminal justice education in the U.S.', *Journal of Criminal Justice* 7: 252–60.

Billig, M. (1982) *Ideology and Social Psychology*, Oxford: Blackwell.

Bittner, E. (1965) 'The concept of the organisation', *Social Research* 32: 239–55.

—— (1967) 'The police on skid row: a study of peace-keeping', *American Sociological Review* 32(5): 699–715.

—— (1978) 'The functions of the police in modern society', in P. K. Manning and J. van Maanen (eds) *Policing: A View from the Street*, Santa Monica, CA: Goodyear Publishing.

Black, D. (1980) *The Manners and Customs of the Police*, New York: Academic Press.

Box, S. (1981) *Deviance, Reality and Society*, 2nd edn, Eastbourne: Holt, Rinehart & Winston.

Bramshill Police College (n.d.) Leadership and Management Course: Personnel Management.

Brim, O. (1966) 'Socialization through the life cycle', in O. Brim and S. Wheeler (eds) *Socialization after Childhood*, New York: John Wiley.

Brown, C. L. (1983) 'The future face of police training', *Police Journal* 56(2): 121–7.

Brown, C. L. and Cochrane, R. (1984) 'Selection, training and work of tutor constables', unpublished Police Foundation Programme Proposal, London: Police Foundation.

Brown, J. and Howes, G. (eds) (1975) *The Police and the Community*, Farnborough: Saxon House.

Bull, R. (1986) 'An evaluation of police recruit training in human awareness', in J. C. Yuille (ed.) *Police Selection and Training*, Dordrecht: Martinus Nijhoff.

Burns-Howell, A., Jones, J. M. *et al.* (1982) 'Policing strategy: organizational or victim needs?', unpublished report, Bramshill Police Staff College.

Butler, A. (1982) 'An examination of the influence of training and work experience on the attitudes and perceptions of police constables', Paper given at the International Conference on Psychology and Law, Swansea.

Butler, A. and Cochrane, R. (1977) 'An examination of some elements of the personality of police officers and their implications', *Journal of Police Science and Administration* 5(4).

Butler, A. and Cochrane, R. (1980) 'The values of police officers, recruits and civilians in England', unpublished paper.

Cain, M. (1973) *Society and the Policeman's Role*, London: Routledge & Kegan Paul.

Chatterton, M. (1979) 'The supervision of patrol work under the Fixed Points System', in S. Holdaway (ed.) *The British Police*, London: Edward Arnold.

—— (1983) 'Police work and assault charges', in M. Punch (ed.) *Control in the Police Organisation*, Cambridge, MA: MIT Press.

Cohen, N. and Chaiken, J. M. (1972) *Police Background Characteristics and Performance*, New York: Rand Institute.

Colman, A. and Gorman, L. (1982) 'Conservatism, dogmatism and authoritarianism in British police officers', *Sociology* 16(1): 1–26.

Comrie, M. D. and Kings, E. J. (1975) *Study of Urban Workloads: Final Report*, London: Police Research Services Unit, Home Office.

Constabulary Annual Report (1980) Derbyshire Constabulary.

Cook, P. (1977) 'Facing the future', *Police Review*, August.

Cruse, D. and Rubin, J. (1973) *Determinants of Police Behaviour*, Washington, DC: US Dept. of Justice.

Davis, F. (1968) 'Professional socialization as subjective experience', in

H. Becker *et al.* (eds) *Institutions and the Person*, Chicago: Aldine.

Ehrlich, M. (1973) *The Social Psychology of Prejudice*, New York: John Wiley.

Ekblom, P. and Heal, K. (1982) *The Police Response to Calls from the Public*, Research and Planning Paper No. 9, London: Home Office.

Ericson, R. V. (1982) *Reproducing Order*, Toronto: University of Toronto Press.

Evans, P. (1974) *The Police Revolution*, London: Allen & Unwin.

Fielding, N. G. (1981) 'The credibility of police accountability', *Poly. Law Review* 6(2): 89–93.

—— (1984a) *Probation Practice: Client Support under Social Control*, Farnborough: Gower.

—— (1984b) 'Police socialisation and police competence', *British Journal of Sociology* 35(4): 568–90.

Fielding, N. G. and Fielding J. L. (1987) 'A study of resignation during British police training', *Journal of Police Science and Administration* 15(1): 24–36.

Gilbert, G. N. and Mulkay, M. (1984) *Opening Pandora's Box*, Cambridge: Cambridge University Press.

Gross, E. (1969) 'The definition of organisation goals', *British Journal of Sociology* 20: 277–94.

Hall, S. *et al.* (1978) *Policing the Crisis*, London: Macmillan.

Hanley, J. (1979) 'The rhetoric of police recruit selections', M.Phil. dissertation, University of York.

Hargie, O., Saunders, C. and Dickson, D. (1981) *Social Skills in Interpersonal Communication*, London: Croom Helm.

Harris, R. (1973) *The Police Academy: An Inside View*, New York: John Wiley.

Hartley, R. (1968) 'Personal characteristics and acceptance of secondary groups as reference groups', in H. Hyman and E. Singer (eds) *Readings in Reference Group Theory and Research*, New York: Free Press.

Hogarth, J. (1982) 'Police accountability', in R. Donelan (ed.) *The Maintenance of Order in Society*, Ottawa, Ministry of Supply & Services.

Holdaway, S. (1983) *Inside the British Police*, Oxford: Blackwell.

Homans, G. C. (1961) *Social Behaviour: Its Elementary Forms*, New York: Harcourt, Brace & World.

Hopper, M. (1977) 'Becoming a policeman: socialization of cadets in a police academy', *Urban Life* 6: 149–70.

Hough, J. M. (1980) *Uniformed Police Work and Management Technology*, Research Unit Paper 1, London: Home Office.

Hughes, E. (1971) *The Sociological Eye*, Chicago: Aldine.

Hughes, E. C. (1958) *Men and Their Work*, New York: Free Press.

Jancowicz, D. and Walsh, P. (1984) 'Researching the sergeant's role', *Gardie News*, October, p. 6.

Jones, J. M. (1980) *Organisational Aspects of Police Behaviour*, Farnborough: Gower.

Jones, J. M. and Winkler, J. T. (1982) 'Beyond the beat: the facts about policing in a riotous city', *Journal of Law and Society* 9(1): 103–14.

Joseph, N. and Alex, N. (1972) 'The uniform: a sociological perspective', *American Journal of Sociology*, 77: 719–30.

Knorr-Cetina, K. (1981) 'The micro-sociological challenge of macro-sociology', in K. Knorr-Cetina and A. V. Cicourel (eds) *Advances in Sociological Theory and Methodology*, London: Routledge & Kegan Paul.

Levi, M. and Jones, S. (1985) 'Public and police perceptions of crime seriousness in England and Wales', *British Journal of Criminology* 25: 234–50.

McCabe, S. and Sutcliffe, F. (1978) *Defining Crime: A Study of Police Decisions*, Oxford: Blackwell.

McClure, J. (1980) *Spike Island*, London: Macmillan.

McNamara, J. (1967) 'Uncertainties in police work: the relevance of police recruits' backgrounds and training', in D. Bordua (ed.) *The Police*, New York: John Wiley.

Manning, P. K. (1972) 'Observing the police: deviants, respectables and the law', in J. Douglas (ed.) *Research on Deviance*, New York: Random House, 213–68.

—— (1977) *Police Work*, Cambridge, MA: MIT Press.

—— (1978) Review of G. Kirkham, 'Signal Zero', *Criminology*, May: 136.

—— (1980) *The Narcs Game*, Cambridge, MA: MIT Press.

—— (1981) 'Careers in criminal justice', in N. Morris (ed.) *Encyclopedia of Crime and Justice*, New York: Garland.

—— (1982) '"Modern" police administration, the rise of crime-focussed policing and critical incident analysis', in R. Donelan (ed.) *The Maintenance of Order in Society*, Ministry of Supply, Canada.

—— (1987) 'The police occupational culture in Anglo-American societies', in V. Strecher *et al.* (eds) *Encyclopedia of Police Science*, New York: Garland.

Manning, P. K. and van Maanen, J. (1978) 'Background to policing', in P. K. Manning and J. van Maanen (eds) *Policing: A View from the Street*, Santa Monica, CA: Goodyear.

Marshall, G. (1965) *Police and Government*, London: Methuen.

Martin, J. P. and Wilson, G. (1969) *The Police: A Study in Manpower*, London: Heinemann.

Martin, S. (1980) *Breaking and Entering*, London: University of California Press.

Mawby, R. (1979) *Policing the City*, Farnborough: Saxon.

Merton, R. and Barber, E. (1976) 'Sociological ambivalence', in R. Merton, *Sociological Ambivalence and Other Essays*, New York: Free Press.

Merton, R. and Rossi, A. (1968) 'Contributions to the theory of reference group behaviour', in H. Nyman and E. Singer (eds) *Readings in Reference Group Theory and Research*, New York: Free Press, 28–68.

Moore, W. E. (1969) 'Occupational socialization', in D. Goslin (ed.) *Handbook of Socialization Theory and Research*, Chicago: Rand McNally.

More, W. W., Jr. (1976) *The American Police: Text and Readings*, St Paul, MN: West Publishing.

Muir, W. K. (1977) *Police: Streetcorner Politicians*, Chicago: University of Chicago Press.

Norris, C. A. (1983) 'Policing the Quiet: an observational study of the Surrey police', unpublished Masters dissertation, University of Surrey, Guildford.

Packer, H. L. (1968) *The Limits of the Criminal Sanction*, Stanford: Stanford University Press.

Police Foundation (1982) 'Neighbourhood policing evaluation', unpublished report, London: Police Foundation.

Police Training Council Working Party (1983) *Police Probationer Training*, London: Home Office.

Pope, D. and Weiner, N. (eds) (1981) *Modern Policing*, London: Croom Helm.

Punch, M. (1979a) *Policing the Inner City*, London: Macmillan.

—— (1979b) 'The secret social service', in S. Holdaway (ed.) *The British Police*, London: Edward Arnold.

Punch, M. and Naylor, T. (1973) 'The police: a social service', *New Society*, 24: 358–61.

Ramparts (the newspaper of the Derbyshire Constabulary) vol. 3, 1980.

Reiner, R. (1978) *The Blue Coated Worker*, Cambridge: Cambridge University Press.

—— (1985) *The Politics of the Police*, Brighton: Wheatsheaf.

Reuss-Ianni, E. (1983) *Two Cultures of Policing*, London: Transaction.

Royal Commission on the Police (1962) Final Report, Cmnd. 1728, London: HMSO.

Rubinstein, J (1973) *City Police*, New York: Farrar, Straus & Giroux.

Sacks, H. (1972) 'Notes on the police assessment of moral character', in D. Sudnow *Studies in Social Interaction*, New York: Free Press.

Salaman, G. (1974) *Community and Occupation*, Cambridge: Cambridge University Press.

Scarman, Lord (1981) *The Brixton Disorders 10–12 April 1981*, Cmnd. 8427, London: HMSO.

Schall, M. S. (1983) 'A communication-rules approach to organisational cultures', *Administration Science Quarterly* 28: 557–81.

Schein, E. (1961) 'Management development as a process of influence', *Industrial Management Review* 2: 59–77.

Schutz, A. (1967) *The Phenomenology of the Social World*, Chicago: Northwestern University Press.

Sherman, L. (1978) *The Quality of Police Education*, San Francisco: Josey Bass.

Skolnick, J. (1966) *Justice without Trial*, New York: John Wiley.

Smircich, L. (1983) 'Concepts of culture and organisational analysis' *Administration Science Quarterly* 28: 339–58.

Smith, D. (1983) *Police and People in London*, vol. 1, London: Policy Studies Institute.

Southgate, P. (1980) 'Policewomen in a Canadian city', unpublished Masters dissertation, University of Surrey, Guildford.

—— (1982) *Police Probationer Training in Race Relations*, Research and Planning Unit Paper 8, London: Home Office.

Southgate, P. and Ekblom, P. (1984) *Contacts between Police and Public: Findings from the British Crime Survey*, London: HMSO.

Speier, M. (1971) *How to Observe Face to Face Communication*, Los Angeles: Goodyear.

Sterling, J. (1972) *Changes in Role Concepts of Police Officers*, Gaithersburg, MA: International Association of Chiefs of Police.

Strauss, A. (1959) *Mirrors and Masks: the Search for Identity*, New York: Free Press.

Strong, P. and Dingwall, R. (1983) 'The limits of negotiation in formal organisations', in G. N. Gilbert and P. Abell (eds) *Accounts and Actions*, Aldershot, Gower.

Sykes, R. and Brent, E. (1980) 'The regulation of interaction by police', *Criminology* 18(2): 182–97.

Sykes, R. and Brent, E. (1983) *Policing: A Social Behaviourist Perspective*, Princeton, NJ: Rutgers.

Taylor, M. (1982) 'Police training: towards a new model', *Police Journal* 55: 1–18.

Teahan, J. (1975) 'A longitudinal study of attitude shifts among black and white police officers, *Journal of Social Issues* 31: 35–47.

Thornton, R. and Nardi, P. (1975) 'The dynamics of role acquisition', *American Journal of Sociology*, 80: 870–85.

Tifft, L. (1974) 'The "Cop Personality" reconsidered', *Journal of*

Police Science and Administration 2(3): 266–78.

van Maanen, J. (1973) 'Observations on the making of policemen', *Human Organisations* 32(4): 407–18.

—— (1974) 'Working the street: a developmental view of police behaviour', in H. Jacob (ed.) *The Potential for Reform of Criminal Justice*, Beverley Hills, CA: Sage, 83–130.

—— (1975) 'Police socialization: a longitudinal examination of job attitudes in an urban police department', *Administration Science Quarterly* 20: 207–28.

—— (1976) 'Breaking in: socialization to work', in R. Dubin (ed.) *Handbook of Work, Organisation and Society*, Chicago: Rand McNally, 67–130.

—— (1977) 'Experiencing organization: notes on the meaning of careers and socialization', in J. van Maanen (ed.) *Organisational Careers, Some New Perspectives*, New York: John Wiley, 15–45.

—— (1984) 'Doing new things in old ways', *Review of Higher Education* 23: 301–13.

van Maanen J. and Schein, E. (1979) 'Toward a theory of organisational socialization', in B. M. Staw (ed.) *Researching Organizational Behaviour*, New York: JAI Press, 209–69.

Weick, K. (1969) *The Social Psychology of Organizing*, Reading, MA: Addison-Wesley.

Weinstein, E. A. (1969) 'The development of interpersonal competence', in D. Goslin (ed.) *Handbook of Socialization Theory and Research*, Chicago: Rand McNally.

Weinstein, E. A. and Deutschberger, P. (1964) 'Tasks, bargains and identities in social interaction', *Social Forces* 42: 451–6.

Westley, W. A. (1970) *Violence and the Police: A Sociological Study of Law, Custom and Morality*, Cambridge, MA: MIT Press.

Whitaker, B. (1979) *The Police in Society*, London: Eyre Methuen.

Wycoff, M. and Susmilch, C. (1979) 'The relevance of college education for policing: continuing the dialogue', in D. Petersen (ed.) *Police Work: Strategies and Outcomes in Law Enforcement*, London: Sage.

Index